D0209712

Criminal Justice

Recent Scholarship

Edited by
Marilyn McShane and Frank P. Williams III

A Series from LFB Scholarly

Crime and Justice in the Age of Court TV

Hedieh Nasheri

LFB Scholarly Publishing LLC
New York 2002

Library of Congress Cataloging-in-Publication Data

Nasheri, Hedieh.
Crime and justice in the age of Court TV / Hedieh Nasheri.
p. cm. -- (Criminal justice recent scholarship)
Includes bibliographical references and index.
ISBN 1-931202-56-7 (alk. paper)
1. Television broadcasting of court proceedings--United States. 2.
Courtroom Television Network. I. Title. II. Criminal justice (LFB
Scholarly Publishing LLC)
KF8726 .N37 2002
347.73'12--dc21
2002008105

ISBN 1-931202-56-7

Printed on acid-free 250-year-life paper.

Manufactured in the United States of America.

Contents

Preface

As this book is coming to completion, recent attention on the topic of televised trials has centered around the question of whether the trials of accused terrorists of the September 11, 2001 attack on New York should be televised. This case may have broad implications for the future use of cameras in the courtroom.

On January 18, 2002, a federal judge refused to allow TV cameras into the trial of Zacarias Moussaoui, one of the September 11 putative terrorists. Judge Leonie N. Brinkema, in a 13-page ruling, denied the request of the Court TV cable network to broadcast the trial of Moussaoui, who is charged with six terrorism conspiracy counts and scheduled to go on trial in October 2002. In her ruling, Brinkema wrote that she had no authority to reject a federal court ban on cameras in courtrooms. Even if she did, she would not, she wrote, because, "given the issues raised in this indictment, any societal benefits from photographing and broadcasting these proceedings are heavily outweighed by the significant dangers worldwide broadcasting of this trial would pose to the orderly and secure administration of justice." Her ruling embraced concerns raised by prosecutors that broadcasting the trial would intimidate witnesses, endanger court officers and provide Moussaoui with a platform to vent his political beliefs. Moussaoui's lawyers favored televising the trial, with restrictions. They argued that the broadcasts would give their client an added layer of protection in getting a fair trial on charges that could result in the death penalty.

The Supreme Court has upheld the public's right of access to the judicial system, but has stopped short of saying the right to a public trial means the right to a televised one. Justice David Souter testified in 1996 before a Senate subcommittee: "The day you see cameras come into our courtroom", he said, "it's going to roll over my dead body." Until recently, the justices did not even allow the live audio broadcasting of arguments, though they did permit archival audio taping. In the landmark case of Bush v. Gore - the case that awarded Bush the presidency after the 2000 election - the justices finally relented and permitted the real-time audio transmission of the final arguments. It was a good first step, but many Americans wondered why the justices were prepared to be heard but not seen. Today's television cameras require no special lighting and can be placed discreetly behind walls so as not to interfere with courtroom proceedings. Bush v. Gore was a wonderful civics lesson, but it was somewhat incomplete because the television cameras were excluded.

The Sunshine in the Courtroom Act was approved by the Senate Judiciary Committee late in 2001 and is pending in the Senate as of the completion date of this book. The bill would give judges in federal trial and appeals courts discretion to permit cameras in their courtrooms, but it would require them to afford witnesses the option of having their faces and voices obscured.

Televising of many state trials since the O.J. Simpson case has increased the level of knowledge and sophistication most Americans have about the US legal system. It also made instant celebrities out of many of the lawyers who participated in the case.

To argue in favor of televising trials is not to ignore the possible dangers in some cases. Court proceedings ought to be as open as possible. Federal court rules specifically prohibit the televising of any federal criminal trial. But the rules of state courts are more flexible; all states now allow some judicial proceedings to be broadcast and 38 states permit the showing of state criminal trials. Still, resistance to the idea remains firm. The U.S. Judicial Conference, the policymaking body for the federal courts, says cameras in courtrooms raise privacy concerns for witnesses in sensitive cases and put traditionally low-profile, but powerful, federal judges at risk. This book is intended to serve as a reference source on the topic of televised trials, for the use of judges, lawyers and academicians who are confronting these issues. It also is intended to present the evidence pro and con so that the general interest reader can decide for themselves.

Acknowledgments

I am grateful to the following organizations: the American Bar Association, the Federal Judicial Center, Society of Professional Journalists, National Center for State Courts, and Courtroom Television Network for providing information, surveys, studies and in some cases support services, as I sought to gather and analyze materials for this book. My thanks also go to numerous authors before me who have described and interpreted the role of cameras in the courtroom. I have drawn on what has been written on the topic of cameras in the courtroom and have attempted to advance my own interpretation and understanding of the portrayal of our justice system in the high-tech society in which we live. Thanks also to David Shock and Brenda Kaminsky for their research assistance. My thanks also goes to librarians and academic libraries that assisted with this project. Finally I would like to thank my colleagues, friends and family for their support and encouragement.

Chapter 1

AMERICA'S LOVE AFFAIR FOR ALL THINGS LEGAL

The role of cameras in court has been debated by lawyers from the 1936 kidnapping trial involving Charles Lindbergh's baby through the 2000 presidential showdown at the U.S. Supreme Court. The public along with the courts, lawyers, and defendants have debated for years whether cameras should be allowed in courtrooms to provide greater access to various important trials and legal disputes. The case for televising a trial as a means of serving a larger public interest hardly could find a better example than the case of suspected terrorist Zacarias Moussaouri whose trial is just months away as this book nears completion. This case will put the debate to the test. Zacarias Moussaouri, who is facing charges connected with the September 11, 2001 terror attacks on the World Trade Center and the Pentagon. Moussaouri is believed to have been the 20th hijacker in those attacks although never making it on board in time to join the 19 others on their suicide missions. Moussaouri has asked for a televised trial, but government prosecutors wish to keep the cameras out. The debate over televised trials could well enter a new phase as a result of this case and others likely to follow out of the September 11th events.

Although cameras are an increasing presence in courtrooms throughout the nation, there are still isolated pockets of resistance. One is New York State, where a ban on cameras in the courts remains on the books, even though several judges have recently allowed trials in their courtrooms to be televised. While almost every state allows cameras in some proceedings and 38 states permit them at criminal trials, a 56-year old-rule promulgated by judges and approved by Congress bars the filming of trials in federal court. A change in the rule would require an act of Congress or an amendment by the Judicial Conference, a federal judiciary's 27-judge policymaking body. Legislation to allow individual federal judges to decide whether to permit cameras in their courtrooms languished in Congress in 2000 and was reintroduced in 2001. The foundation laid by Court TV founder Steve Brill was as simple as it was controversial: gavel-to-gavel courtroom proceedings, much of it live. It was C-SPAN for legal junkies.

From the Salem Witch trials in 1692 to the Scopes Monkey trial in 1925, to the more recent O.J. Simpson trial, the American public has long been intrigued by the inner workings of courtrooms. This fascination has become a near-obsession in recent years, as demonstrated by the growth of trial-related television shows, dramas, newscasts and best-selling novels. The craving for all things legal has turned previously successful but relatively unknown lawyers, such as Johnnie Cochran, Marsha Clark and Greta Van Susteren from the O.J. Simpson trial, into high-profile media figures hosting shows of their own. With programs such as the People's Court and Judge Judy rivaling ratings juggernaut Oprah Winfrey in popularity, the courtroom bandwagon shows little sign of slowing down. Shows such as "Ally McBeal" and "The Practice" confirmed there are ratings to be gained in law related shows.

Those involved in law-related media say public interest in their field has always been high. They note that court-related movies such as To Kill a Mockingbird and Inherit the Wind are considered classics, and that television dramas such as Perry Mason and The Defenders were popular long before the O.J. Simpson case. The media has devoted a tremendous amount of attention to televising high profile cases for one single reason: people are fascinated by this brand of human interest story.

Courtroom cameras are among many technological advances that have revolutionized our courts and court proceedings, especially in the 1990s.[1] So what was new in the 1990s? According to one of the lawyers turned media star, Ms. Van Susteren, the difference "is not in interest, it's in access." A new niche of media, such as the Courtroom Television Network (Court TV), has made court proceedings and trials accessible to anyone who has access to cable television.

The concept of Court TV has prompted a public debate on broader issues raised by this new form of media. According to Steven Brill, who launched Court TV in 1991 and later moved to the position of Chairman and editor of Brill's Content magazine, "the public has always been fascinated with courts and trials". In fact every 10 years Time Magazine does a story about America's rabid interest in legal affairs. Brill believes that two major events this decade have helped satisfy the public's hunger like never before: cameras in the courtroom and cable television.

The appearance of justice to the public, accurate or not, may be as important as justice itself. Televised trials may fuel a negative perception of our criminal justice system, including the perception that justice is bought by those who can afford an expensive defense team. Televised trials and courtroom procedures may be able to provide for the kind of accountability that our democracy needs. Is it purely a question of profit, or is education also a factor? Do cameras in the courtroom infringe on the right to a fair trial, or does the right to free speech mandate open access? Do cameras interfere or enhance our court proceedings? These are just a few of the issues under debate regarding Court TV, and, more generally, televised coverage of trials.

JUST FEAR OR REALITY? ALL THE O.J. HOOPLA

The debate over cameras in the courtroom reached new height in 1995 as the O.J. Simpson criminal trial in Los Angeles reached a verdict of "not guilty" on the charges of murder.[2] The trial had been an emotional circus, with thousands of journalists from around the world covering a trial that appeared at times would never come to a conclusion. The final verdict in favor of O.J. Simpson simultaneously sparked celebrations and sparked pleas for judicial reform. At the center of the controversy was the issue of cameras in the courtroom. The central issue raised by the trial was whether justice had been undermined as a result of televising the criminal proceedings. The O.J. Simpson case may have created a permanent audience for televised trials.[3] Some have called the case against the former professional football player the "Media Mother of all Trials."[4] The Simpson trial rekindled the debate about the role of the electronic media, especially video cameras, in this nation's courtrooms. "For cameras in the courtroom, the O.J. Simpson trial may be the worst case of all."[5]

For months after the Simpson trial, judges across the country banned, or greatly restricted, television coverage in their courtrooms. They based their decisions, in large part, on what they considered to be the slipshod way the Simpson trial was handled. Even now, most judges who allow coverage of trials put forth extensive written rules for the media in the form of a court order, meaning that any violators could be held in contempt of court. In some particularly high-profile cases, judges will even meet with members of the media before the trial to clarify how coverage must be handled. Nevertheless, these court-mandated limitations do not appear to have diminished American's appetite to know what's going on inside our courtrooms.

It is clear that the O.J. Simpson trial lead to increased cynicism. Still, there is debate as to whether the O.J. Simpson case taught the American public any valuable lessons about the system. On the positive side, televising the trial "provided tremendous insight into courtroom rules and procedures, DNA, and physical evidence". It has been argued that such high-profile cases can accurately show the public what really happens inside the courtroom, as opposed to tabloid coverage of those trials. Court TV shows the public ordinary criminal and civil trials, and thereby educates the public about the adversarial system and how it functions.[6] In high profile cases, there is a greater interest and a greater opportunity for the public to be educated.

Shortly after the O.J. Simpson trial, public confidence in lawyers, the judicial system and the media was reported to be down,[7] and the backlash against cameras in the courtroom across the country resulted in the closure of the courtroom to several high-profile cases, such as the trial of Susan Smith who was found guilty of drowning her two small children in the back of the family car, and the retrial of the Menendez brothers' who were charged with the brutal shotgun murder of their parents as they sat watching television.[8] This backlash may have been an overreaction because "it was not the courtroom cameras that dragged the Simpson trial into the tabloids. The case had all the elements of a circus before it started, and Judge Lance Ito proved an ineffectual ringmaster once it was under way."[9] Moreover, the media tended to persecute Simpson even though the jury found him not guilty, and the media fanned the race issue by tracking the race composition of the jury, of the prosecution team and of the defense team.[10] Even without cameras in the courtroom, the Simpson case could easily have been front page news. After all, cameras were prohibited during the subsequent civil trial of O.J. Simpson but it still remained a front page news story.[11]

THE DEBATE OVER CAMERAS
GOES BACK MANY YEARS

Legal experts on both sides of the issue agree Simpson's "trial of the century" was the greatest blow to efforts to integrate cameras into courts since the original "Trial of the Century"- the Lindbergh baby kidnapping

- which prompted many judges to first banish photographers in 1935. The media circus that engulfed the Simpson case will not be soon forgotten. More than seventy million Americans saw the trial.[12] There were more than eight hundred phone lines installed in the press rooms of the Los Angeles courthouse for use by more than one thousand reporters, and more than fifty miles of cable for television cameras which carried a combined two thousand hours of live gavel-to-gavel coverage on stations such as Court TV, CNN, and E! Entertainment.[13] As a result of the trial, proposals have been introduced such as the abolition of the unanimous jury verdict requirement in California.[14] Then California Governor Wilson further proposed that cameras be banned all together from the courtroom. Supporters of cameras in the courtroom say their detractors won their case in subsequent years, in part because of the perception left after the O.J. Simpson trial that justice became a "media circus". Yet, in his address to the Arkansas Bar Association's annual meeting in June of 1999, Philip Anderson, president of the American Bar Association, continued to urge judges to allow cameras in their courtrooms in order to alter misconceptions created by the O.J. Simpson criminal trial.[15]

The first murder trial covered by cameras was the 1935 trial of Bruno Hauptmann, accused of the kidnaping and murder of national hero Charles Lindbergh's child.[16] As a result of the media circus that ensued during the Hauptmann case, the American Bar Association (ABA) adopted Canon 35 of the Code of Judicial Ethics, which urged a ban on photographing court proceedings. In 1952, Canon 35 was amended to specifically mention television cameras.[17]

The issue once again became a public focus in the 1960s with *Sheppard v. Maxwell*.[18] In Sheppard, the United States Supreme Court held that the defendant was denied his Sixth and Fourteenth Amendment rights to a fair trial due to the widespread media publicity surrounding his trial.[19] In this same era, in 1962 the Federal Government permanently barred cameras from its courtrooms. When the Code of Judicial Conduct replaced the Code of Judicial Ethics in 1972, the prohibition on cameras of Canon 35 was restated in Canon A(7).[20]

Over the years, the courts have routinely guarded the rights of the accused to have a fair trial, even if doing so forecloses the right to a free press.[21] The Supreme Court, however, has declared that gag orders that prevent the media from publishing material about the proceedings should not be the first option courts choose in an attempt to ensure a fair trial.[22] As a middle ground, courts have elected to relocate the trial proceedings to other jurisdictions if local publicity might prevent a fair trial.[23] Nevertheless, some lower courts have refused to abide by such prohibitions on gag orders, either by disregarding the rulings altogether and thereby placing a gag order on the press, or by skirting the spirit of the rulings and placing a gag order on all participants of the trial instead of on the press.[24] And, in reality, gag orders have not always worked. An example of a failed gag order occurred in the case of Charles Manson and his followers, who were tried for the 1969 multiple murders in Los Angeles. Then-President Richard Nixon declared to reporters that Manson was "guilty, directly or indirectly, of eight murders without reason."[25]

The potential impact on a fair trial cannot be treated lightly. On one hand, some legal scholars believe cameras adversely affect a defendant's due process rights.[26] These critics of cameras in the courtroom claim that the camera was the cause of "every imaginable evil associated with the [O.J. Simpson] trial."[27] These scholars believe that the length of the trial and "attorney grandstanding"[28] was directly caused by the cameras' presence. On the other hand, some legal scholars maintain that any detrimental effects of cameras in the courtroom are only illusory.[29] They claim that any negative effects in the Simpson case were caused not by the television cameras in the courtroom, but by statements made outside of the courtroom.[30] Moreover, they cite cases in which cameras were barred from the courtroom that had taken just as long, if not longer than the O.J. Simpson trial, and had incidents of attorney misconduct[31] Some members of the legal community, including Simpson's defense team, believe that cameras can actually aid the defendant in receiving a fair trial, rather than violate his or her due process rights.[32]

The O.J. Simpson trial was the latest in a string of more than two dozen "trial of the century" cases in recent history.[33] Media trials,[34] although small in number, are vehicles whereby knowledge of the justice system is circulated, and television, being the most predominate form of media, influences the public's perception of those trials, the justice system, and crime in general.[35] Further, media trials combine the realm of news and entertainment, and exploit the entertainment value in order to get viewers. This coupling of news and entertainment is made easier by the appearance to viewers of a theatrical production whereby the judge, attorneys, and witnesses are the actors, the courtroom is the stage, and the trial is the show.[36]

As of April 1, 2001, 50 states had adopted rules and/or statutes allowing cameras into courtrooms, 40 of them permitting the televising of trials, 37 of them criminal trials.[37] The federal judiciary's governing body, the Judicial Conference, has allowed the appellate courts to decide for themselves if they will allow cameras to record civil appellate arguments.[38] Currently, no federal district court allows cameras in the courtroom, and only the Second and Ninth Circuits permit civil appellate arguments to be televised. None of the federal appellate courts presently allow criminal appeals to be recorded.[39] There are indications that this practice may change, however, as the House Judiciary Committee approved the Judicial Reform Act in March, 1998 that would allow cameras in both the district courts and the appellate courts at the discretion of the presiding judge.[40] The bill would require a three-year experiment in the district courts, while the use of cameras would be permanent in the appellate courts.[41]

The difficulty facing the judiciary regarding cameras in the courtroom is balancing the perceived First Amendment rights of a free press, the defendant's Sixth and Fourteenth Amendment rights to a fair trial, and the right to privacy issues of the witnesses and jurors. The link and tension between the First Amendment and the Sixth Amendment was apparent to the Founding Fathers of the Constitution.[42] "[In an early version of the First Amendment, James Madison combined both freedom of the press and the right to a fair trial by jury, but it was rejected by the U.S. Senate."[1]

For the past several decades, the media has devoted a great deal of attention to televising high profile cases for one single reason: people are interested. As a result, the media will closely follow eases of interest to the public whether or not there is a live broadcast. A sensational trial showcases the role that media has come to play in the criminal justice system. The public becomes obsessed with high profile eases and now the public has a twenty-four hour outlet for such interests -- Court TV.

This book seeks to provide useful and relevant information to aid judges, lawyers, legal scholars, media groups and the public at large in making decisions about the appropriateness of permitting live electronic coverage of courtroom trials both as general rule and in individual cases. To aid in the discussion of cameras in the courtroom, this book will focus on the electronic trial coverage conducted by the Courtroom Television Network (Court TV).

Chapter 2 will provide a historical background analysis of cameras in the courtroom. An in-depth overview of the early and modem history of cameras in the courtroom is conducted. In addition, special attention is given to the O.J. Simpson criminal trial. The Simpson trial, more than any other case, has propelled the cameras in the courtroom debate onto the public agenda. While the issue was debated by the attorneys before the Simpson trial, the subsequent debate has occurred mostly in judicial and academic circles. The current federal ban on cameras in federal courts also is discussed, as well as the current status of cameras in courtrooms at the state level and federal experimentation.

Chapter 3 describes the development of Court TV. It explains some of the history behind its beginnings and the method of operation. It also explains the way that trials are chosen for broadcast and some of the bumps along the way in its brief history. Chapter 4 addresses Criticism of Cameras in the Courtroom. It explores the potential impact of coverage on the trial process and participants, including judges, lawyers, witnesses and jurors. It also considers issues of public impact and confidence in the justice system.

Chapter 5 discusses the public perception of the judicial system. It reports on various studies of public perception and their findings as they relate to concerns over televised coverage of the process. Chapter 6 reports on various empirical studies of the effects of television coverage on the trial process and on public impact. This includes numerous state studies and the federal pilot project. Chapter 7 summarizes and discusses conclusions that can be drawn from the issues raised throughout the book. In addition, this chapter discusses the future of cameras in the courtroom and offers some recommendations about the future course of public policies regulating cameras in the courtroom at the state and federal levels.

Chapter 2

BACKGROUND OF CAMERAS IN THE COURTROOM AND THE PRESENT DAY RULES

OPEN TRIALS AS THE NORM

There is no evidence that criminal trials were ever held in private under the English common law, even at the request of the defendant.[1] The concept of a public trial was seen as "a means of protecting the integrity of the & look trial and a guard against the partiality of the court."[2] Open criminal trials can be traced back to Anglo-Saxon trials that were conducted before, and judged by, the "freemen" of the community.[3] Following the Norman conquest, Norman kings added the jury system to public trials.[4] Colonists in the New World maintained the jury system and open trials by placing these concepts in colonial charters and state constitutions.[5] When the colonies declared independence from England, the tradition of determining a person's guilt or innocence by a public jury trial remained in the form of the Sixth Amendment to the Constitution.[6]

With the opening of the courts in post-revolutionary America, the actual rooms were built to accommodate large groups of people. The size of the courtroom was designed to give any interested citizen space to observe the judicial process in action. Because communities were relatively small in the early days of the nation and the focus on news and crime generally localized, it was possible for everyone to attend in person.

What our Founding Fathers couldn't anticipate, in all their wisdom, was the exponential growth of the U.S., in both population and territory, side by side with technological and communications advances. The escalation in population raised the challenge of maintaining a spirit of inclusion, since courtrooms increasingly were built to hold fewer people, and logistical considerations made easy access problematic. At the same time, major trials became a topic of not simply local, but national interest.

Fast-forward to the late 20th Century. Television's ability to place the viewer at remote locations and bring an unbiased eye to the proceedings are major factors in resolving this concern, with the lower courts in the last decade embracing the camera.[7]

SCOPES AND HAUPTMANN - THE SIMPSON OF THEIR ERA

Until 1935, cameras and newsreel photographic equipment were widely permitted in trial court proceedings. For example, cameras, newsreel photography and radio microphones were permitted at the 1924 trial of Leopold and Loeb, represented by Clarence Darrow, and the 1925 trial of John T. Scopes in which Darrow and William Jennings Bryan served as opposing counsel.

The "monkey-trial" of John Scopes, held in 1925 in Dayton, Tennessee, has been described as one of the greatest media circuses of all times.[8] The nine-day trial before Judge John Raulston was a challenge to a Tennessee law forbidding the teaching of evolutionary theories that denied biblical creation.[9] Despite the fact that many of his colleagues on the bench were banning cameras, Judge Raulston welcomed both cameras and radio coverage of the Scopes trial.[10]

In or about 1935, attitudes toward in-court coverage of judicial proceedings changed dramatically, when Bruno Richard Hauptmann was accused, convicted and subsequently executed for the kidnapping and slaying of the 18-month old son of Charles Lindbergh. The *Hauptmann* trial generated immense public interest, and immense photographic and radio coverage, both in-court and out-of-court. Hauptmann was accused of the kidnap and murder of the infant son of famed aviator Charles Lindbergh.[11] Because Lindbergh was the first person to make a successful transatlantic flight, the case drew world-wide interest.[12] More than 700 members of the international press descended upon Flemington, New Jersey to cover the trial.[13] Crowds of citizens, as many as 20,000 per day, lined the streets around the courthouse,[14] and savvy entrepreneurs sold souvenirs such as a mini-ladder that represented the ladder used in the kidnaping.[15] The courtroom, which had a seating capacity of 260, had up to 275 spectators and witnesses crammed within its walls.[16] Attorneys for both sides issued subpoenas to their friends, with the notion they may be called as witnesses, in order for them to be present in the courtroom.[17] The local sheriff collected "donations" from people who sought a seat in the courtroom.[18] When the governor demanded that he cease, scalpers in New York began selling seats for $100 to $500 each.[19] Due to the number of people, the courtroom filled with noise on several occasions, prompting the judge to threaten to have the room cleared.[20]

Even though the judge banned cameras from being used during the trial proceedings, *Hauptmann* was "the first [case] to show trial proceedings by audiovisual technology to a remote public. . .".[21] Promising to film only during recesses, cameramen persuaded Judge Thomas Trenchard to allow a camera to be placed overlooking the witness stand and jury box.[22] Judge Trenchard permitted a silent camera to be placed on the floor of the courtroom and a sound camera in the balcony.[23] The judge permitted four photographers to take still photographs and the newsreel cameras to film before the court session began, at the noon recess, and after the evening adjournment.[24] No restrictions were made upon newspaper reporters and there was no gag order placed on any of the trial participants.[25] There was only one confirmed violation of the newsreel restriction and one still photographer who knowingly violated the judge's order.[26] The sound camera was so quiet that no one knew it was running until coverage began to show up in the newsreel theaters during the trial, and the photographs were taken without anyone's knowledge until they were published in the newspapers the next day.[27] Swift action was taken by the judge to discipline the offending cameramen.[28]

Hauptmann was convicted and sentenced to death by electrocution.[29] On appeal, Hauptmann claimed the disturbances in the courtroom denied him a fair trial, but the appellate court disagreed and stated that Hauptmann should have objected to the media presence at the time of the trial.[30] The Governor of New Jersey had his doubts about Hauptmann's guilt and granted Hauptmann a last minute reprieve.[31] The public was outraged at the issuance of the reprieve and called for the governor's impeachment.[32] Reportedly still convinced that Hauptmann was innocent, but fearful of being removed from office, the governor did not renew the reprieve when it expired and Hauptmann was put to death pursuant to his sentence.[33]

Much like the O.J. Simpson trial, the circus was not really caused by cameras inside of the courtroom, but by factors outside of the courtroom.[34] The New Jersey state attorney general chose to prosecute the case himself, becoming a media star.[35]   Attorneys for both sides held daily press conferences where promises were made about iron-clad evidence that would prove Hauptmann's guilt or innocence.[36] Hauptmann's attorney even had his letterhead and business cards changed to include a red ladder and declaration of his involvement in Hauptmann trial.[37] The jurors were even offered vaudeville tours, which they all declined, but they did not accept monetary compensation for interviews to a newspaper syndicate.[38]

THE RESPONSE AT THE TIME

In response to what one observer called the "Roman Holiday" surrounding both the in-court and out-of-court media coverage of the Hauptmann trial, a national backlash emerged against the use of photographic equipment in, and the radio broadcasting and photographic publishing of, court proceedings. As part of that backlash, in 1937, the House of Delegates of the American Bar Association adopted Canon 35, which admonished judges to prohibit the taking of photographs in courtrooms and the broadcasting of court proceedings. According to Canon 35, such activities "degrade the court and create misconceptions with respect thereto in the mind of the public and should not be permitted."

This was the first time the American Bar Association (ABA) addressed the role of cameras in the courtroom.[39] Following *Hauptmann*, the ABA appointed the Special Committee on Publicity in Criminal Trials to investigate the actions of the media in that trial.[40] The committee, chaired by former Minnesota Supreme Court Justice Oscar Hallam, issued sixteen recommendations, including a ban on cameras in the courtroom punishable by contempt of court citations.[41] Once Hauptmann's appeal was over, the report was delivered to the ABA's Executive Committee, which then created a special subcommittee comprised of members of the media and the bar.[42] The goal of the subcommittee was to create standards for courts to use in highly publicized trials.[43] The report that came out of the subcommittee was much more favorable to the use of cameras in the courtroom than the report Hallam had prepared.[44] Hallam's document purported to ban all cameras from the courtroom, but the subcommittee report stated cameras should be used in a courtroom only when the presiding judge had expressly approved of their use.[45] Without taking the subcommittee report into consideration, the ABA's Committee on Professional Ethics and Grievances amended Canon 35 of the Canons of Professional and Judicial Ethics to included a ban on courtroom cameras.[46] As created, Canon 35 read:

Proceedings in court should be conducted with fitting dignity and decorum. The taking of photographs in the courtroom, during sessions of the court or recesses between sessions, and the broadcasting of court proceedings are calculated to detract from the essential dignity of the proceedings, degrade the court and create misconceptions with respect thereto in the mind of the public and should not be permitted.[47]

Following the ABA's lead, Congress enacted Rule 53 of the Federal Rules of Criminal Procedure which banned all camera or radio coverage of criminal cases before a federal court.[48]   In 1952, audio-visual technology was crude, and when placed in courtrooms, cameras and other recording devices could intrude upon the dignity and conduct of the proceedings. In 1952, participants might claim to feel self-conscious, intimidated or distracted by the presence of the obtrusive technology. In 1952, Canon 35 was amended to specifically prohibit television cameras in the courtroom.[49] However, under the 1952 revision, television cameras were permitted for naturalization proceedings.[50] The press was upset with both Canon 35 and the new federal rule for what it believed was an interference with its First Amendment rights.[51] The media argued that photographs and broadcasts could take place without interrupting the criminal proceedings.[52]

By the 1950s, Canon 35 was adopted in all but Colorado, Oklahoma, and Texas, where experiments with cameras continued.[53] The first case to be broadcast on television was State v. Manley[54] on December 13, 1953 in Oklahoma City.[55] Television cameras were placed in a e special booth in the back of the courtroom, a microphone was hidden near the front of the room, and special lights were placed in the chandeliers.[56] Judge A. P. Van Meter had a button on his desk that he could push if he chose to stop camera coverage.[57] The swearing in of the jurors, part of the trial testimony and sentencing were the only events seen on local Oklahoma television stations.[58] On September 3, 1958, the Oklahoma Court of Criminal Appeals upheld the use of cameras in the courtroom on the ground that a criminal trial is a public event.[59] The court determined that the use of cameras in the courtroom were within the discretion of the presiding judges, "subject to certain general standards of dignity and decorum."[60]   The court went on to state that Canon 35 was an unwarranted "presumption" and that the ABA should not try to legislate the courts.[61]

Although Oklahoma was experimenting with cameras in the courtroom, Colorado was the first to allow the permanent use of cameras.[62] The presiding judge had the authority to decide on a case-by-case basis whether to allow camera coverage and no camera footage could be taken of a witness or juror who objected to such coverage.[63]

The presence of cameras during trial has not been the only issue regarding cameras that many defendants have claimed violated their rights. Defendants have also claimed that camera coverage made prior to trial violated their due process rights under the Sixth and Fourteenth Amendments. They have argued that pretrial publicity contaminated the jury pool and created a presumption of guilt in the minds of the jurors. They also have argued that the members of the jury carried these presumptions to the deliberations despite orders to determine guilt based only on the evidence presented in court.[64] An example of this phenomenon occurred in *Rideau v. Louisiana*[65] where the defendant claimed that the broadcast of his confession recorded on "motion picture film with sound track" prejudiced the jury pool beyond the point where he could receive a fair trial. The majority of the Supreme Court agreed. In *Rideau*, the defendant was charged with robbing a bank, kidnaping and murder.[66] Following his arrest, a twenty-minute "interview" conducted at the jail by the sheriff in which the defendant confessed to the crimes was recorded and broadcasted on television three times prior to his court date.[67] The defendant asked for a change of venue because he did not believed he couldn't receive a fair trial based on the vast numbers of people that saw his confession.[68] The trial court denied his motion and he was subsequently convicted and sentenced to death.[69] Justice Stewart, writing for the Supreme Court, declared:

> It was a denial of due process of law to refuse the request for a change of venue, after the people of [the] Parish had been exposed repeatedly and in depth to the spectacle of Rideau personally confessing in detail to the crimes with which he was later to be charged. For anyone who has ever watched television the conclusion cannot be avoided that this spectacle, to the tens of thousands of people who saw and heard it, in a very real sense was Rideau's trial — at which he pleaded guilty to murder. Any subsequent court proceedings in a community so pervasively exposed to such a spectacle could be but a hollow formality.[70]

FIRST AMENDMENT IMPLICATIONS

Media involvement again reached the Court in a different form several years later. In a case of first impression, the conflict between the First Amendment right to a free press and the due process rights of the accused was examined by the Supreme Court in 1965. The case against Texas businessman Billie Sol Estes[71] on charges of swindling was subjected to vast regional pretrial coverage.[72] The pretrial hearings were broadcasted live via both television and radio.[73] The Court noted that there were at least twelve cameramen in the courtroom with their equipment and wires "snaked across the courtroom floor."[74] There was no doubt in the Court's mind that the cameramen caused considerable disruption.[75] At a pretrial hearing, the defense asked for, but was denied, a ban on camera and radio coverage of the trial. Instead, the defense was granted nearly a month continuance, during which a special booth for cameras was built in the back of the courtroom.[76] Live broadcasting with sound of the trial was not permitted for much of the trial, but silent recording was allowed although not utilized, throughout the proceedings.[77] In fact, only the State's opening statements, closing statements, the return of the verdict and the judge's receipt of the verdict were carried live.[78]

The Court, in a plurality decision, decided that Estes was denied a fair trial because of the presence of the cameras in the courtroom and overturned his conviction.[79] It was noted by the Court that coverage of the actual trial was more in compliance with due process, but it was determined that the widely publicized pretrial hearings, some conducted within the presence of the jury, were enough to violate due process.[80] Beginning with the Sixth Amendment right to a public trial, the Court reiterated the fact that the public trial was a right guaranteed to the accused, not to the press, for the purpose of preventing secret hearings. Looking next at the argument furthered by the media -- that to exclude cameras meant to limit the First Amendment rights guaranteed to the press -- the Court responded by saying the freedom of the press is subjected to fairness within the justice system.[81] Justice Clark explained that all members of the press should be permitted to report whatever occurs in open court, but the presence of the press should not be an undue burden on the goal of fairness central to our judicial system.[82] Justice Clark went on to reason that when advances in technology made the use of cameras in courtrooms less disruptive, a different ease would present itself.[83]

The Court came close to establishing a per se ban on cameras in the courtroom in the *Estes* case. In fact, many courts across the nation acted as though a per se ban on cameras had been handed down and enforced a prohibition on camera coverage.[84] The plurality believed cameras caused inherent unfairness in the judicial system.[85] In particular, the Court was concerned with the impact television cameras would have on jurors, witness testimony, the trial judge, and the defendants.[86] The Court made assumptions regarding the impact of cameras instead of doing empirical studies on the effects of cameras.[87]

Justice Harlan believed the circumstances surrounding the *Estes* case were unconstitutional, however he did not agree with the plurality that cameras were per se unconstitutional. In his concurrence, he wisely stated, "the day may come when television will become so commonplace an affair in the daily lives of the average person as to dissipate all reasonable likelihood that its use in courtrooms may disparage the judicial process."[88] His concurrence, therefore, limited *Estes* to its facts, as would be evidenced in later cases before the Supreme Court.[89]

Perhaps the most evident example of the conflict between the freedom of the press and the right to due process is the Sam Sheppard[90] murder case. Sheppard was accused of killing his pregnant wife in a suburb of Cleveland, Ohio in 1954.[91] The press had front page editorials and headlines for more than twenty days leading up to the trial.[92] Five volumes worth of news clippings were compiled that highlighted the incriminating evidence against Sheppard, the discrepancies in his story, and affairs he allegedly had with several woman.[93] Sheppard was not granted a change of venue nor was his jury sequestered.[94] A table was placed inside the bar between the counsel table and the jury box for the press to utilize.[95] Cameras were not permitted to be used during the proceedings, but were allowed during recesses.[96] The judge, witness and jurors were all photographed and interviewed extensively.[97] Despite a loud-speaker system in the courtroom, witnesses and attorneys often had trouble being heard because of the movements of the media representatives.[98] Furthermore, reporters made it difficult, if not impossible, for Sheppard to speak confidentially with his attorney during the trial.[99]

U.S. District Court Judge Weinman ruled that the trial was "a mockery of justice." He said the trial "fell far below the minimum requirements of due process of law." Actions which Judge Weinman said violated Sheppard's constitutional rights included: the failure of the trial judge to grant a change of venue due to extensive pretrial publicity; the inability of the court to empanel unbiased jurors; the failure of the trial judge to remove himself when there were questions of his impartiality; improper admittance of lie detector evidence; and unauthorized communication with the jury.

The Supreme Court accepted the Sheppard case on the pretrial publicity issue. In an eight-to-one decision that Sheppard was denied a fair trial, Justice Clark stated:

> While we cannot say that Sheppard was denied due process by the judge's refusal to take precautions against the influence of pretrial publicity alone, the court's later rulings must be considered against the setting in which the trial was held. In light of this background, we believe that the arrangements made by the judge with the news media caused Sheppard to be deprived of that "judicial serenity and calm to which (he) was entitled.[100]

The Court believed the majority of the blame for Sheppard not receiving a fair trial rested with the presiding trial judge.[101] As a result of the media's actions and the court's failure to control the media, Sheppard's conviction was reversed.

Following the *Estes* and *Sheppard* cases, the ABA once again reviewed the issue of cameras in the courtroom. The new code included a ban on camera coverage much like Canon 35. In fact, Canon 3A (7) was really just a revision of Canon 35.[102] The revised canon now permitted camera coverage for limited purposes, such as making a court record, and coverage could only be viewed by students for educational purposes or by court personnel.[103]

PRIOR RESTRAINTS BEFORE TRIAL

The trial court judge is the person assigned the role of securing a fair trial for the defendant. The actions the judge may take must be weighed between the fairness to the defendant and the fairness to the press.[104] Recognizing that prior restraints on media coverage are serious infringements on First Amendment rights, the Supreme Court in 1976 held that prior restraints could be imposed in certain limited situations.[105] In *Nebraska Press Association v. Stuart*,[106] the Court struck down a restrictive order issued by the trial court and amended by the Nebraska Supreme Court. The underlying case centered on the murder of six family members in a small town of about 850 people.[107] Both the State and the defense requested an order restricting pretrial media coverage of the case.[108] The trial court granted the requested motion. Members of the press, seeking to have the gag order vacated, went to the district court and sought to intervene in the case.[109] The district court allowed the press to intervene and entered its own restrictive order prohibiting the reporting of five specific topics until after the jury was seated.[110] The press then appealed to the Nebraska Supreme Court, which modified the order to prohibit reporting of three issues.[111] The five-member majority of the United States Supreme Court held that the requirements of prior restraint were not satisfied.[112] To ease the uncertainty of the constitutionality of prior restraints, the Court created a three-pronged balancing test.[113] Chief Justice Burger wrote that the Court had to:

> examine the evidence before the trial judge when the order was entered to determine (a) the nature and extent of pretrial news coverage; (b) whether other measures would be likely to mitigate the effects of unrestrained pretrial publicity; and (e) how effectively a restraining order would operate to prevent the threatened danger.[114]

Using this test, the Court found that the pretrial coverage could have been dealt with using less restrictive means than a prior restraint.[115] Therefore, if less restrictive alternatives are available to the trial court, prior restraints on the media are not an option.[116] Notwithstanding this ruling, many courts have attempted to side step this holding by prohibiting not the press coverage, but prohibiting the participants in the ease from speaking to the press.

Retreating from the favorable First Amendment stance taken in *Nebraska Press Association*, the High Court has retained the ability to close pretrial hearings to the public and to the press.[117] Closing court proceedings prevents the media from publishing prejudicial material due to the fact that the media is not exposed to such information.[1] It is this lack of access that the press contends is unconstitutional.

Although members of the press have asserted a constitutional right to be present, not only at a criminal trial, but also at any pretrial hearings under the First, Sixth and Fourteenth Amendments, the Court has declared that no such right exists. In *Gannett Co. v. DePasquale*,[119] a five to four majority recognized that the Sixth Amendment "permits and even presumes open trials as a norm,[120] but opined that the Constitution does not require a pretrial be open to the public when the trial participants agree that closure is the best way to assure a fair trial.[121] The Court noted that the purpose of a pretrial hearing, to screen out inadmissible evidence, would be undermined if potential jurors received that evidence by media publicity.[122] The Court stated that:

> When such [inadmissable prejudicial] information [about the defendant] is publicized during a pretrial proceeding...it may never be altogether kept from potential jurors. Closure of pretrial proceedings is often one of the most effective methods that a trial judge can employ to attempt to insure that the fairness of a trial will not be jeopardized by the dissemination of such information throughout the community before the trial itself has even begun.[123]

The Court then reiterated the right to a public trial was personal to the accused and that the Sixth Amendment did not guarantee the public nor the press any right of access to the proceedings.[124] Additionally, the Court determined that the press had no First Amendment claim to access to the pretrial proceedings because the denial of access was only temporary and a transcript of the hearing was made available to the public after the danger of prejudice had passed.[125]

In the mid-1970s, state courts began authorizing broadcast coverage of judicial proceedings, on either an experimental or permanent basis. In 1979, the Florida Supreme Court conducted its own one-year experiment of the effects of using electronic media in the courtroom, whereby many of the concerns raised in the *Estes* case were empirically tested.[126] Based on the findings of that study, documented in *In re Petition of Post-Newsweek Stations, Florida. Inc.*,[127] the Florida Supreme Court decided to open the Florida courts to electronic media coverage on a permanent basis.[128] In so doing, the Florida Supreme Court revised Canon 3A(7) of the Florida Code of Judicial Conduct to allow cameras and other electronic media devices subject to the discretion of the presiding trial judge.[129] It was the opinion of the court that neither the First nor the Sixth Amendment mandated the use of electronic media, but those amendments also did not forbid per se the use of electronic media in the judicial system.[130]

Throughout the 1980s, several cases challenged the federal courts' prohibition on electronic media coverage.[131] The challenge to the constitutionality of the revised Florida Canon 3A(7) came in 1981 with the case of *Chandler v. Florida*.[132] Basing their appeal on the interpretation that *Estes* declared that electronic coverage was inherently a violation of due process, the defendants, claimed without an express showing of prejudice, that the presence of one television camera and the broadcast of a portion of their trial denied them their constitutional rights.[133] In writing for an unanimous Court, Chief Justice Burger declared *Estes* was distinguishable from *Chandler*, and because of Justice Harlan's limiting concurrence, should be read only in light of the facts of that case.[134] The Court declared that "[t]he risk of juror prejudice in some cases does not justify an absolute ban on news coverage of trials by the printed media and broadcast coverage.[135] Furthermore, since the circus-like atmosphere surrounding the *Estes* case was not present in *Chandler*, the Court refused to agree with the defendants that electronic coverage of their trial was unconstitutional.[136] Instead the Court held that, "[a]bsent a showing of prejudice of constitutional dimensions,"[137] electronic media could be permitted in the courtroom.[138] The Court went on to conclude that the Constitution did not prohibit states from conducting experiments with electronic equipment in their courtrooms.[139] Combining the decisions of *Estes* with that of *Chandler* provides the general ruling that the Constitution neither requires nor prohibits the use of television cameras in the courtroom setting.[140]

In the 1980 case of *Richmond Newspapers, Inc. v. Virginia*,[141] the Supreme Court recognized for the first time that the right to attend criminal trials was implicitly guaranteed in the First Amendment.[142] Recounting the rich common-law history of open trials and the importance of the public having knowledge of the judicial system,[143] the Court ruled that a criminal trial must be open to the public absent a stated overriding.[144] The High Court observed, however, that the right of the public to attend criminal trials was not absolute and could be limited in the interests of the fair administration of justice.[145] The Court later upheld the ruling of *Richmond Newspapers* in *Globe Newspaper Co. v. Superior Court*,[146] when it struck down, on First Amendment grounds, a Massachusetts law requiring the exclusion of the public and press during trials involving sexual crimes against minors.[147] The *Globe* Court held that the state must show a compelling governmental interest before it can constitutionally close a trial to the public and press.[148] The Court held that, the right of access to trial rests on the necessity that the public, and the press as its surrogate, know as much as is possible about how the judicial process functions, both in particular cases, and, as a whole:

> [T]he right of access to criminal trials plays a particularly significant role in the functioning of the judicial process and the government as a whole. Public scrutiny of a criminal trial enhances the quality and safeguards the integrity of the fact-finding process, with benefits to both the defendant and to society as a whole .... And in the broadest terms, public access to criminal trials permits the public to participate in and serve as a check upon the judicial process - an essential component in our structure of self-government.

Until 1983, defendants almost always objected to trials subject to the electronic eye. However, in *United States v. Hastings*,[149] the defendant, federal judge Alcee Hastings, requested cameras to be permitted at his trial on the charges of accepting bribes so that his reputation could be restored.[150] He claimed his Sixth Amendment right to a public trial demanded cameras be allowed.[151] Members of the press then intervened asserting they had a First Amendment right to televise the trial based on the Supreme Court's decision in *Chandler*.[152] The district court denied the request to have cameras in the courtroom, stating that Rule 53 of the Federal Rules of Criminal Procedure prohibited the use of cameras in Federal courts.[153] The Eleventh Circuit Court of Appeals agreed, declaring that the *Chandler* Court determined that the use of cameras was not inherently unconstitutional, not that cameras were constitutionally mandated.[154] The court went on to define the First Amendment right of the press to attend trials did not include bringing recording devises with them.[155] The court asserted that the trial was public without the inclusion of electronic equipment and that the trial was in no way closed from public viewing if cameras were banned.[156]

In 1983, a group of interested media and other organizations petitioned the Judicial Conference to adopt rules permitting electronic media coverage of federal judicial proceedings, and the Conference appointed an ad hoc committee to consider the issue. In its September 1984 report, that ad hoc committee recommended denial of the requested change. On September 20, 1984, the Conference adopted the Committee's report, denying the permission of electronic media.

Shortly after the *Chandler* decision the American Bar Association made significant revisions to Canon 3A(7) of its Model of Conduct to permit judges the authority to broadcast, televise, record, or photograph civil and criminal proceedings subject to appropriate guidelines. The Canon was ultimately removed from the ABA's Code of Conduct based on a determination that the subject of electronic media coverage in courtrooms was not directly related to judicial ethics and was more appropriately addressed by administrative rules adopted within each jurisdiction.[157]

The Supreme Court again returned to the issue of pretrial closure one year later with the 1984 case of *Waller v. Georgia*.[158] In that ease, the Court determined that the Sixth Amendment right to a public trial extended to a pretrial suppression hearing.[159] The Court stated that such a hearing resembles a bench trial and often is, due to plea bargaining, the only trial a defendant has.[160] The Court reiterated that closure can only be justified when there is an overriding interest expressed and that closure must be narrowly defined to protect those interests, and further stated "the explicit Sixth Amendment right of the accused is no less protective of a public trial than the implicit First Amendment right of the press and public."[161] Therefore, when the defendant objects to closure of a pretrial suppression hearing, the party seeking closure must show an overriding interest will be prejudiced or the hearing must be open.[162] In *Waller*, the closure of the entire suppression hearing was excessively broad to meet the acceptable standards laid out by the Court. If the lower court found that a portion of the suppression hearing met the correct standard, then that portion alone could be closed.[163]

The Supreme Court reiterated the fact that the public and the press have a valid First Amendment right to be present at pretrial hearings when it decided *Press-Enterprises v. Superior Court*[164] because of the tradition of open pretrial hearings and the important role open proceedings have in the judicial system.[165] In this case, the defendant claimed he would be denied a fair trial if his pretrial hearing was open to the public and press. The Court stated:

> If the interest asserted is the right of the accused to a fair trial, the preliminary hearing shall be closed only if specific findings are made demonstrating that, first, there is a substantial probability that the defendant's right to a fair trial will be prejudiced by publicity that closure would prevent and, second, reasonable alternatives to closure cannot adequately protect the defendant's fair trial rights.[166]

The Court further stated a risk of prejudice alone was not enough to warrant closure and that the right of the public and the press as guaranteed under the First Amendment "cannot be overcome by the conclusory assertion that publicity might deprive the defendant of that right."[167]

In *Mu'Min v. Virginia*,[168] a case of first impression, the Supreme Court examined the issue of how extensively the defendant may inquire about prior knowledge of a case due to pretrial publicity in voir dire. The Court decided the trial court need only determine that the potential juror has not formed a prior opinion of the defendant's guilt or innocence.[169] The court held that there was no need for the lower court to empanel a jury that was "totally ignorant" of the case, merely a jury that could base their verdict on the facts heard in the courtroom.[170]

In 1988, the Judicial Conference appointed a second Ad Hoc Committee on Cameras in the Courtroom "to review recommendations from other Conference committees on the introduction of cameras for the courtroom, and to take into account the American Bar Association's ongoing review of Canon 3A(7) of its Code of Judicial Conduct".[171] In September 1990, after receiving input from news organizations and a letter from U.S. Representative Robert Kastenmeier, then Chair of the House Judiciary Committee's Subcommittee on Courts, Intellectual Property, and Administration of Justice, the ad hoc committee recommended that the Judicial Conference: (1) strike Cannon 3A(7) from the Code of Conduct for United States Judges, and include a policy on cameras in the courtroom in the *Guide to Judiciary Policies and Procedures*; (2) adopt a policy statement expanding permissible uses of cameras in the courtroom; and (3) authorize a three-year experiment permitting camera coverage of certain proceedings in selected federal courts.[172]

In September 1990, the Judicial Conference adopted these recommendations[173] and authorized the three-year pilot program allowing electronic media coverage of civil proceedings in selected federal trial and appellate courts, subject to guidelines approved by the Judicial Conference. The Federal Judicial Center (FJC) agreed to monitor and evaluate the pilot program. In its final report to the Conference in March 1991, the ad hoc committee recommended the following pilot courts for the experiment: the U.S. District Courts for the Southern District of Indiana, District of Massachusetts, Eastern District of Michigan, Southern District of New York, Eastern District of Pennsylvania, and Western District of Washington; and the U.S. Courts of Appeals for the Second and Ninth Circuits. The pilot courts were selected from courts that had volunteered to participate in the experiment. Selection criteria included size, civil caseload, proximity to major metropolitan markets, and regional and circuit representation. The use of size, civil caseload, and location in metropolitan areas as criteria reflected a concern that smaller and less metropolitan courts would not have enough cases with high media interest to support evaluation of the program.

After the ad hoc committee selected the pilot courts and approved the FJC's proposed evaluation methods, the Conference discharged the ad hoc committee and assigned oversight of the pilot program to the Judicial Conference Committee on Court Administration and Case Management.

PILOT PROGRAM GUIDELINES

The pilot program began on July 1, 1991, and ran through December 31, 1994.[174] The program authorized coverage only of civil proceedings and only in the courts selected for participation in the pilot program. The guidelines adopted by the Judicial Conference required reasonable advance notice of a request to cover a proceeding; prohibited photographing of jurors in the courtroom, in the jury deliberation room, or during recesses; allowed only one televison camera and one still camera in trial courts (except for the Southern District of New York, which was permitted to allow two cameras in the courtroom for coverage of civil proceedings) and two television cameras and one still camera in appellate courts; and required the media to establish "pooling" arrangements when more than one media organization wanted to cover a proceeding. In addition, discretion rested with the presiding judicial officer to refuse, terminate, or limit media coverage. At the end of the three-years, the response by the judges involved with the experiment was favorable to opening of the courtroom to the electronic media, however, after only twenty-minutes of deliberations, the experiment was suddenly ended.[175] In 1996, however, the Judicial conference reversed itself and currently allows the circuit courts to decide for themselves whether to allow cameras.[176] Presently only the Second and Ninth Circuits have decided affirmatively to allow cameras to televise arguments.[177]

As a result of the Simpson trial, the public and politicians have grown less confident in the judicial system, and the blame for that lack of confidence has been passed onto the cameras in the courtroom. Following the trial, discussions arose about the necessity of an unanimous jury verdict, the ability to have a fair trial in a multiracial society, and the presence of camera observation of trials.[178] The Simpson civil trial was drastically different from the criminal trial in that Judge Fujisaki not only banned cameras from the courtroom, but placed a gag order on all the participants.[179]

Since the O.J. Simpson trial, State governments have been reviewing their laws regarding cameras. In California, then Governor Pete Wilson proposed a bill that would have ended the threat of another O.J. circus by forbidding cameras to observe trials.[180] However, the California legislature did not agree and, as a result, cameras are still permitted in the courtroom, subject to the judge's discretion.[181] Although the legislature allows cameras, judges have been forbidding cameras more frequently, and in cases that they would probably have allowed them prior to the Simpson trial.[182] Following the Simpson case, New York allowed a tenyear-old law allowing cameras in the courtroom to expire with no sign that a replacement will be forthcoming, and thereby closing the doors on cameras in that state.[183] Local television news stations and Court TV have been clamoring to get their cameras back in New York since they were tossed out 1997. Thus far, only five states, including New York, have officially banned cameras from the courts.

Surveys were sent to selected people in all fifty states, Washington, D.C. and Guam in a study conducted two days after the Simpson case ended.[184]   The results covered the spectrum. Idaho, Missouri, North Dakota and Tennessee expanded the access to cameras.[185] In Maryland and Mississippi both had failed attempts at expanding camera coverage.[186] California, Georgia, and Oklahoma reviewed legislation that would ban cameras in the courtroom.[187] Expansion or experiments with cameras were delayed in Delaware, Louisiana, and Utah.[188] New Jersey, New York (immediately following the Simpson case), and Pennsylvania all seemed to have been slightly impacted, if at all, by the case.[189] In the three states that do not allow any camera coverage -- South Dakota, Indiana, and Mississippi -- the Simpson trial had no real impact on maintaining the camera ban.[190] Interestingly, twenty-one states plus Guam reported there was no significant effect on cameras as a result of the Simpson case.[191]

State courts have been far more receptive to expanding access to public trials than the federal courts. Forty-seven states allow some form of audio-visual coverage of court proceedings at the judge's discretion. The federal courts have lagged behind the states in opening the doors to cameras. While forty-seven states allow some form of camera coverage, most federal courts are still closed. Rule 53 of the Federal Rules of Criminal Procedure remains an absolute ban on cameras, with the exception of the three year experiment of camera coverage of civil trials authorized by the U.S. Judicial Conference.[192] Recently, the House Judiciary Committee approved a bill that would allow cameras in the federal courtrooms at both the district and appellate court levels upon the discretion of the judge.[193] The tide maybe changing as the federal court that tried the Oklahoma City bombing ease illustrates. In that case, the judge ordered a closed-circuit camera to broadcast the trial so that victims in Oklahoma could see the trial even though the case was being tried in Denver.[194] The Supreme Court, although petitioned several times, refused to allow cameras to televise the oral arguments in that case.[195]

LACK OF UNIFORMITY

There is a lack of uniformity today among the state and federal courts on whether to allow cameras in their court proceedings. For example, the majority of the states allow cameras into the courtroom under certain restrictions, while the federal courts generally disallow cameras, distinguishing between the right to attend a trial and the right to broadcast the trial. At the federal appellate court level, the judge is given the discretion to decide whether the trial will be broadcast or not. Some states allow defendants to object, but require that a defendant prove that he will be substantially harmed by such coverage. It is difficult to gather such evidence, let alone prove. Other states allow defendants to object to the cameras, and such objection is considered sufficient to prevent the cameras. One commentator concludes that cameras should remain out of the courtroom until there are uniform and substantial protections for all trial participants, regardless of their status in society.[196]

The Supreme Court, in *Richmond Newspapers*, stated that the print media has a First Amendment right to be present at a criminal trial, but declared that the right was not without some limitations.[197] Nevertheless, the Court refused to extend to the broadcast media the same First Amendment right.[198] Instead, the Court distinguished the print media from the broadcast media, which traditionally has been more subject to regulation.[199] The Court later defined the *Richmond Newspapers* ruling when it struck down a law that mandated the public and the press be excluded when a minor victim of sexual abuse was on the witness stand.[200] Through Justice Brennan, the Court stated the right of public access to criminal trials was protected by the First Amendment because historically trials had been open to the public, and because public access is essential for the proper functioning of the judicial system.[201]

Despite that numerous proceedings conducted within the legislative and executive branches have been televised for several years without a significant problem, the judicial branch has been slow in opening its doors to the camera. The First Amendment argument of the public's right to know, which is persuasive over both the legislative and executive branches, is less of a factor over the judiciary for two reasons: 1) courts tend to focus on personal lives rather than on governmental action, forcing the disclosure of the most personal of facts, and 2) justice is, and must be, blind.[202] That is, detached neutrality is a cornerstone of a fair trial.[203] The camera, some argue, threatens that neutrality.

Although the Supreme Court has implied that cameras are neither per se acceptable nor per se unacceptable in the courtroom under the Constitution, several lower federal courts have declared there is no First Amendment right to televise courtroom action.[204] That is why media organizations have been lobbying for the privilege, not suing for the right. Despite this trend in the lower federal courts, the Ohio Court of Appeals suggested in *Cosmos Broadcasting v. Brown*[205] that a limited First Amendment right to televise does, in fact, exist.[206]

> [U]nder the First Amendment, the concept of equal access to courtroom proceedings and the effective reporting of courtroom events means at least this: unless there is an overriding consideration to the contrary, clearly articulated in the trial court's findings, representatives of the electronic news media must be allowed to bring their technology with them into the courtroom, even if only to a small degree (e.g., a single camera).[207]

Additionally, a number of federal courts, including the Supreme Court (in Justice Stewart's concurrence in *Richmond Newspapers*) have declared the denial of cameras in the courtroom is a legitimate time, place, manner restriction.[208] The rationale has been that the restriction on cameras does not preclude the public from personally observing the proceedings, nor does it preclude the public from learning about the courtroom action by alternative methods.[209] However, Diane Zimmerman, a professor of law at New York University School of Law, argues that the restriction of cameras is not merely a time, place and manner restriction. Rather, she asserts that the refusal to allow cameras in the courtroom is a restriction on the type of content because the content of a broadcast is fundamentally different than content distributed through the print media.[210]

As Mercy Hermida stated, "Freedom of the press, in its simplest form, involves the concept that people should be able to express themselves by communicating their thoughts on paper. The media's primary purpose is to gather the news and relate what it has received to the public.[211] However, members of the media maintain that the public's right to know is sufficient to justify their "hot pursuit of criminal cases" and access to criminal trials[212] Leo Wolinsky, metro editor of the Los Angeles Times stated, "our reason for being here is not to assure whether someone gets a fair trial but to get facts out to the public in such a way that's accurate and fair. Not to report is a disservice, because the public needs to know whether the police are operating fairly."[213]   According to Jonathan Gradess, the executive director of the New York Defenders Association, which actively opposes the use of cameras in the courts, "the fundamental question is if a defendant is going to get a fair trial." He warned that the media favor high-profile cases and often offer only snippets of those cases -- doing more to exploit the grief of victims than to educate the public.[214]

THE SUNSHINE IN THE COURTROOM ACT

In March 1999, Representatives Steve Chabot and Bill Delahunt, introduced the Sunshine in the Courtroom Act to allow federal judges of every sort to permit cameras in their court, which is now banned by the Judicial Conference, the governing body of the Federal courts. Senators Chuck Grassley and Charles Schumer followed with a similar bill in the Senate. Congress has made attempts in recent years to open Federal courtrooms to cameras[215] triggered by "the Sunshine in the Courtroom Act". Delahunt believes that cameras in Federal courts would offer the public "an unfiltered, unvarnished glimpse of the judicial process. The bill would allow cameras in both appellate and trial courts. Most arguments against such a permanent authorization was the so-called circus of the O.J.

Simpson murder trial. Opponents of the bill believe that television was what made their trial a travesty, with lawyers on both sides "performing" for the cameras. It was their contention, apparently, that, if you remove the impetus for misbehavior, lawyers will behave properly. The proponents argue that the public needs to witness what goes on in courts, as opposed to being told about it or reading about it. They further argue that the court system is the creation of the public, the domain of the public and the business of the public. Trials need to be seen, blemishes and all, in order to be able to properly assess the operation of the courts. Courts are no more above public scrutiny than the executive and legislative branches.[216]

STATE LEGISLATURES

For more than a decade, state legislatures experimented with legislation allowing cameras, both still and video, into courtrooms. Most states have not been willing to fully open up their courts and allow their proceedings to be documented by still and video cameras. All but two states and the District of Columbia do provide some access to their courts, but many still require the consent of all parties, which means cameras access is rarely granted.[217]

Ruling in the spring 1999 on a series of lawsuits brought by three television stations, including Fox News in Albany, New York, judges found the 47-year old state law keeping all recording devices out of courtrooms does not violate freedom of speech and equal rights protections. The Fox lawsuit sought to get cameras in courts to cover a high-profile police brutality trial in which two Albany police officers were charged with severely beating a handcuffed student. The cameras were kept out. Even the judge who ruled in the Fox case called the law archaic. But without a public clamoring for the heightened access, even sympathy among some lawmakers has not persuaded political leaders to act.

In addition to the Fox News case in Albany, two cable stations in Manhattan challenged the 1952 law in an attempt to cover the trial of four New York City officers charged with murdering Amadou Diallo, an unarmed immigrant shot 40 times in the vestibule of his Bronx home.

The legal arguments in the lawsuits centered on the question of public access to the courtroom. According to Michael Grygiel, an Albany attorney behind all three cases", what if there are 125 seats in a courtroom and I'm the 126th and I can't fit in? The presence of cameras expands the gallery space infinitely. Should my constitutional access rights be contingent on seating arrangements in the courtroom?" Albany County

Judge Larry J. Rosen ruled to keep cameras out. His decision indicated that the law banning cameras would give lawyers ground to appeal the verdict. He further believed that if cameras were allowed in the courtroom, it would have potentially jeopardized the outcome of the case. In the same decision, however, the judge sharply criticized the ban. In urging the legislature to revisit the issue, Rosen stated that the present law discriminates against the electronic media and labeled it "hopelessly anachronistic" and in need of "permanent shelving".[218]

Grygiel maintains that the state constitution requires that the modern tools of reporting -- like cameras and recorders -- be allowed into what is otherwise an open courtroom. Grygiel and his client, Fox News, argued that blocking cameras denies direct, firsthand and unmediated access to the thousands of citizens who cannot attend a trial leaves and one stuck with second hand subjective interpretations of what occurred."[219]

The Courts are full of real-life drama that everyone can relate to. The judge is a player, the jurors are players and even the media is a player. The law becomes a format for the human drama. It is the place where there are rules and we watch the game played out. According to Steven Brill, trials with lawyers holding two opposing positions, a judge acting as an arbiter and a jury to bring closure to the matter, are "perfectly east in an understandable way". According to Henry Schleiff, the CEO of Court TV, it's only a matter of time before judges are convinced cameras can be a passive observer.[220]

Chief Justice William Rehnquist sits atop one of our three equal branches of government. He is a powerful figure who exercises immeasurable influence over all our lives. Yet when he appeared in the Senate Chamber to preside over the impeachment trial of President Clinton, it was the first time that most Americans had ever seen him in action or heard his voice. Rehnquist was a novice to television. We live in an age dominated by visual images -- but not at the Supreme Court and the lower federal court system. Rehnquist and several other Supreme Court justices adamantly oppose allowing television cameras to record the Court's public proceedings; not a single justice actively favors allowing cameras in the court. The result: the Justices, unlike officials of the other two branches, operate virtually behind close doors.

Over the years, studies have been conducted to test a wide variety of claims that cameras are harmful to the judicial system. Most studies, which will be discussed in more detail in subsequent chapters, have concluded that cameras do not cause the harm that the *Estes* Court feared. There seems to be little evidence that cameras have a negative impact upon the judge,[221] jury[222], witnesses,[223] or attorneys.[224] Further, there is evidence that television cameras are beneficial to educating the public about our judicial system.[225]

Chapter 3

THE DEVELOPMENT OF COURT TV

It is evident that cameras in the courtroom remains a controversial topic. The latest, and predictably controversial, step in the broadcast of court proceedings was the creation of the Courtroom Television Network (Court TV). Court TV, which specializes in extended gavel-to-gavel coverage of criminal and civil trials, is a 24-hour a day cable legal news network that reports on the judicial systems in both the United States and abroad.[1]

It is evident that Court TV is a different network than most others. When Court TV was asked "why a network dedicated to our legal system?" Court TV responded:

> At Court TV, we feel strongly that trials can be educational as well as entertaining. The framers of our constitution intended that trials that were important to a community be open to that community.... While [conventional news] reporting can be valuable in helping us to sort out the issues involved, it can never replace the understanding we can gain from viewing actual proceedings. Consequently, many of us have become jaded or just plain misinformed about the workings of our judicial system.

> Frankly, Court TV's goal is to substitute real law for *L.A. Law*. We want to teach people that constitutional rights aren't technicalities used by soft judges and slick lawyers, but are the bedrock of a system of rule of law that is the envy of the world.[2]

Although Court TV - the most prominent member of the genre - has altered its format and by adding law-related dramatic programming in order to improve profits, it still offers viewers coverage of live trials and analysis each weekday.

When the network premiered in 1991, it was a pioneer. Led by Steven Brill, the founder of *The American Lawyer*, Court TV got its cameras into the courtroom by convincing judges it was providing a public forum for debate. The breakthrough set a controversial standard for television coverage of trials. According to Timothy Sullivan of Court TV, who worked with Steven Brill from its inception, Brill and his colleagues created a revolution in the broadcast media in this country. They changed television journalism entirely. Before Court TV came along it was extremely rare to see courtroom television-a real courtroom-with real events. Subsequent to Court TV's creation, all cable news networks have rushed to cover trials. For cases such as Louise Woodward (the British nanny accused of murder) and O.J. Simpson, every television Network in America covered some parts of these trials. Court TV is still the only Network that covers the entire trial. Not even CNN covered the entire O.J. Simpson trial. According to Sullivan, cable news networks such as Fox, MSNBC and CNN, now feel pressured into covering the courts. According to one Court TV executive, half of what they do is covering courts. As a result of Court TV, the criminal justice system as a whole is covered in greater detail by all media.[3]

Court TV's first big splash was the William Kennedy Smith rape trial, which drew viewers more accustomed to watching soap operas. The network went on to televise the lurid double-murder trial of the Menendez brothers. Court TV has televised more than 750 court cases, including the William Kennedy-Smith case, the Simpson case, the Lorena Bobbitt case, the Menendez brothers case, the Rodney King case, the Jeffery Dahmer case and the Louise Woodward case.[4] In recent years, cases like these have helped lift the network's viewership from *2.5* million to 14 million households. Its shining moment came with the O.J. Simpson murder trial. The nation closely followed the case, and Court TV was there with gavel-to-gavel coverage. Advertisers began to pay attention, and it seemed that the network would keep its viewers past the sensational trial. (See Appendix I for a listing and brief description of trials and hearings aired from 1999 to 2001 to see the variety of cases televised).

THE CABLE INDUSTRY

There are two sides to the cable business in the United States. One side is the cable business that the average subscriber pays $20 or $40 a month to get a multitude of channels which include the national broadcast channels, government access channel of some sort, local channels, and basic cable channels like Court TV, CNN, MTV, ESPN and A&E. There are also pay TV channels like HBO, Showtime, Cinemax and pay-per-view channels.

The other half of the cable business is the advertising side of the business which pays for programming. Historically in this country we have only had CBS, ABC, and NBC and later PBS. There have always been independent stations around the country. After World War II the cable industry started. There were large areas of the country outside the reach antenna reception. This led to the eventual development of cable networks. One of the first networks was HBO. In 1972 HBO launched in Wilkes Barre, Pennsylvania as a pay TV service. The defining moment for the cable programming business began in 1975 when HBO launched its satellite - and subsequently got cable operators all around the country to install big dishes to receive HBO. As a result of this, cable operators were selling more than reception for the first time. Operators were selling a proprietary programming service, the first real national cable channel. Ted Turner, owner of the Atlanta station, WTBS, heard what Gerald Levin was doing in the cable industry and, after visiting him, started the development of WTBS, as a superstation nationally. At this time the race was on in the cable business, with the likes of ESPN, the Weather Channel and, CNN, another Ted Turner branch out of a 24-hour newschannel. Showtime, launched in 1976, followed with pay service, and Court TV eventually launched in 1991.[5]

The basic cable television networks all derive their revenue from the fees that the cable operators pay and from advertising revenue that any network advertisers pay to be on a particular network. For example, MTV makes significant money even with small ratings because its audience ranges from 18-24 year, which is the hardest audience to attract and it delivers almost exclusively. Newer networks get lower fees, while older established networks tend to garner higher fees. An example is ESPN, which started years ago, allowing ESPN to charge a fairly high fee to the cable operator to distribute its signal.

The Cable industry is a business of leverage. If the cable operator has all the leverage, it can decide at its discretion whether to distribute a particular network or not, or whether to accept the network's fees.

Eventually, if the network is successful and builds a huge consumer franchise, the leverage shifts away from the cable operator to the programmer who may say "look if you don't pay my fees we won't have a deal and you can't be on - you can't show my network."[6]

HISTORY OF COURT TV

Court TV was the creation of Yale-educated lawyer Steven Brill. Following law school, Brill began writing articles about the law for magazines such as *New York Magazine* and *Esquire*.[7] Brill's *Esquire* column about lawyers was such a success that he decided to develop his own legal magazine. Taking his journalistic knowledge and the help of his boss at *Esquire*, Brill created the legal publication *The American Lawyer*.[8] By 1985, Brill's legal newspaper was so well received that he began to expand by buying and improving local legal newsletters all across the country. As he did, quality and subscriptions of these papers rose.[9]

Wanting a new challenge, Brill had the idea to switch from print media to broadcast media.[10]

> [Brill] founded Court TV in large part because as a reporter covering trials closely [he] often was stunned by how jurors — who, unlike other members of the public, had actually seen the system up close and for real — usually came away respecting and appreciating it, and how surprised they were at how that positive view differed from the media view they had been given of law and lawyers before they had come to court.

> [Brill] really believed that if all Americans could see real instead of "L.A. Law," or Clint Eastwood movies, or apocryphal and often false accounts of litigation gone haywire, and if they could see real lawyers in public defenders' offices, and prosecutors' offices, and in small and large firms doing the work of everyday justice, they would sometimes see something to be angry about but more often see a dignified, fair — indeed inspiring — proceeding that was a model for the world.[11]

While sitting in a New York City taxi, Brill heard a confusing radio sound bite about a criminal trial. He had already demonstrated that publications that focused on legal issues could be successful. Brill "suddenly got the idea that the way to reach non-lawyers about how the system really works would be television because you can now televise trials."[12] Brill did not believe the networks would be the most appropriate place to air his vision. He wanted to show the entire trial, "the real guts of it had to be the notion of showing gavel-to-gavel or long-form coverage of trials."[13]   Brill took his idea of a network devoted to courtroom television coverage to Time-Warner. He told Steven Ross, then-chairman of Warner Communications, that his idea would be "a cross between C-Span and [a] soap opera."[14]   Time-Warner then bought out Brill's *American Lawyer* partner, Associate Newspapers.[15]

At the same time Brill was developing Court TV, Rainbow Programing Holdings (a subsidiary of Cablevision Systems Corporations) with the help of NBC also was forming a network, "In Court," devoted to live courtroom television.[16] Sharon Patrick, the CEO of Rainbow, was to run the new network.[17]

While Patrick had experience with cable, Brill had the contacts in the legal system.[18]   Cable companies, worried that the market could not support two courtroom television networks, urged the competitors to merge.[19] In late 1990, Brill convinced NBC to "fold their operation into Court TV.[20]   Brill then was able to bring in Tele-Communications Incorporated (TCI), which then controlled one-fourth of the country's cable market.[21]

Brill had intended the 1991 trial, known as the Central Park Jogger's case, to launch his new endeavor, a case against a group of black teenagers accused of the rape and near-fatal beating of a young white upscale jogger in Central Park. The initial idea was to televise the entire case. However, Court TV was denied access. The district attorney's office had joined the defense's objection to the camera's presence.[22]

Brill was convinced that the television black-out would not protect the rights of the accused or the victims. He believed that the sound-bites and interpretations coming from the courtroom would provide an "incomplete, distorted view of the courtroom and the charges brought in the case."[23]

The first day on the scene, Court TV brought a 25 year-old Florida murder case that was reopened by the defendant's son, an Ohio rape case involving a basketball star, and live coverage of a federal age discrimination case in Pennsylvania.[24] However, it was the case against William Kennedy-Smith[25] that brought Court TV into the limelight. The rape case in Palm Beach County, Florida, was carried live, and the coverage was fed to the rest of the media.[26] The national interest in the case, because of the involvement of a Kennedy and the legal issues involved, meant that the full coverage of the case by Court TV resulted in increasing the network's visibility in the public's awareness.[27] From the time the charges were filed in the case, the public wanted more and Court TV seized the opportunity to bring it to them.[28] "As Court TV was the only network broadcasting live unedited coverage of the trial proceedings, millions of Americans who were starving for information about the case tuned into Court TV for the first time."[29]

The momentum continued with the Lorena Bobbitt case. David Kaplan's *Newsweek* article detailed how millions of Americans sat glued to the television, transfixed by the Bobbitts. As more important events occurred, such as President Clinton's first major tour of Europe, Americans were more interested in what was occurring in a courthouse where Lorena Bobbitt emotionally testified. She testified to the years of physical abuse in her marriage prior to the notorious night of June 23, 1993. On that night, she testified, John came home after a night of bar hopping and raped her. She then cut off his penis with a kitchen knife as he was passed out.

Sixteen satellite-uplink trucks were positioned outside the courtroom to follow Lorena's trial. As many as two hundred reporters lined up for seats inside the courtroom. CNN carried the trial live in simulcast with Court TV. CNN doubled its ratings and was flooded with viewer complaints when it broke away from the trial to cover a Russian summit. A *Newsweek* poll found that sixty percent of the country was following the trial. John's rape trial was not even televised whereas Lorena's trial came into our living rooms every day. The nation watched as the trial played more like a daytime soap opera. Rush Limbaugh chastised the American public for their fascination with the trial but it proved too tough to resist.

By 1994 when O.J. Simpson was brought to trial on charges he brutally murdered his ex-wife and her friend, Court TV had earned "a strong reputation for serious reporting and good courtroom manners and had attracted a devoted following."[30] NBC, ABC, CBS, and CNN moved from their regularly scheduled programming to use the same live video feed as Court TV. The networks even used the same gavel-to-gavel coverage interspersed with expert commentary as Court TV used. "In a sense, anyone who watched the Simpson trial watched Court TV, proving that Court TV just about owns the television courtroom news business."[31] The Menendez[32] trial, in itself, was one of the most intensely followed legal proceedings of modern times, second only to the Simpson trial.

In 1997, Brill resigned as CEO of Court TV and sold his minority interest in American Lawyer Media to Time-Warner. The only asset Time-Warner planned to keep was Court TV, which had grown to 30 million subscribers since its creation.[33] In 1997, Time Warner bought Brill's stake in the network.

THE O.J. AFTERMATH AND COURT TV'S INTERNAL STRUGGLE

According to Dan Levinson, the Executive Vice President of Marketing of Court TV, when Court TV got started in 1991, and rapidly gained distribution system by system, it had a series of really exciting trials in the beginning - the William Kennedy Smith trial, the Menendez brothers' trial, the O.J. Simpson trial. As a result it gained huge ratings for Court TV. It just swamped the country with interest and put Court TV on the map. After the O.J. trial, America's appetite for courtroom coverage declined. It shrank dramatically and the company floundered for awhile under Brill's leadership. As the ratings fell, the partners of Court TV began bickering about the direction the network should take. Hoping to rekindle interest in trials just before Brill left, Brill hired Eric Sorenson from CBS News and Levinson to build more programming life into the model and to market trials effectively to consumers.

Levinson and others planned to narrow the focus of Court TV to be more news oriented. Levinson and Sorenson attempted to incorporate more news breaks and legal news, which would market Court TV trials more aggressively. Brill took Levinson out of HBO, where he had been for 14 years. Brill wanted to cover local trials, an idea that NBC supported but Time Warner vetoed.[34] Threats were made by several cable companies to drop Court TV and Court TV was not getting launched anywhere new. Court TV had three partners at the time, Time Warner, NBC and Liberty (which at the time was part of TCI). The three partners allegedly pushed out Brill, and Thayer Bigelow was brought in to be acting CEO. The three partners, however, continued to fight. NBC wanted to own Court TV by itself and to make Court TV a part of its news organization. On the other hand, Time Warner did not want NBC to get Court TV and instead wanted to put Court TV into its own news organization. As a result of their bickering back and forth, the partners stopped funding Court TV. Once the funding stopped, Court TV tried to manage its business for approximately a year and half. It was during this period that things started to get bad and a few cable systems dropped Court TV. In the summer of 1998, things were looking bleak for Court TV. At this point, NBC agreed to leave the partnership, but pressured the right to buy back in. Time Warner and its partner Liberty, still in the program, decided to give Court TV a shot. They hired Henry Schleiff as the CEO. Schleiff had a terrific career in the entertainment world. A lawyer by training, he worked at Viacom, and at HBO for a number of years. Schleiff had never run a network before, but ran a television operation for some of the studios and made and syndicated shows that are on television. Schleiff is considered a veteran broadcaster who most recently oversaw several issue related talk shows. Schleiff plans to inject more entertainment into Court TV's programming. Schleiff was named president and CEO of Court TV in October of 1998.[35] With Schleiff's arrival, Court TV presented a five-year plan to all of it partners, financial people and the board which consisted of Dick Parsons, who is the president of Time Warner, Terry McGuirk, president of TBS Turner Networks and Dob Bennett, the president of Liberty Media. They presented a new prime time lineup, a new generalized positioning of the network, beyond just trials and legal news. The Plan was approved by the Board of Directors. Court TV was able to secure the rights from Lifetime to the NBC show "Homicide: Life on the Streets". Court TV announced its new programming to its partners, which left the daytime trial coverage intact, but changed the network's Prime Time toward a coverage of the Criminal Justice System.[36] According to Glenn Moss, Court TV's Vice President, Business Affairs and Affiliate Relations, the most fundamental change in Court TV is its CEO, Henry Schleiff, who unlike Steven Brill, is a television guy, where as Brill was a print guy. According to Moss, Brill never felt comfortable being in the television world. Moss describes Brill as a man with a vision that if the legal system was presented in the right manner, people would come to it. According to Moss, this is not how television works, because in order to survive in the cable business you have to market it.[37] The network's fate is now currently in the hands of Schleiff. Having survived dueling owners and the lowest ratings on cable, the legal-issues network has proven that it can lure more viewers even when it is not broadcasting a sensational trial.

COURT TV'S PRIME TIME

Everything that Court TV airs between 9:00 a.m. to 5:30 p.m. is trial-oriented with reporters and expert guests that spend all day explaining the proceedings to the viewers. According to Moss, the day time programming revenues are not primarily generated by ads, as it is difficult to market and promote a trial. The schedules are not always set, and therefore requires expensive spot marketing. Moss points out that there is still a delicate balance between, on the other hand, how much a network promotes while maintaining the integrity of just reporting, and on the other hand, how it avoids turning into a perceived carnival.[38] At night Court TV broadcast programs such as Catherine Crier live talk show for a half hour. Schleiff's philosophy to embrace a more diverse audience and a larger audience for prime time schedules which complement the day time schedule of live trials. The day time schedule provides a complete picture, as opposed to "highlights", taking a sound bite and a tabloid approach. The prime time either features fictional series like "Homicide" or Court TV's original series "The System", which looks at all aspects of the legal system. By providing a full flavor for the entire trial proceeding, these programs provide original and compelling documentaries. The cable operators, as opposed to the advertiser, want to see the network provide something unique and distinctive. These programs are not anti-educational. It is not fiction and it is real.

Prime time is how the cable industry evaluates cable networks according to Dan Levinson. Court TV has different audiences. One audience only wants information, the other wants entertainment and the third wants a combination of information and entertainment. According to Schleiff, there are a variety of ways of satisfying each constituency with a mix of programming, including classic off-network series, along with Court TV's original produced products. It is significant to Court TV executives that Court TV is understood by those diverse constituents, viewers, advertisers and cable operators, that the network is about investigation. What Court TV has been able to do in 1999 is to expand its appeal and enhance its importance to the cable operators and advertisers. In the process Court TV has made its owners Time Warner and Liberty satisfied with the network's progress. Schleiff has taken what Brill had in place, smart live trial coverage, with experienced, un-biased anchors and reporters, and has build upon that foundation. The new management at Court TV told its partners in 1998 of its desire to redefine the network as a network devoted to crime and justice issues, including trial coverage and coverage of the American system of justice as a whole. As a result of the new Prime time programming the network ratings have increased steadily since 1998. In 1998 Court TV was rated as the last place network among the 38 networks that were rated. Court TV's new strategy is further evidenced by its programming crew that is in the process of producing new crime and justice related documentaries which aired first in year 2000. The following programs are examples of Court TV's new programming efforts.

Court TV, in conjunction with Cable in the Classroom, National Middle School Association (NMSA), and the nation's leading cable companies, has launched a broad-based public service initiative aimed at young adolescents. The initiative, called Choices and Consequences, spotlights the issues facing children aged 10 to 15 as they make pivotal decisions during the transition period from childhood to adolescence.

Choices and Consequences is a response to the National Television Violence Study, which stresses the negative results of violence portrayed on television without consequences. In Choices and Consequences, Court TV and the participating organizations and major cable companies have designed a response that boldly underscores the consequences of violence and includes information and resources that help young people make the all-important connection between the choices they make and the consequences that follow.

Young adolescents are the target of this initiative because this age group, more than any other, is poised to make choices and decisions that can have lifelong consequences. The study found that the curriculum decreased adolescents' verbal aggression and curbed their physical aggression. Exposure to the curriculum also increased adolescents' empathic skills and increased their knowledge of the legal system. The study divided 21 classrooms of seventh and eighth grade students from three California middle schools into experimental and control groups. Seven teachers presented the curriculum to their students in regular social studies classes. The 513 young adolescent students participating in the study came from diverse racial and socioeconomic backgrounds. In a pretest conducted prior to administering the curriculum, students in both the experimental and control groups scored relatively the same on measures of verbal and physical aggression, empathy, and legal knowledge. After half the students received the curriculum, the verbal and physical aggression scores were four percent lower in the group that received the curriculum than those in the control group. Empathy scores were eight percent higher in the curriculum group and legal term knowledge was ten percent higher. Through a broad spectrum of programs and events, Court TV and its partners hope to highlight the significance of this period in a young person's life and to foster a better understanding of the developmental needs and characteristics of the these individuals.

The initiative was announced in Washington, D.C. by Leo J. Hindery, Jr., president and chief operating officer of TCI, on behalf of leading cable companies including, Cablevision Systems Corporation, Time Warner Cable, and others who have helped carry out the initiative in local communities across the country.

HOW COURT TV OPERATES IN
THE COURTROOM

As mentioned previously, Court TV creates all of its programming and specializes in extended, "gavel-to-gavel" coverage of civil and criminal trials, both live and on tape, and supplemented by attorney commentators who explain the proceedings to a lay audience. Court TV attempts to be non-disruptive. Prior to any proceeding, Court TV works with court personnel and the presiding judge to ensure that all requirements as to placement and camera coverage are satisfied. Routinely, Court TV uses one very small, silent, stationary camera, which requires no additional lighting other than existing courtroom lighting. Placed away from the proceedings, the camera can, if necessary, be operated by remote control by a Court TV technician far from the proceedings. The wiring is unobtrusive and microphones are small and are not placed in such a way as to record conversations between attorneys and their clients. Microphones are turned off during off-the-record bench conferences and during other parts of the proceedings that are not part of the public record.[39]

Court TV provides the trial judge control over the manner in which a proceeding is transmitted or taped.

Court TV also supplements its on-air coverage with an anchorperson, who is an attorney with prior experience, and with guest attorney and judge commentators, who are present "to assist the viewers in understanding the basic procedural reasons for certain in-court events, to explain the possible range of reasons for particular substantive events, and to place the proceedings in their social and political context."[40]

Coverage is usually that of a courtroom with all the typical courtroom participants present. Court TV provides the viewers with on-screen background information in the form of subtitles, such as the name of the case and the charge, as well as the role of the current witness. This is done because many viewers do not (or cannot) watch the entire case from beginning to end.[41]

Court TV's anchorpersons are attorneys with prior knowledge of the field. They provide voice-over commentary or appear on camera to explain the status of the case (i.e., the change of witnesses, etc.) or to converse with a guest commentator, himself an attorney or judge.[42] Unlike C-Span, Court TV uses expert litigators to explain the trial proceedings. The anchorperson questions experts, whom are chosen on the basis of their expertise in the type of case being aired, during breaks in the case, recesses or at the end of the trial.[43]

COURT TV'S DAYTIME PROGRAMMING AND CASE SELECTION PROCESS

Like other commercial networks, Court TV relies on commercials for a large portion of revenue.[44] Unlike other networks where the programming is centered and created around commercials, Court TV's daytime programming does not lend itself to commercials very easily. "Breaks in the flow of a trial come when appropriate for the case or its participants, not the network and its advertisers."[45]   Court TV tries to avoid breaking into live coverage when important testimony is being given.[46] Court TV even assumes it will lose about twenty percent of their scheduled advertising due to the fact that they do not break into the trials in order to have a commercial break.[47]

Court TV faces the difficult editorial decision of what cases to air. While some cases, like the Simpson case, are obvious to be covered, most chosen for broadcast are not as obvious. Some cases make national headlines. However, the majority of cases do not, and it is up to numerous trial trackers teams to find these cases.[48] Once the case has been brought to Court TV's attention, the newsworthiness of the case must be determined. In choosing the cases that will be covered on Court TV, five criteria are routinely examined:

1) the importance of and public interest in the case;
2) the notoriety and newsworthiness of the case and the participants;
3) the quality of the story;
4) the educational value of the case; and
5) the likely duration of the case.[49]

As the name suggests the trial tracking department at Court TV, is responsible for tracking trials. Once the trials are near fruition, the trackers write a report. Every Monday Wayne Loewe, Coordinator Producer for Trial Coverage, brings the executives and producers at Court TV a packet of trials. The trial tracking department gives its sales pitch for the trials it selects. The meeting is usually attended by daytime programming staff, the field producers, the reporters, the anchors and, the documentary unit. The attendants include approximately ten producers. This stage of the selection process includes several factors: a) the interest of the stories, b) the best selection that will work on television and c) what will the viewers will find the most interesting to watch. The producers look for drama, melodrama, issues that normal people relate to, good lawyers, and lawyers with charisma and interesting to watch. The producers tend to look for trials that are short rather than long, unless it is a high profile case, such as the O.J. Simpson case which aired for nine months. Court TV's programming unit attempts to present the most interesting trials that are available. Some focus groups studies have been conducted to determine what kind of trials people are interested to watch. According to Irving Duncan, the former Coordinator Producer for Trial Coverage, the results are never surprising. Duncan, an English man from London who has had twelve years of journalism experience, states that people are interested in murders, death penalty cases and inter-family homicides. What would make it a good story, does not always make good a trial, according to Duncan, a common sentiment that he heard every Monday morning in his trial tracking department meeting. Thirty percent of the cases thrown out every week fall into the "lousy trial" category. Duncan points out that "in a perfect world we would cover all kinds of cases, even probate cases, however, Court TV is also a business that is trying to make a living. That being said, Duncan, does not think that the network will ever turn into a great profit making business.[50] According to other Court TV executives, Duncan's statement with respect to profit, proved to be wrong at least by 2002.

COURT TV'S GOAL AND IMPACT

Court TV's goal is to educate the public about a branch of government that few people are familiar with, the judicial system. Court TV emphasizes the educational value in live trial coverage. The trial coverage of the O.J. Simpson case gave people a taste of life in the courtroom and provoked a debate about media coverage that will forever be in existence. It further reminds us that if cameras were not included in the courtroom, the public would frequently know about the trial only through supermarket tabloids.

Court TV gives strong support for having the camera as a part of the courtroom. "All the reasons to have the cameras in the courtroom are there: it provides a check and balance on the judicial system and its players, it allows the public to see what goes on in the courtroom -- (the) camera inside the courtroom acts as an antidote to the abuses of the (media) circus by allowing viewers to make their own judgments independent of the circus elements."[51] Court TV is a strong believer that what goes on outside the courtroom, not inside, is the problem. The circus atmosphere that was created in the O.J. Simpson case was used to prohibit coverage in the *Selena, Polly Klass*, and second *Menendez* trials.[52]

With the majority of the states allowing cameras in their courtrooms, the impact of the heightened exposure of Court TV is considerable. Many observers believe that Court TV clearly has its advantages. These advantages include portraying a better view of justice for its viewers.[1] This improved view of justice, some believe, is created in four ways. First, Court TV essentially shows the complete trial. Its coverage is generally to be gavel to gavel, although it performs some minimal editing to fit the program on television. This allows the viewer to see and come to understand all of the significant aspects of a trial. The second advantage comes from the fact that Court TV allows public monitoring of elected officials. The public can view the trial and assess the operation of the system. This allows the public, for example, to evaluate those judges they have elected. When it comes time for reelection, they can use this information to aid their decision. Third, Court TV provides an examination of significant social issues, like acquaintance rape. The public needs to be exposed to some of these issues and may gain an enhanced view of the system by seeing that these issues are addressed. Fourth, Court TV lets the public see the significance of legal technicalities, such as rules of procedure and rules of evidence. The public can learn how and why the courts exclude some evidence from a trial. Krygier argues that, in this respect, the video camera constitutes a "thirteenth juror." The camera, he argues, helps to ensure a fair trial by making it public. In effect, Court TV educates the public.[54] Court TV's coverage has also been praised by the Yale Law Professor John Langbein, who mentioned that "cameras are an absolute godsend because the public has been educated to think that criminal trials are what they saw on *Perry Mason*, and it ain't true."[55]

Although Court TV purports to educate the public, several critics claim the network falls short of this goal in at least five ways: 1) the network leads the public to think every legal dispute is resolved inside the courtroom; 2) the network broadcasts only sensational cases; 3) Court TV ignores civil cases; 4) a majority of cases on Court TV involve violent crimes such as murder; and 5) the focus on ratings prevents Court TV from truly educating the public.[56] In an unscientific survey of 120 people in Columbus, Ohio, Angelique Paul discovered Court TV was not fulfilling its goal of educating the public. According to this survey, between sixty-six and ninety-five percent of all cases are settled out of court. Court TV focuses only on the courtroom aspect of the system. A plea bargain solves the majority of criminal cases. According to some,

Court TV, therefore, does not give the viewer a complete picture of the criminal justice system. Critics may be correct in stating that Court TV leads the public to believe most cases are handled before a judge and jury.[2] Critics also believe that Court TV focuses on sensational cases to attract audiences and boost ratings. These critics believe the ratings game have made Court TV abandon its educational goal. According to Harte, Court TV selects violent cases in order to entertain the public and gain a profit. The public's interest in violence encourages a broadcaster like Court TV to pick homicide trials to publicize, even though these cases are not as common as other cases.[58] Court TV selects cases that will provide the highest profit. They must attract a large audience. Broadcasters must edit to fit the program on television. These limits impact the quality and balance of the programming, thereby creating a distorted view of the criminal justice system.[59] It appears, however, that many people understand the fact that the sensational cases are not the norm.[60] The network also has been criticized for focusing on criminal rather than civil trials. The fact that many viewers do not yet understand the civil litigation process would suggest the need for more focus on civil cases, according to critics.[61] Fourthly, critics believe the level of violence shown on Court TV furthers the myths that violence is on the rise.[62] Finally, some experts believe Court TV's commercial nature itself draws the educational value away because the search for ratings causes the network to air trials that will grab viewers, not educate them.[63]

Another disadvantage, according to some, is that Court TV is believed by some to increase public mistrust of the system.[64] This negative outlook occurs because, as the public views the trial, it may come to its own conclusions, which may differ from that of the jury. Members of the public may then believe that they could do a more effective job than the jury. The publics' trust for the jury and the criminal justice system diminishes. One critic has stated:

> Steven Brill's newborn project, Court TV, which televises entire commentated trials, claims to provide a public service by educating viewers about the court and demystifying the judicial process. It is hard to accept that Court TV's primary goal is education, however, when financing for the televised trials was admittedly obtained by promoting the trials as a "a cross between C-Span and soap opera" The requirements of constitutional law do not necessarily make for the wonderful "education" that Mr. Brill preaches. The promise of televised trials advancing anything more than a public spectacle seems remote indeed.[65]

In response Brill made the following remarks:

> Sure it may mean that some trials replace soap operas and freak-of-the-day talk shows as daily entertainment fare.... But assuming any of us can define entertainment, let alone constitutionally distinguish it as something less worthy than news, is that trade-off of soap-opera fiction and talk-show sleaze for nonfiction justice bad, let alone something the Founding Fathers — who regularly saw trials captivate the throngs in the town square — would have wanted the government to define and prohibit?. . . No way.
>
> They understood that the dignity of the courts came from the courtroom itself and from the values on display there, and that those values would be invigorated, not undercut, by having the so-called masses there to watch...[66]

When told a network devoted to legal issues would be boring, Brill combined the same mixture of "hard reporting and dicey gossip" that had made his legal newspaper a success.[67]

Alan Dershowitz, Brill's most scathing adversary in the media vs. Courtroom area, has accused Court TV of "monopolizing the televising of trials" which he claims leads to "dangers of censorship". Dershowitz is a long time advocate of televising court proceedings, but disagrees with Court TV's emphasis on sensational, audience-grabbing cases which he believes seem to have destroyed any realistic likelihood that our judicial branch will be televised with dignity."[68] His comments address the fact that Court TV is in charge of the "pool camera" in the courtroom. All other networks get the "raw feed" from this camera, but only after the Court TV producers have decided which shots to take and which to leave out.[69] Dershowitz has proposed a C-Span-like channel, with no commercials and no commentary, would be the most dignified way to broadcast courtroom activities. According to Dershowitz:

> Just as Congress established C-Span, [I] had hoped that the judiciary might follow suit and establish "J-Span," which would cover judicial arguments and decisions in much the same way. It would be a noncommercial operation, not driven by ratings, available as a public service to the citizens interested in seeing how an important branch of our government functions.[70]

It is interesting to note that even though Dershowitz has been critical of Court TV in the past, he recently has signed up with Court TV to serve as an anchorman.

If the media were to report only the facts surrounding the issues in court proceedings, then the public would have a well balanced understanding of how our justice system works. The media, however, generally focuses more on stories about the trial's participants as they are outside the courtroom, especially if such "background" story grabs the public's attention. The fact that the story has nothing to do at all with the case or the court proceeding is irrelevant. As Roscoe C. Howard put it: "This means that the media reports stories that capture the 'public's fancy.'... [and that] the media report details... that will titillate and entertain,..."[71] These media stories are a natural attempt to sell newspapers and magazines in order to make money. This fact may be lost on the public as the public associates these accounts with the justice system. Televised coverage of trials on Court TV, in contrast, gives a more direct view of the process and its participants. Such direct access is controversial, but the controversy is not new.

COURT TV'S RESPONSE TO REACTIONS & CRITICISM

None of the executives at Court TV would disagree that their network is more commercial, profit oriented and entertainment oriented these days. On the other hand Timothy Sullivan, the Deputy Executive Producer for the day time programming, who started with Brill at Court TV, points out that "there is still quite a few of us here who still have the same goals we had when we started working for Steve, which is that, Court TV would be a serious journalistic exercise that covers the criminal justice system in a way that upholds the highest standard of journalism and I still do that. There is no question in my mind that we cover trials or that we cover criminal justice issues better, more knowledgeably and with more sophistication than any other news organization." Sullivan points out that the impeachment trial of President Clinton was covered by every network in America and obviously Court TV cannot compete with CNN or CBS when it comes to scale or breath of coverage. However, when it comes to focusing on their specialty which is the legal system, nobody can do it as well as Court TV.

Has Court TV contributed to or created a negative perception of our justice system? The perception is accurate according to the network's executives, however, Court TV takes no responsibility for its creation. The perception is created by witnessing how the courts operate by watching trials and becoming aware of the shortcomings in our criminal justice system. Sullivan states that Court TV shows people the system which led them to the conclusion that the system does not work. According to the network's executives, Court TV airs cases that are of interest to its viewers-- the general public. This boils down to a lot of sensational trials. Some executives like Timothy Sullivan are quick to point out that for example, the weather channel covers hurricanes, floods, tidal waves and tornados. They will not broadcast a show that consistently covers nice days all day long. Trials in general are rare in the American justice system. Misdemeanors, purse snatchers, burglaries and, most domestic violence cases do not go to trial. Most criminal trials are about serious crimes and most of them consist of murder cases. Sullivan states that it is not an accident that Court TV mostly covers murder cases. However, what most critics forget, is that, with or without cameras in the courtroom, sensational cases exist and are litigated in our courts across the country everyday. Court TV's function is simply to cover some of these trials. Sullivan suggests that Americans, including members of the media had little understanding of the justice system, until the creation of Court TV. Once Court TV launched its trial coverage in 1991, all other networks and news stations followed the same pattern.[72] Henry Schleiff Court TV's CEO believes that his network plays a very significant role, arguably a leading role, given that it reaches as many as 72 million households. Schleiff argues that judges who have allow Court TV into their courtrooms overwhelmingly support the experience. According to Schleiff open access removes any mystery or suspicion surrounding the proceedings and, if fact, encourages solid professional behavior because of the broader scrutiny. The benefits of opening up the courts to cameras today are similar to those of 230 years ago. Court TV, which pioneered the use of cameras in the courtroom, already has seen how effective televison can be in reaching out beyond the confines of the actual space to ensure an informed public.[73] Schleiff further believes that allowing cameras in the courtroom also offers a unique opportunity to educate the public about the judicial process and enable the American people to see directly the consequences of bad choices and inappropriate behavior.[74] In contrast to Schleiff, Levinson who is the Executive Vice President of Marketing for Court TV does not see his network as having much influence on the justice system. The only influence that Court TV has on the justice system, according to Levinson, is that people tend to better behave. Levinson believes that there is a consensus that everyone in the courtroom behaves better when the cameras are in the courtroom and people are watching the entire process. Cameras are only a fraction of the

American Courts around the country and do not contribute to the existing deficiencies in our judicial process. Levinson believes that defense attorneys as a group may tend to look poorly at cameras in the courtroom. One of the tasks of any defense counsel is to get one's client acquitted and to provide the client with a vigorous defense. Many members of the defense bar believe that the camera is an inappropriate intrusion upon their clients' rights--it makes their client look guilty to the general public. When Levinson asked whether he thought that Court TV educates the public or not, he responded that "when we go to trial, we are a conduit for the people to see what is going on in the trial, but by the same token we are educating people. We are not educating people in the sense that we are offering them our point of view. We are not picking trials that reflect some existing bias about the justice system. Court TV does not try to influence the audiences' opinion nor do they pick trials that will educate and influence the viewers one way or the other. If Congress was debating an issue related to abortion rights, C-Span would not take a position on it. Levinson, points out that CNN is not trying to reform the world, nor is Court TV's agenda to reform the justice system. Sullivan differs in his views when asked whether the network had a philosophical agenda to reform the system. Sullivan believes that if they shed enough light on the system and explain the process to the people, it will eventually improve things. He points out that the coverage of the Watergate proceedings led to reforms in our governmental system. Coverage of Congress leads to reforms in our government. Educating the people about the courts may lead ultimately to some reforms in the courts, Sullivan believes. However, Sullivan like Levinson does not believe that it is Court TV's responsibility to fix it, but to show it. Levinson comments that Court TV is a conduit-- people can just look in on the justice system and see what is going on. Viewers naturally educate themselves about the justice system by watching any trial proceedings. The more aware and educated people are the better. However, this is not Court TV's goal nor is it the Court TV's role according to Levinson. Court TV's role according to its executives, is to shine a light on the justice system and let the people decide for themselves -- that is democracy. According to Duncan Irving, the justice system is a public domain and Court TV demystifies the legal process and further provides a channel of awareness about the justice system. Many lives are at stake and people, therefore, should see the legal process at work. Court TV is a unique feature in United States, he points out, which to date has not been developed in other countries.

THE FUTURE OF COURT TV

The network, which reached its peak covering the O.J. Simpson trials, has stumbled badly ever since the verdict. It was stymied by disagreements among its three owners, a painful battle that ended in May of 1998 when Time Warner Inc. and Tele-Communications Inc. bought out the interest of NBC Corp. TCI gave Time Warner control of Court TV's board, and the two partners agreed to pump in million of dollars to revamp programming and fund a much needed advertising campaign. The eleven-year old network has a long way to go to become the powerhouse that its new CEO is hoping to develop.

It is available in 72 million homes nationwide, about half as many as receive USA Networks or TNT, and it faces increasing competition as it seeks space on other cable systems. While cable giants Time Warner and TCI have committed to expanding Court TV to another 5 million households on their systems, the network needs a fast rating boost to convince other operators to increase distribution.[75] According to Doug Jacobs, Executive Vice President and General Counsel of Court TV, during its history of televising over 750 trials and proceedings, Court TV is not aware of a single appellate decision overturning a verdict based on the presence of cameras at trial. Jacobs further states that the question is not whether trials generate publicity. The question is whether public information about trials is to come solely from second-hand summaries on the news, "spin control" press conferences, and prejudicial and inflammatory characterizations by interested third parties; or whether the public will be permitted to observe the entirety of the actual in-court proceedings - dignified, somber and under the control of the Court. It is submitted that the latter option is plainly preferable.[76] Like it or leave it, Court TV has made a major impact, and provides the viewer one and the best opportunity presently available to witness the justice system.

Chapter 4

CRITICISM OF CAMERAS IN THE COURTROOM

Any discussion of cameras in the courtroom initially focuses on the constitutional tension between the First and Sixth Amendments. The balance of a free press, as guaranteed in the First Amendment, is often in direct conflict with the rights of a fair trial before an impartial jury, as guaranteed to the defendant under the Sixth Amendment. Historically, criminal proceedings were open to the press and to the public. In the Colonial era, trial attendance was mandatory and the attendants, known as "freemen", were the ones to render the decisions. Open trials later were included in the Sixth Amendment under the Bill of Rights in order to protect the accused against unfair trial proceedings. Exceptions to the Sixth Amendment include "housekeeping" items such as preventing overcrowding of proceedings, controlling disturbances and ensuring a fair trial. Open trials provide a "check" on the system of judicial proceedings by safeguarding against an unfair trial, ensuring that the judges are doing their job properly, and helping to prevent perjury.[1]

The Sixth Amendment rights may conflict with the First and the Fourteenth Amendments which generally provide that Federal and state governments are forbidden from curtailing the freedom of the nation's communication media. The rights of an accused "a speedy and public trial may also conflict with the First and Fourteenth Amendments."[2] These rights are granted, not to the public, but to an accused.[3] Specifically, the Sixth Amendment requires that an accused be provided with "an impartial jury of the state and district wherein the crime shall have been committed."[4] Generally, freedom of the press cannot be restricted unless the publications are "a serious and imminent threat to the administration of justice."[5] This interpretation of the freedom of the press is based on the theory that "a trial is a public event, and what transpires in the courtroom is public property."[6] While the purpose of a public trial is to prevent injustice by secretive governmental persecution, the court has not declared that the Sixth Amendment guarantees the right to broadcast a criminal trial.[7] In fact, the court has ruled a trial may only be broadcast if the trial court takes sufficient measures to protect the accused's Sixth Amendment rights.[8]

More than 50 years since television swept the country, many lawyers still adamantly oppose allowing cameras in the courtroom. Why? "The objection of some members of the legal profession to televised trials might well be based on their subconscious commitment to mystification," observes author and attorney Ronald L. Goldfarb. "Most groups prefer to operate in the dark. Remember that the judges and lawyers who are resistant to televised trials are members of the very groups that would be exposed to more public scrutiny by these cameras, and thus would be more accountable for their own contributions to the vagaries of our Justice System."[9] While this criticism has some appeal, it is clear that many of the objections to televised trials warrant careful consideration.

THE IMPACT OF TRIAL PUBLICITY

Some argue that pretrial publicity contaminates the jury pool, creating a presumption of guilt in the minds of the jurors. Some also argue that the members of the jury carry these presumptions in their deliberations despite orders to determine guilt based only on the evidence presented in court.[10] Even if a new trial is ordered by an appellate court, some state that the jury pool for the second trial will be contaminated by knowing the evidence presented in the first trial as a result of extensive pretrial and trial coverage.[11] Bluntly stated, it is theorized that the accused cannot receive a fair trial if cameras are permitted in the courtroom because of the impact of television on the jurors.

This criticism however, cuts both ways. In the *Simpson* case, for example, the defense took an opposite approach, arguing that cameras during the trial would, in fact, provide a fairer trial.[12] Despite the potential downfalls of trial publicity, there have thus been cases in which the defendant may receive a more just trial due to the fact that the trial is not held behind closed doors and is in the presence of the broadcast media.[13]

The task of determining if cameras should be permitted in courtrooms is made more difficult when the court must also be concerned with the privacy rights of witnesses and jurors.[14]   The Supreme Court has determined that jury privacy is an area where camera coverage can readily be denied.[15] Juror privacy is closely guarded for fear of embarrassment by publication of highly personal details and the fear of harassment of the potential juror.[16]

Supreme Court Justice William O. Douglas viewed televised court proceedings as an invasion of people's privacy and endangerment of the defendant's Sixth Amendment constitutional right for four reasons. First, televised court proceedings influence the administration of justice by intimidating and distracting the witnesses and by arousing the emotions of the community. Furthermore, televised court proceedings add to the accused's anxiety, causing a form of psychological punishment. Second, television transforms our trial process into a demonstration where the passion of drama replaces the judicial search for truth, making the trial into a spectacle similar to an event at Yankee Stadium or the Roman Coliseum. Third, the Sixth Amendment's guarantee is a benefit created for the accused, not the press. The purpose of a public trial is to create a small, close, non-secretive environment so that the accused would receive an impartial trial. The Sixth Amendment was not created to make a trial into a city, state, or nation-wide press conference. Fourth, television corrupts the government by denying the divine dignity of the courts, transforming the justice system into a theater for the amusement of nosy viewers.[17]

Other opponents of courtroom cameras also hypothesize that cameras change the nature of the proceedings. According to George Gerbner, the Dean of the Annenburg School of Communication, the purpose of the court is neither education nor public entertainment, but justice. Gerbner notes that: "it's very difficult for participants in a courtroom who are speaking to a global audience of tens or maybe hundreds of millions of people not to be affected by that. It makes and breaks reputations, it creates instant celebrities, it encourages what has been called 'trash for cash', or 'cash for trash' syndrome."[18]

In this vein, opponents of cameras also declare that the strict upholding of the constitutional rights guaranteed to the press prejudices the constitutional rights of the defendant.[19] Defense attorneys are frequently concerned that their clients (the accused) would suffer the most because much of the footage viewed by the public benefits only the prosecutor, and not the defendant.[20]

As mentioned by Justice Douglas among the fears of those opposed to cameras in courts are that the media would be an obtrusive presence and that witnesses and jurors might be intimidated. Those opposed to electronic media coverage believe the presence of cameras creates a circus-like atmosphere much like the one that surrounded the *Estes* case an atmosphere that threatens the dignity and decorum of the courtroom. They point to the *Simpson* case as a prime example of the circus that camera coverage creates. It is their contention that everything that was wrong in that case — attorney grandstanding, the length of the trial, and the inability of the judge to control the proceedings — was caused by having the one camera inconspicuously placed in the courtroom. They argue that the right to a fair trial is also undermined because witnesses may be less likely to come forward to testify. These cameras affect the proceedings just by their presence.[21]

But are cameras really the kind of distraction today that they once were? Technological advances have made cameras quieter, smaller, lighter, needing little if any cable, and no longer a surprise in our lives. In fact, cameras have become such a part of our everyday lives, they barely go noticed by the average citizen. In 1965, Justice Harlan stated "the day may come when television will have become so commonplace an affair in the daily life of the average person as to dissipate all reasonable likelihood that its use in courtrooms may disparage the judicial process."[22] According to proponents of cameras, that day has arrived, and people should have an opportunity to see their government at work.[23] Those favoring media coverage of the judicial branch urge opponents to recognize that many trials have been long, draw-out processes even without cameras being present in the courtroom.

SUPPOSED IMPACT ON THE TRIAL PARTICIPANTS

If one thinks about it, televised trials represent a unique and complex communication exchange. Trial participants are able to interact with their own performances, though the distinction between actor and audience is eliminated.[24] The courtroom player becomes a viewer of his own actions. He is able to scrutinize his own comments, body language, and overall performance as reflected off the television monitor.

Although not an empirical study, Paul Thaler conducted a detailed analysis of the Steinberg[25] trial and its impact on the trial participants. According to Thaler, critics of cameras in the courtroom fear that televised trials magnify public opinions and intensify public reactions that may find their way into the courtroom and into the minds of jurors. Strict rules forbidding trial participants to engage in out-of-court activities concerning the trial often prove futile when the public is immersed in a sensational televised trial. Trial participants risk being exposed to comments and opinions from family members, friends, and colleagues who have watched the television coverage. According to Thaler, this exchange of information is referred to as *mediated feedback* and threatens the impartiality of the case, particularly a case such as the *Steinberg* trial, which received intense, extensive televison coverage.[26]

Christo Lassiter's study entitled, "TV or not TV", discusses three prejudicial effects of a feedback loop operating between the trial participants and the remote public. He comments that when trials are televised, they take on a greater importance than the actual matter before the court. As a result, the judicial process becomes corrupted when the public is substituted for the fact finders in the courtroom. Secondly, he argues that the adversarial system is transformed into a politically motivated prosecution. Public outcry leads to a political vice of judicial disposition against a disfavored minority.[27] By working high profile cases, some believe that both the media and public view the entire justice system as being on trial, which contributes to the public's notion of mistrust in the justice system.[28]

ALLEGED IMPACT ON THE JUDGES

William J. Harte, an experienced litigator, points out that trial court judges play a very specific role in court proceedings -- Judges are to monitor and protect the due process and equal protection rights of the defendant. Under current state laws, trial judges are generally given much discretion in determining if television and broadcasting may be allowed in the courtroom. One pressure involved with the use of cameras is the complex rules involved with the use, and the proper procedure and placement of, the electronic devices in the courtroom. Another initial burden for the judge is the question of whether the jury needs to be, or should be, sequestered to protect them from the influence of the media and others and for each individual juror's safety.[29]

Dean Erwin Griswold argued years ago that judges should be protected from having to decide if television and broadcasting should be present in the courtroom. He theorized that judges may enjoy and encourage the publicity surrounding a broadcasted trial, which he foresaw as a problem. Also, he feared that judges not approving the use of cameras, would succumb to the pressures of others to allow access into the courtroom.

To add credence to Griswold's predictions, there have been many judges who have welcomed the publicity, as many believe was the case with Judge Ito in the O.J. Simpson trial. Judge Ito reveled in the public spotlight. Likewise, the judge at the bail hearing for Joseph Hazelwood, the former captain of the Exxon Valdez, accused of illegally spilling oil in pristine Alaskan waters, increased his bail from $50,000 dollars to one million dollars and included an eloquent speech in front of the cameras emphasizing the importance of the case. Similarly, the judge in the trial for Jeffrey Dahmer hired a press agent, was approached for movie rights, and also began writing a book. In this instance, the judge encompassed not only the traditional role of protecting the defendant's rights to a fair trial, but oversaw the media activities during the pretrial motions, during the trial, and for himself.[30]

Harte points out that there may be added pressure on elected judges when deciding whether to allow television and broadcasting in the courtroom. The goal of the judiciary is to have an objective, non-political court. However, elected judges who turn down the chance to allow cameras in the courtroom run the risk that the media may cast a negative shadow on their re-election efforts. These judges may be ridiculed as being old-fashioned, discriminative, and unconcerned with pleasing the public. Illinois, for example, has 55% of the judges elected.[31] Re-election pressure may be too much for some judges to resist.

According to Anderson, once a judge allows cameras in his or her courtroom, he or she has also opened the door to possible judicial corruption. The cornerstone of the judicial system is the judge. If people lose confidence in the integrity of a judge then the public confidence in the court system is doomed. Anderson states that in this day and age it is impossible for a judge to ignore the public because they are concerned about reelection and reappointment factors. Name recognition and political image is an important factor in today's society for any elected judge. Anderson argues that publicity affects a judge and creates competitive positions. He states that to counter at least part of this problem, a judge other than the presiding judge on the case should decide whether cameras should be allowed in the courtroom. The decision to allow cameras in the courtroom can help or hinder a judge. If the judge desires exposure, it may help the judge to have the cameras in his or her courtroom. On the other hand, if the judge does not allow cameras, it may be a hindrance because the judge is allowing the media to speculate about the case.[32]

All in all, elected judges are asked to bear added pressures when cameras are in the courtrooms including, jury concerns, interests of personal gain, and job security caused by the presence of cameras in the courtrooms.[33]

ALLEGED IMPACT ON WITNESSES AND VICTIMS

Harte argues that, when considering the impact of cameras and broadcasting of a trial, it is necessary to understand that broadcasting may change the content of testimony or the giving of evidence. Television increases witness exposure and causes greater nervousness for a witnesses as opposed to newspaper coverage of the courtroom. Likewise, the witness may become more distracted by the electronic equipment in the courtroom and the knowledge that they are on national television. Further, television and broadcasting may cause a witness to fear for his or her own personal safety as well as the fear of being ostracizing from his or her own community.[34] As an example, in 1987 two inmates witnessed an in-jail murder but were concerned for their safety if their testimony was covered by television cameras. They feared that their faces would be seen and possibly recognized.[35] Likewise, widespread public exposure may lead to trauma and embarrassment for a victim and his or her family. For instance in the Jeffrey Dahmer trial, Dahmer's parents were publicly chastised for the actions of their son. In the William Kennedy-Smith trial, the victim was subjected to humiliation as her pain became entertainment for others and the trial became a spectacle. This could have a chilling effect on other witnesses.[36]

Harte further argues that television coverage negatively affects witnesses in two ways. First, witnesses may embellish their testimony due to excitement. Secondly, witnesses may experience difficulty in responding to questions. As a result, the testimony will be distorted and the jury may therefore find the witness untrustworthy by misreading the witness's nervousness.

Additionally, witnesses may become influenced by the fame of being on television. In the Kennedy-Smith rape trial, for instance, witness Anne Mercer sold her story for $40,000 to "A Current Affair", which then lead to the subsequent impeachment of the witness's credibility.[37]

Moreover, there is the concern with witnesses viewing the court proceedings. Witnesses may become biased after hearing a commentator's version of the court proceedings. Subsequently, witness's testimony may be distorted due to viewing the court trial prior to testifying.

Critics of in court cameras fear that court participants will watch media coverage of the trial and change their behavior, attitude, and judgment to fit a self-styled image that they wish to project on television.[38] For example, Anderson argues that publicity may cause a witness to change his or her testimony in order to make himself or herself more attractive to the media. Furthermore, media coverage and publicity may contribute to witnesses developing their own agenda during the trial, such as book deal contracts or talk show appearances.[39]

POTENTIAL IMPACT ON JURORS

Not unlike the rest of the players in a courtroom, Harte also argues that cameras in the courtroom also distract jurors. Although cameras have become less obtrusive than in the past, there is still pressure on jurors in knowing that a national audience is watching. Furthermore, the tremendous responsibility a juror has in a trial is likely increased in a highly publicized case. Jurors may become nervous and feel pressure due to the knowledge that a "jury of millions" is watching, analyzing, and predicting their actions.[40]

Similar to the effect on witnesses, cameras place an increased burden on the jury by tempting jurors to look into the possibility of personal gain when considering the verdict in a celebrated case. Likewise, if there is a mistrial, it maybe difficult to find an impartial jury to retry a highly publicized case.[41]

Similarly, the need to sequester jurors is increased in a celebrated case. Without sequestering a jury, it is easy for jurors to view themselves or the trial on television and thus to rehear certain portions of the trial causing a bias. There is also an increased possibility in a highly publicized case that a juror will discuss the trial with others. One example is when "Hard Copy", in the case of William Kennedy-Smith, offered a prospective juror gifts for her story.[42]

Lastly, the issue of safety is an area of concern for jurors in televised trials. An example in the Kennedy-Smith case is when two jurors were threatened after the news broadcasted their faces. Likewise, Court TV broadcasted the face of an alternate juror in the O.J. Simpson trial which raised doubts about the protection of jurors. In conclusion, it is argued that cameras in the courtroom bring pressure, risk of bias, sequestering issues, and safety concerns for the jurors participating in a televised trial.[43]

Another concern is that even though jurors are instructed to ignore news coverage of the trial, they may nonetheless be exposed to prejudicial news reports through the highly accessible television medium. The fear is that this exposure will then affect the juror's judgment and ultimately influence his or her vote.[44] It is imperative that jurors be impartial, which means that jurors cannot have a personal interest in the case. Media coverage and publicity may create an interest for the juror.[45]

Kathleen M. Krygier's conclusions differs from Anderson in that according to Krygier, studies show that the electronic media does not have a negative impact on the participants and does not interfere with the administration of justice. The potential impact on the jurors was a specific concern. The studies found "no or little effect" of the electronic media coverage upon jurors." Krygier suggests that the electronic media may actually have a benefit in the state courts. Since state court judges are elected officials, the media coverage may serve as a "safeguard against corruption and judicial abuse of power."[46]

Mercy Hermida raises two major issues concerning the witnesses and victims since the advent of the media's expression of its First Amendment rights. First, a witness knows she or he may become famous by having his or her testimony aired and face on national television. Second, witnesses may hear a different version of the story through the media, and this will change their story so that it is more compatible to another witness. This is especially true if the other witness's story grabs greater media coverage. Furthermore, a victim's privacy is compromised in a situation where a witness would use the victim's name in order to complete the story. The victim is subjected to harassment and simply would become a victim over again by that harassment from the media. There is no law or restriction that would allow prior approval from the victim(s).[47]

IMPACT ON LAWYERS

Lawyers, while trying a case that is televised, may be distracted by the cameras in a number of ways. For example, lawyers inevitably will become the subject of intense scrutiny and criticism by television commentators, especially in high profile cases. Lawyers may also become nervous which may ultimately affect their ability to argue the case.

Likewise, Harte argues that cameras can cause a lawyer to change his or her strategy. For instance, one of the first nationally televised cases, the William Kennedy-Smith rape trial, gave everyone the chance to examine the benefits and disadvantages of televising a trial and emphasized how a lawyer's strategy may be changed due to the cameras in the courtroom. Roy Black, Kennedy's attorney for the case, discussed the way televison, and having a national audience at the trial, altered his strategy and performance on a key cross-examination. During the cross-examination, he found himself unable to ask detailed sexual questions because all he could think of was his mother watching him during the examination. If serious enough, a client maybe able to appeal on the grounds of inept cross-examination.[48]

Similarly, lawyers aware of the cameras can turn a trial into a spectacle. The obvious example is in the O.J. Simpson trial. In this trial, the attorneys directed part of their cases to the viewing public rather than to the judge and jurors.

It has also been argued that there is a definite conflict for lawyers between self-interest and the interest of the client as a result of the cameras. An attorney in a high profile case may forget his or her duty to the client in an attempt to gain more business due to the new found publicity. For example, Robert Shapiro, a member of O.J. Simpson's defense team, started a 1-800 number for "anyone seeking legal representation from Robert Shapiro's offices", as its last option. There is the legitimate concern that attorneys may use their exposure to advance their careers which, as a result, could affect their representation of the client.[49]

Likewise, there is the concern that tabloid television, looking for higher ratings, will search far into a lawyer's personal life, under the guise of educating the public. A key example is Marsha Clark, the lead prosecutor in the O.J. Simpson trial. The media picked her life apart ranging from inspecting her two marriages, analyzing her religious beliefs and commenting on her clothing and make-up.[50]

Lastly, it is important to note that it is not yet known the true extent of the impact that the cameras have on lawyers especially concerning the long-term effects of attorney-client relations, or for the attorney's career and reputation due to the media and television commentators.[51] According to Arnella, a lawyer may become preoccupied by the pressure of cameras in the courtroom and could very easily lose his or her focus. The time that should be devoted to the client is taken away from the client by the fact that the lawyer not only has to persuade the jury but he or she has to persuade the public as well.[52]

The notion of lawyers as actors is not a new concept, according to Ms. Tuma, who has covered numerous trials. She states that lawyers are acting from the minute the jury sits in the jury box, and they are almost committing malpractice if they don't. We have to get rid of that notion that there is no acting in the courtroom. According to Estrich, a professor of law at the University of Southern California, "the courts are a place where you can get a great story, you can always get lawyers to fight with each other. It's easy TV. You don't have to frame the issue; they're framed.[53]

IMPACT ON THE DEFENDANT

Harte argues that in considering the impact of cameras in the courtroom it is of most importance to look at the impact on the defendant. First, the defendant is the individual most likely to suffer from the publicity endured as a result of television and broadcasting in the courtroom. The defendant has the right to equal justice and due process under the law, which the cameras threaten to jeopardize. Among the various problems faced by the defendant are nervous judges, lawyers, and witnesses due to being filmed. Likewise, defendants also face the problems of improper editing and biased commentary by the media. Further the jurors, with the duty to judge the facts in the case, are faced with the unique pressure of speaking to the media during highly publicized trials as well as the problem of finding an impartial jury, if the need for a retrial arises. In conclusion, Harte states that it is apparent that the defendant has the most at stake when cameras are allowed in the courtroom.[54]

THE ENTERTAINMENT ASPECTS

Another criticism raised against cameras in the courtroom is that camera coverage is not journalism, but merely entertainment.[55] Those opposed to cameras maintain that cases that are widely followed in the media are only those cases that grab the viewer's attention. As Rosco C. Howard put it, "the media reports stories that capture the 'public's fancy.' . . . [and the] the media reports details. . . that will titillate and entertain. . . . "[56]

Additionally, there is an argument that what the public sees is a manipulated and distorted view of the trial rather than an actual account of the proceedings. It has been claimed that what is finally televised has been modified according to the discretion of the editors and the cameramen.[57] Many opponents believe that editors carve up the trial to appeal to the masses and cameramen use lighting and camera angles to shape the public's perception of the case.[58] They further argue that because most people do not realize these "distortions" are made, camera coverage creates an impression in the minds of the public of the defendant's guilt.[59] A recent example of this "distortion" would be the pre-trial *Time Magazine* cover of O.J. Simpson which had Simpson's photograph shaded to make him appear more sinister and guilty.

But is it not true that the entertainment value of trials has always been present? In colonial times, people would travel from miles around to see a criminal trial.[60] Hence, the reason for the large galleries in older courtrooms. There was no television or radio to keep the public entertained, let alone informed about the trial. Moreover, other forms of media coverage, such as print media also seek to entertain. Sex and crime sell papers and advertising time and this is not a new phenomenon. Generally, these elements fascinate the public and are what the public wants.

PUBLIC CONFIDENCE IN THE JUSTICE SYSTEM

Some opponents of cameras also believe that cameras cause the public to lose respect for the judicial system. Susanna Barber, a professor of Mass Communications at Emerson College, argues that televised trials affect people's perceptions of social reality. For those individuals who lack knowledge about the operation of the justice system, televised trials shape their perceptions and opinions about the justice system. Opponents argue that this perception may be distorted because the media does not broadcast all trials, only selected ones.

Is it not possible, however, that public confidence actually is increased by the ability to see the system in action? Lassiter argues, for example, that in high profile cases, it is even more critical that the public receive the maximum amount of information about the process by which a particular result has been achieved[.]"[61] Similarly, in *Richmond Newspapers*, the Supreme Court noted that "[p]eople in an open society do not demand infallibility from their institutions, but it is difficult for them to accept what they are prohibited from observing."[62]

Cameras are not the cause of the problems with the judicial system, cameras merely show the public the problems that are already present within the system. Although the public may not like what it sees, proponents state that this is no reason to order cameras out of the courtroom. The same attorney grand-standing or lackadaisical judge is present with or without cameras, as anyone who has attended a court case can attest.

Perhaps the best argument available to supporters of televised trials is that live continuous coverage educates the public and makes people more aware of the complexities of the process. Opponents counter that there has been no real scientific studies of the phenomena, so it is impossible to say that these trials truly educate, and that most of the studies that do exist are flawed.

Proponents further theorize that, in an age where most people get their information about current affairs from television, the camera is a necessary tool in educating the masses about the least understood branch of our government. Television is turned on more than seven hours a day in the typical American household, and, like it or not, the majority of Americans get their news from television and not from print media.[63] Therefore, some believe that having a camera in the courtroom is a strong educational tool. Televised trials can show the public how the system works or explain to a lay public why, for example, a person was charged with second-degree murder instead of first-degree murder. Students, lawyers and the public benefit from media coverage of court cases.[64] Even Justice Harlan believed that "television is capable of performing an educational function by acquainting the public with the judicial process in action."[65] The argument is that, without television coverage, people are left to their imaginations and to fictional dramas to shape their understanding of the courts. The misconceptions formed from the fictional accounts can be frustrating to a public when the truth is revealed that not every case ends in a *Perry Mason* acquittal or a *Law & Order* conviction. Only an educated public can elect competent judges and prosecutors. Cameras in the courtroom can ensure that the electorate will see their elected government officials in action.

Proponents go on to expound that there is a tradition of open trials in America dating back to colonial times. To have a truly open trial during this technology age, cameras must be present in the courtroom.[66] The camera overcomes barriers such as physical space limitations and geographical distances that have prevented trials from being completely open as in the past. Cameras allow more people to witness and observe trials without being in the courtroom to disrupt the proceedings, as happened in the *Hauptmann* trial where there were repeated outbursts from the gallery that plagued the proceedings. According to Attorney General Janet Reno, cameras in courtrooms "give people the opportunity to see justice in action", which Reno believes helps build public confidence. Unlike the hysterical and hostile reactions of some judges to media attention, Reno acknowledges that "the potential that television has for properly informing the people is great".[67]

Chapter 5

THE PUBLIC PERCEPTION

High profile, celebrated criminal cases, including the Lorena Bobbitt, Lyle and Erik Menendez, John Hinckley, Rodney King and O.J. Simpson cases, have had a profound impact on the American public's image of the criminal justice system. Criminal trials express our society's deep values and our commitments to justice and equality. A community trusts that when a loss is suffered, a criminal trial will repair the damages. However, public faith in the system exists only when the trials are perceived to be just and fair. Many believe that our current justice system is on shaky grounds, and that the public is close to losing faith in the system. Trials are being viewed by many more as entertainment -- products of clever lawyers -- than as a method of restoring justice.

RECENT SURVEY RESULTS

On May 13-15, 1999 in Washington, D.C. five hundred leaders from state and Federal courts, bar organizations, the media, and citizen groups convened in the first ever conference of its type addressing the serious issue of public trust in the justice system, at the National Conference on Public Trust and Confidence in the Justice System (The National Conference on Public Trust). Frank A. Bennack, Jr., President and Chief Executive Officer of Hearst Corporation made the following comments at the conference:

... Suppose you have no direct experience with the courts. Where do your perceptions come from? Television, newspapers and drama have stayed roughly the same since 1983 as sources of information about courts. For example, six of ten still say they get court information from electronic media and half regularly receive it from print media. About a fourth get it from dramas and comedies with a legal theme, which is actually an increase. Perhaps we can thank Mr. Grisham for that. The big change, however, has been court television. Let's face it—people wait for Judge Judy to come down on an evasive defendant the same way they wait for the furniture to start flying on Jerry Springer. It's justice as entertainment. Is that bad or good? Apparently neither. There is no strong pattern connecting sources of information, including Court TV, with ratings or degree of knowledge.[1] See Appendix III.

At the same conference Governor Mario M. Cuomo made the following comments:

My Mother and Father never changed how they felt about judges, but in recent years many other Americans appear to have. Television is probably one of the reasons. In thousands of hours of programs, it tore away the veil, even disrobed some of the judges. It created a different image of them - it made them less distant, more profanely present, tangible and fallible. Even the recent live coverage - which I admit to having advocated - has created distortions because viewers seldom witness an entire proceeding, and most of them lack the familiarity with the law necessary for a full understanding of what is happening in the nightly glimpses on the screen. The O. J. Simpson episode is a good example. For many viewers, the O. J. trial was the most they had ever seen of the law at work. It proved to be a devastating blow to the favorable image the courts had preserved for so many years. Surveys indicated that millions of Americans who watched the trial had lost respect for our judges and our judicial system: only a small number said it enhanced their opinion. That wasn't because the system didn't work in the O.J. trial. It's because the people didn't understand how the system works. In fact, the whole wide world of explosive technology has dramatically changed how both our political and judicial systems are regarded - and how they are being treated. Thanks to television, movies, radio and computers, we have been saturated with information about everything imaginable from the mating habits of tsetse flies to the possibility of life on other planets - often without adequate interpretation. As a result we have become better at facts than at philosophy; more knowledgeable without necessarily becoming wiser; certainly more self-assured and less willing to accept opinions or decisions from experts or established authorities.

The agenda at the National Conference on Public Trust was a national survey conducted by the National Center for State Courts Survey and funded by the Hearst Corporation (The State Court Survey). Early in 1999, 1,826 Americans were asked in connection with the State Court Survey to express their opinions regarding "the courts in your community". The objectives of the State Court Survey were to:

- establish what the American public thinks about the performance of state and local courts in key areas such as access to justice, timeliness, fairness and equality, and independence and accountability;
- clarify what the public believes about basic aspects of court performance and explain different levels of confidence in and satisfaction with the courts;
- provide a model survey that can be used by individual states and localities wanting to undertake a systematic inquiry into what their public thinks about court performance; and
- enhance and refine the knowledge accumulated through surveys conducted by others between 1977 and 1998.

Earlier surveys of public opinion about the courts include three major national surveys and 27 surveys commissioned by the judicial branches of 24 states. Care was taken to adequately represent the views that members of minority groups hold about the courts. In addition, all respondents were given an opportunity to express their views in their own words, in response to questions inquiring about the most important thing that the courts were doing well or poorly. Previous surveys had hinted at differences among racial and ethnic groups in how the courts are perceived. The State Courts Survey attempted to contribute to this body of knowledge by explicitly searching for points of view that are broadly shared by all Americans and points of view that differ across racial, ethnic and other demographic groups. The survey also examined some new topics related to court performance and investigated in greater depth some of the areas where there is widespread public agreement that the courts need to improve their performance.

The 500 attendees at The National Conference on Public Trust met to identify the issues affecting public trust in the justice system and to enhance and support state court strategies addressing these issues. The conference was held under the auspices of the Conference of Chief Justices, the American Bar Association, the Conference of State Court Administrators, and the League of Women Voters. The conference was funded by the Bureau of Justice Assistance, United States Department of Justice, the State Justice Institute, and the American Bar Association.[2] Prior to the conference, most of the participating states and territories submitted prioritized lists of public trust issues resulting in a preliminary identification of public trust issues common to most states.

Although the mission of the judiciary was not court popularity, the conference planners recognized that there are some very real public concerns. In explaining to the conference why his corporation funded the State Courts Survey, Frank A. Bennack, President and Chief Executive Officer of the Hearst Corporation, stated:

> If Alexander Hamilton was right when he said the chief duty of society is justice, the judicial system is the bedrock of our ability to meet that responsibility. Think about it – it would be nice if everybody had complete trust in the media. Those of us in the media earnestly want that trust but it's doubtful that we'll ever have it. . . .
> And what about complete trust in politicians? Not likely. We learned a long time ago that those tracks all over our trust in institutions have been left by feet of clay. But the courts- that's something different. Here trust is essential. Here, knowledge is essential. Here, society and institution come together in ways that really define who we would like to think we are as a society – fair, open, and protective of the rights of every individual.[3]

The State Courts Survey revealed that 23% of the respondents have a "great deal" of trust in the courts of their community and an additional 52% have "some trust," thereby placing courts in the middle range of trust among American institutions. This fairly lukewarm endorsement was reflected in survey responses on a number of issues. For example, only 10% of the respondents felt that the courts in their community handled cases in an "excellent" manner. Respondents were particularly critical of how courts handled family and juvenile cases.[4]

In addition to broad issues of public trust and confidence, the State Courts Survey addressed four major areas of court responsibility: (1) access to justice; (2) expedition and timeliness; (3) equality, fairness, and integrity; and (4) independence and accountability. The State Courts Survey revealed some public dissatisfaction in each of these areas. The level of dissatisfaction among African-Americans was higher in practically every category of the survey, but most markedly on issues of equality and fairness. The results are summarized below:

ACCESS TO JUSTICE

Only 32% agreed that "it is affordable to bring a case to court." Respondents overwhelmingly identified legal fees as the cause. But 74% agreed that "courts make reasonable efforts to ensure that individuals have adequate attorney representation." 58% agreed with the statement that " it would be possible for me to represent myself in court if I wanted to." 74% agreed that "court personnel are helpful and courteous.

TIMELINESS

Respondents severely criticized the timeliness of the courts, mostly with respect to lack of speed that cases are processed through the system. 52% agreed that "courts adequately monitor the progress of cases". 61% agreed that "judges do not give adequate time to each individual case". 80% agreed with the statement "cases are not resolved in a timely manner".

EQUALITY AND FAIRNESS

On the favorable side, 85% agreed that "courts protect defendants' constitutional rights. Also, 79% agreed that "judges are generally honest and fair in deciding cases" but answers to other questions seem to undercut this affirmation.

On the unfavorable side 40% did not agree that "court rulings are understood by the people involved in the cases". This lack of understanding among parties to a case appears very high. 56% agreed that "juries are not representative of the community." 59% agreed that "courts do not make sure that their orders are enforced." 66% agreed that "when a person sues a corporation, the courts generally favor the corporation over the person." And 80% agreed that the wealthy are treated better than other groups.

68% of African-Americans felt that they were treated worse by courts than other groups and almost 45% of the respondents in other groups agreed with this perception. Yet, 68% of African-Americans agreed that "judges are generally honest and fair in deciding cases." This apparent discrepancy suggests that the concerns of African-Americans about fairness were directed more at the system than at judges, who still retain some credibility.

COURT INDEPENDENCE AND RESPONSIVENESS
44% of all respondents agreed that "courts are 'out-of-touch' with what's going on in their communities." However, more than 50% of both African-American and Hispanic respondents felt that courts were out of touch.

A vast majority of respondents (81%) agreed with the statement that "judges' decisions are influenced by political considerations." 78% agreed that "elected judges are influenced by having to raise campaign funds."[5]

The State Courts Survey summarized the key issues contributing to low or declining public trust and confidence in the Justice System, and ranked them in order of priority, as follows:

I.   BARRIERS THAT DECREASE PUBLIC ACCESS TO THE
        COURTS
The top barrier to public access identified by the State Courts Survey was the cost of litigation. This is a problem both for the poor and for the middle class. The next most important barrier was the complexity of court procedures and the arcane language used in court proceedings. This leads to the next most commonly identified difficulty which was the problems experienced by pro se litigants having difficulty representing themselves even on a simple dispute and the difficulties experienced by non-English speakers and people from other cultures. Finally, the State Courts Survey identified inconvenient court business hours, inconveniently located courthouses, limited or outdated facilities, limited parking, lack of wheelchair ramps and others as impediments to access to the courts.

II.   ACTUAL OR PERCEIVED BIAS IN THE SYSTEM
Survey respondents frequently identified actual or perceived bias in the system as a major problem with our court system. These actual or perceived biases cut across various classes of society. The top bias problem identified in the State Courts Survey was a bias against the poor and in favor of the rich. Next there were perceived biases based upon race

or ethnicity. A lesser degree of the problem was in the area of bias based upon gender or based upon disability.

III. TIME AND EXPENSE REQUIRED TO MOVE A CASE THROUGH THE JUSTICE SYSTEM

The third category of problems revealed in the State Courts Survey was the issue of time and expense required to move through the system. Contributors to this problems are the following public sentiments, the inherent slow pace of court cases, the complexity of the process, which some members of the public believe is designed by lawyers for the benefit of lawyers, and the indecisive or inaccessible judges. Others viewed it as a problem of too many cases for too few or inefficient judges. Finally, some saw it as a matter of dilatory and unprepared lawyers or lawyers and clients who use discovery and other litigation phases to delay the proceedings and add expense to their opponents.

IV. INTEGRITY OF THE JUDICIAL PROCESS

The fourth broad category of problems identified in the State Courts Survey involved the integrity of the judicial process. The number one problem in this category was a lack of accountability to the public by the judiciary, notwithstanding the fact that many judges are elected officials. Ironically the second concern in order of priority was over the quality of the judiciary, methods of judicial selection, judicial discipline and difficulty in replacing ineffective judges. This was followed by concerns over the influence of politics in individual case decisions and by the ability of some attorneys to manipulate the court system. Respondents expressed an interest in making judges truly independent by removing them from the political process and in curtailing the use of expert witnesses. Finally, concern was expressed over the influence of financial contributions to judicial candidates on judicial decision making.

V. LACK OF PROTECTION FOR SOCIETY

The fifth category was a concern about the lack of protection for society. The issues in this category included concerns over criminals being released on technicalities and, to a lesser degree, lenient sentencing and a corresponding revolving door for repeat criminals. Finally there was concern over inadequate or ineffective responses to certain types of cases such as family disputes, juvenile cases and low level crimes. This included a concern over a lack of constructive sentencing options, such as referrals to social services and other more holistic responses.

VI. LAWYERS

The next category identified in the State Courts Survey was concerns over lawyers themselves. The survey results showed that the top concern here was that too many lawyers put winning before justice or truth due to an imbalance between the lawyers's duty as an officer of the court and his or her duty to zealously represent lawyers. Next in line was a concern over lawyers who break and bend the rules and unethical or dishonest lawyers. Next, there was the issue of judges who do not appropriately control lawyers who break the rules as well as a legal profession that does not police itself effectively. Finally, the issue of cost was again expressed as a concern over inadequate free legal services and the high cost of legal representation.

VII. MEDIA EFFECT

It is not until category *seven* that we begin to see any concerns about news media effects on the judicial system. Here the top concern was that media coverage tends to select the most sensational cases and as such tends to reduce the public's trust and confidence in the judicial system. The secondary concern was leaks and comments by lawyers to the news media on pending litigation in order to control the "spin" of coverage. Finally in the area of media concerns respondents expressed concern that media reports were often inaccurate or misleading and focused only on negative stories.

VIII. EDUCATION

The State Courts Survey turned up many perceived shortcomings in the area of education. These include a failure: (i) to educate our children that the judiciary is an independent branch of government and the reasons why; (ii) to educate the public about the rule of law and that our justice process is infinitely superior to ones based upon power or influence; and (iii) to educate the public about obligations which both judges and lawyers have imposed upon them by our system; e.g., the inability of a judge to defend himself/ herself for his/her decisions and the right of the accused to counsel no matter how heinous the crime.

As a result, there was reported to be inadequate public knowledge about courts and legal procedures (including differences between state and federal courts, court procedures, substantive law, function of the courts, rationale for certain procedures, structure and organization of the court) and a lack of public understanding of criminal case decision-making.

Concerns were also expressed over the unpopularity of and dissatisfaction with court decisions.

IX.   JURIES
The next category in order of priority involved juries. Respondents identified juror frustration with summons and selection process as the top problem. Juror frustration as a result of being forced to sit mute in the jury box without the right to ask questions came next in the rankings. Finally, discourteous and inflexible treatment of jurors was cited.

X.   LACK OF COURTESY AND RESPECT
Concerns over courtesy and respect were next. These concerns, in order of priority, listed disrespectful treatment of crime victims, disrespectful treatment of those charged with minor criminal infractions, discourteous or unhelpful court staff, discourteous judges, and discourteous lawyers.

XI.   TRIALS/JUDICIAL PROCESS IN GENERAL
'The final catch-all category involved concerns over trials and the judicial process in general. The respondents felt that as a top priority that there is an increasing public concern that truth, fairness and justice are too often the victims and not the product of our judicial system. There was a need expressed for more specialized courts and that courts be made more user friendly.   Finally, the concern again arose of a lack of two-way communication with the public.

STRATEGIES TO ADDRESS THE KEY ISSUES

Various strategies to the address the above issues were submitted by the states at the National Conference on Public Trust. They were translated into a set of recommended "overarching strategies" as follows:
  • Improve external communication.
This general strategy derives from frequently stated objectives of improving media relations and improving dissemination of court information to the public, particularly court users.
  • Improve education and training.
This strategy includes the many references to school curricula and internal education programs for judges, attorneys, and court staff (the most common topics being bias, sensitivity training and ethics training).
  • Make the courts more inclusive and outreaching.
This strategy includes the creation of court-community collaborative efforts, the appointment of citizens to court advisory committees, the

creation of a user-friendly court environment, and the establishment of more public appearances by judges to illustrate the openness of the courts.
  • Improve management and information technology.
A variety of strategies deal in one way or another with efficiency, planning, an upgrading of information available internally and externally, as well as improving public service. These strategies include:
  • Make changes in existing laws and rules governing court procedure.
  • Enhance justice and the appearances of justice, including changes in the adversarial system and the role of judges in seeing that the truth emerges.
  • Make courts adaptable to social change, particularly in the family area, including, for example, the creation of specialized forums to meet changing needs of society and court users and to accommodate a wider range of rehabilitative services.
  • Simplify courts to make them more accessible to persons without an attorney so that court procedures are understandable to the lay person.
  • Change the economics of courts and the legal profession so that access of litigants (as opposed to lawyers) is enhanced.
  • Strengthen and improve the relations of the judiciary with other branches and court-related agencies.
There also were a number of recommended strategies involving court relationships with the legislative and executive branches and with criminal justice agencies and treatment providers. Another significant strategy included the improvement of *media* understanding of the system.
  • I submit that branch of the media that focuses on those sensationalist trials has overheated public perceptions. . . .
  • . . . if I were proposing a strategy, I would follow Judge McBeth out of the courtroom into the public, into as many newspaper newsrooms as I could, to say –look out, someone is going to propose this, some lawyer is going to spin, some prosecutor, some defendant, and you are going to get burned, and I can't stop it unless you are willing to understand why this runs counter to everything that has traditionally been sacred in the administration of justice.
  • I thought Governor Cuomo made the point. I mean, the First Amendment is there so that you can speak out and protect the Fourth, Fifth, and Sixth. And it is for that reason I suggest to you that a media strategy must be part of any strategy that helps educate the public.[6]

Conference participants, having thus identified key issues and having set strategic priorities, were asked two fundamental attitudinal questions. Both questions were answered strongly in the affirmative: Ninety per cent of the voters concurred that public trust was indeed a problem. Fifty-five per cent felt the primary responsibility for building public trust lay with the judiciary.

BARRIERS TO EFFECTUATING STRATEGIES TO BUILD PUBLIC TRUST AND CONFIDENCE

In an open microphone session moderated by Professor Arthur Miller of Harvard University Law School, the conference participants addressed the reality that there are many obstacles to effectively implementing the conference strategies. Even though many of the speakers identified themselves as judges or lawyers, the speakers overwhelmingly felt that the barriers to implementing effective strategies were internal barriers – impediments found within the judicial and legal professions and arising from the procedural rules governing the system. These barriers included the following:

- Lack of public funding
- Lack of listening and interaction…denial
- Insufficient public accessibility to the proceedings – lack of innovation
- Not sufficiently collaborative or facilitative
- Failure to develop non-judicial and judicial alternative dispute mechanisms
- Failure to make leadership role in public trust and confidence part of the judicial job description
- Lack of data on defining the problems and identifying what works in building trust and confidence
- Failure to educate the public on the importance and role/procedures of the judiciary
- Failure to educate the profession regarding the need to reform
- Lack of quality control in the lower courts
- Failure to aggressively deal with racial and ethnic bias
- Unreasonable expectations of judges
- Tension between fairness values and efficiency
- Failure of bar to get own house in order and to stand up against legislature for encroachment into judiciary functions

- Failure to adopt change
- Lack of diversity and self-discipline in the legal profession
- Failure of legal profession to understand public's lack of trust which is inherent in our form of government
- Lack of understanding of how tribal judiciaries relate to state
  judiciaries
- Lack of public understanding of legal language
- Media misinformation
- Citizen dissatisfaction with government in general[7]

SUMMARY OF FINDINGS

The State Courts Survey showed that Americans' views about the courts in their communities are often contradictory. Overall, the courts received an average rating from the American public. The core of the courts' positive image is the perception that courts meet their constitutional obligations to protect the rights of defendants, litigants have adequate legal representation, and that judges are honest and fair in their case decisions. The American public also approved of the courtesy and respect with which court staff treat those with business before the courts.

The negative image of the courts covers issues such as access to the courts, the treatment given to members of minority groups, and the independence and responsiveness of the judicial branch of government. In terms of access, courts were viewed as too costly and too slow. In terms of fair treatment, juries were regarded as not representative of communities and courts were regarded as not giving equal attention to all cases and not ensuring that their orders were enforced. Survey respondents also believed that members of minority groups were treated worse than Whites/Non-Hispanics. African-Americans were seen as clearly estranged from the courts. In terms of independence and responsiveness, judges were perceived as negatively influenced by politics and by campaign fund-raising efforts. These views held by respondents in states that appoint judges or use merit selection did not differ greatly from those of respondents in states were judges are selected through partisan elections.

The contradictory nature of public opinion exhibited by the State Court Survey is seen in other areas. For example, the public viewed judges as honest and fair in their case decisions, but at the same time believed judicial decisions were influenced by political considerations and the need to raise campaign funds. Indeed, in a Texas survey, the respondents both roundly criticized campaign fund-raising by judges and overwhelmingly chose election as their preferred method of judicial selection.

The comments and recommended strategies coming out of the National Conference also provide some interesting insight. Most of the problems identified in the survey and discussed by the conference attendees have little or nothing to do with media coverage of trials.

THE AMERICAN BAR ASSOCIATION SURVEY

In August of 1998, the American Bar Association sponsored a national survey, "Perceptions of the U.S. Justice System." In the ABA study, 1,000 adults were interviewed via telephone. Relative to previous surveys, the ABA survey findings suggested improvements to the public's image of the courts, increases of public involvement with the courts and a positive relationship between such involvement and confidence in and satisfaction with the courts.

The American Bar Association survey was commissioned to: (1) assess the public's current understanding of and confidence in the justice system; (2) identify the public's sources of information about the justice system; and (3) understand what factors drive public attitudes. The survey, which included 1,000 randomly selected respondents age 18 and older, was conducted by telephone interviews between August 6 and August 31 of 1998 by M/A/R/C ® Research, an independent Chicago research firm. Like the State Courts Survey, this survey put the shaky public image of lawyers and courts into focus with hard numbers. The ABA survey suggests that people want more information about the judicial branch of government in the way that they once wanted more open access to the legislative branch. See (Appendix V).

Some of the key findings of the ABA study include the following:

- People strongly believe in the justice system, though they also identify areas that warrant improvement.
- People have confidence in the overall justice system, though the amount of that confidence varies for specific components of the system. Further, that confidence can be influenced over time and by level of knowledge, positive court experience, and personal demographic traits.
- People's knowledge of the justice system is uneven. Individuals generally recognize some obscure tenets about the justice system but still lack knowledge about many facets.[8]

The ABA survey found that, prior to the impeachment trial of President Clinton, only 17 percent of respondents could identify Rehnquist as the Chief Justice. The survey also concluded that those who were least informed about the courts wanted to know more. Cameras might be the best tool to that end, according to the ABA President.

Only 30 percent of the respondents were "extremely or very confident" in the justice system. Different components of the system fared better. Half the respondents give the United States Supreme Court a high confidence rating -- higher than any other institution or profession measured in the survey.

Lawyers ended at the bottom of public confidence, along with Congress and the news media. Only 14 percent of the respondents gave lawyers a high confidence rating, slightly lower than Congress, but above the media, which received a high confidence rating from only 8 percent of the respondents.

Survey respondents also expressed skepticism about whether justice is dispensed evenly in the United States. Perception of the justice system is not all negative, according to the survey. This country's justice system is the best in the world, said 80 percent of the respondents, who also expressed strong support for the jury system. Nevertheless, 51 percent of the respondents said the justice system needs a complete overhaul and that the country would be better served with fewer lawyers.

OTHER SURVEYS AND SUMMARIES

In addition to the more recent studies discussed in detail above, studies of public perception have been conducted at various levels and with various goals for several decades. The most salient points coming from this work are described in the next few paragraphs. For more details, refer to the sources cited for this chapter in the endnotes.

A major survey was conducted in 1977 entitled "Public Image of the Courts," commissioned by the National Center for State Courts to inform a national conference, "State Courts: A Blueprint for the Future." The methodology used was a face-to-face survey of 1,931 adults. The survey was notable for its gloomy picture of the courts' standing with the American public, the finding that the public was poorly informed about the courts, and its conclusion that "those having knowledge and experience with the courts voiced the greatest dissatisfaction and criticism."

Likewise, in 1983, The Hearst Corporation undertook a national telephone survey of 1,000 adults, "The American Public, the Media and the Judicial System: A National Survey of Public Awareness and Personal Experience." That survey found that Americans were largely ignorant about the legal system, that jury service was experienced by only a small proportion of the population and that public opinion about the courts was strongly influenced by the mass media.

Numerous state surveys were conducted between 1984 and 1999. The results of these surveys reveal significant changes in the public perceptions of the courts and indicate that more and more Americans have direct experience with the courts. In several instances, states conducted more than one survey; the trends over time indicate improvements in public knowledge about the courts and shifts, largely positive, in the public's perceptions of court performance.[9]

COURT TV SURVEY

In 1997, Court TV hired a market research firm to conduct a telephone survey to learn what Americans think about television coverage of trials. The survey interviewed 800 adult Americans between February 10-12, 1997. In general, the results of the survey indicate that Americans believe they enjoy a basic right to see court trials and are willing to have individual federal judges decide for themselves when to allow cameras in their courtrooms. While the public does not support televising all federal trials, they are opposed to the current blanket ban on cameras in federal courts. Support for televising trials seems to stem from a mistrust of the general media's coverage of the legal system, mistrust of the legal system itself, the educational value of witnessing court proceedings, and the belief that it would improve the performance of key actors in the system. For more details see Appendix VI.

JUDGES SHOULD DECIDE WHEN TO ALLOW CAMERAS IN THEIR COURTROOMS

An overwhelming majority of Americans surveyed (80%) believe they have the right to witness court trials. Agreement with this basic principle cuts across every demographic group. However, Americans are largely undecided about televising all federal trials. While 29% favor allowing cameras in courtrooms to broadcast the proceedings of federal trials, 31% oppose this idea and fully 41% are undecided. A blanket policy, either for or against televising trials, seems to have little appeal. In fact, when it comes to cameras in the courtrooms, a plurality (48%) believe that judges should be able to decide for themselves.

Another 12% say all federal trials should be televised. This leaves 60% who believe that cameras should be allowed in courtrooms at least in some instances.

DISTRUST OF BOTH THE MEDIA AND THE LEGAL SYSTEM INCREASES SUPPORT FOR TELEVISED TRIALS

More than a third (36%) of Americans say that general news media coverage of trials has made them less favorable toward the legal system, while only 11% say it has made them more favorable. Those who dislike the general media's coverage are more supportive of allowing cameras to televise federal trials (44% favor, 22% oppose). Fully 69% agree that complete and unedited television coverage of trials would give them more accurate information than relying upon the news media. Indeed, allowing TV cameras in courtrooms permits Americans to see legal proceedings firsthand and not through the filter of the media is a "very convincing" reason to allow cameras in federal courtrooms to 47% of Americans. Forty percent (40%) also find "very convincing" the argument that televising federal trials would allow Americans to see the legal process firsthand, similar to C-SPAN's coverage of Congress.

Further, most Americans agree that televising trials would play an important role in improving the performance of key players in the legal system.   Fully   65% of Americans believe that televising court proceedings would make judges more careful than usual and 62% say it will ensure that lawyers are more careful than usual. A plurality (48%) go one step further in saying it is necessary to televise court proceedings to make it easier to watch over judges who take it upon themselves to change laws.

AMERICANS SEE AN EDUCATIONAL FUNCTION IN TELEVISING TRIALS

People view television coverage of trials as a good educational experience. In addition to a sense that they would get more accurate information by watching complete coverage of trials, Americans find argument about the educational value of watching trials to be compelling reasons to support cameras in the courtrooms. After hearing the argument that television and movies glorify violence and televising trials shows people the real consequences of violence, 40% say they are much more likely to support cameras in the courtroom. Forty percent (40%) say the same after hearing that three-quarters of high school teachers would recommend watching Court TV to their students.

COURT TV WATCHERS SAY THE CHANNEL'S COVERAGE IS MORE LIKELY TO GIVE A POSITIVE IMPRESSION OF OUR LEGAL SYSTEM THAN IS THE GENERAL MEDIA

While just over a quarter of the sample (27%) watches any Court TV, a majority (50%) of those viewers said that the channel's coverage made the legal process easier to understand. Although only a quarter say Court TV's coverage has made them more positive toward the legal system, that is nearly three times the number who can say the same about the general media's coverage. A mere 9% say the general media's coverage has made them more positive toward the legal system while fully 35% have become less favorable toward the legal system as a result of general media coverage.

The results of the Court TV Survey described above are consistent with the National Courts Survey discussed in Chapter 5. The National Courts Survey showed a relatively low level of concern about media coverage of the judicial system. It also showed a perceived need to better educate the public about the operation of the justice system. Similarly, the Court TV Survey showed that the public believes they should be able to witness trials at length and should not have their knowledge of the events filtered and potentially distorted by the traditional news media. Exposure to complete trials or large segments of trials is seen as educational and appears to improve public perception.

Court TV also commissioned surveys of judges whose cases have been covered from the fall of 1997 through January 1999 to see their perceptions of the impact from televising the trial. Some of those questions and responses are as follows:

1.   **Overall, were the Court-TV personnel you and your staff encountered:**
   A) **Courteous**
   B) **Respectful of the court and the process**
   C) **Dressed Appropriately**

Of the sixty-seven judges who returned their completed questionnaires, sixty-six responded favorably on these questions. One judge chose not to respond to these questions. Combined with questionnaire answers that predate Fall of 1997, (total positive response rate):

Question 1A: 364/366 (99%+)
Question 1B: 362/366 (99%)
Question 1C: 336/366 (92%)

2.   Do you feel that the presence of our cameras impeded the fairness of the process?

Sixty-four of the sixty-seven judges (96%) do not feel that the presence of Court-TV cameras impeded the fairness of the legal process in their courtroom. Two responded that they did while one judge chose not to respond to this question. One of the judges who responded that the impeding fairness said that, "TV has an impact on lawyers and witnesses." The other judge who responded negatively had no comment. Combined with earlier years' results (total positive response rate):

Question 2: 353/366 (96%)

3.   Do you think that the presence of our cameras and, to the extent that you are aware of it, Court-TV's reporting, helped convey the events of the trial in a way that contributed to the public understanding of the legal system?

Fifty-four of the sixty-seven judges (81%) thought that the reporting helped convey the events of the trial in such a beneficial manner. Six judges said that it did not, while seven judges did not answer the question. The concerns expressed by the six judges who responded negatively include:

"I believe it served only as entertainment."

"While (the) explanation of legal theories and law may be dull, it should be explained properly. With TV's personnel, even this could be interesting." "Reporting on (the) percentage of (the) jury's request for a lighter sentence was confusing to public."

Combined with earlier years' tabulations (total positive response rate):

Question 3: 268/366 (73%)

4.   Did Court TV's reporters or camera people do anything that you feel they should not have done?

Sixty judges (90%) said that the Court-TV staff behaved in an appropriate fashion. Two judges said they did engage in such activities, while five judges chose not to respond to the question. One of the two who gave a negative assessment did so because the staff "promised me videos, which they forgot about, until they wanted certain information which I wouldn't give to them until the videos came. I finally received them." The other judge said that the staff "left the camera on after the trial concluded for the day."

Combined with earlier years' tabulations (total positive response rate):

Question 4: 33/366 (90%)

Selected Quotes
"All of the Court TV personnel conducted themselves appropriately throughout the trial."
Honorable James C. Spencer, North Carolina Superior Court, Wake County.
Your crew and staff were delightful and a pleasure to work with.
Honorable James Kaddo, Louisiana Superior Court
My conversations with viewers indicated that they were watching not only the trial proceedings, but also had careful follow-up through the commentaries, and had a very full understanding of the issues.
Honorable A. Harris Adams, State Court of Cobb County, Georgia
These people were professionals and they are welcome in my courtroom at any time.
Honorable Jim Hamilton, Circuit Criminal Court 22nd Judicial District, State of Tennessee.
There was no difficulty, your personnel are very professional.
Honorable Frank Allen, 2nd Judicial District Court, Albuquerque, New Mexico.
Your staff were substantially more professional than the local media. It was a pleasure to work with you.
Honorable Ralph Winkler, Court of Common Pleas, Cincinnati, Ohio[10]
The preceding responses from judges who have actual experience with courtroom cameras shows little negative impact.

What insights do these survey results provide for the issues surrounding cameras in the courtroom? It seems that among all of the concerns expressed over the judicial system, media related concerns are low on the list. Is the concern expressed by scholars and lawyers justified? Might their fear for the public impact be overblown? It seems that the main media concern expressed by the public involves a concern that a distorted presentation would decay public confidence in the judicial system. Yet the level of trust and confidence appears to have improved between 1977 and 1998, a period when television coverage increased tremendously and Court TV came into existence. Might it be that the real concern should be over the manner in which trials are televised rather than whether or not they should be televised at all?

Chapter 6

EVIDENCE REGARDING TELEVISION BROADCASTING OF TRIALS

The case of Shirley Egan became a footnote in legal and ethics books when she was charged with shooting her daughter, who then asked to be removed from life support and subsequently died. Egan's trial, which began on August 16, 1999 in Orlando, Florida, set a technological precedent -- it was one of the first trials in the nation to be broadcast by a local court system over the Internet. According to Greg Flemming of the Pew Research Center for the People and the Press, "people like being able to get things directly by going to the source. You are not being filtered through the traditional news media or other types of outlets." Media organizations, as opposed to the court system itself, have aired legal proceedings on the World Wide Web and Court TV's Website has aired 150 trials involving such notables as TV talk show host Jenny Jones and assisted-suicide advocate Jack Kevorkian. In addition, the Internet site broadcast.com, showed President Clinton's grand jury testimony. The Egan trial, however, is the first time a court system has broadcast a trial on its own site. While some privacy advocates say that such broadcasts raise issues of fairness and confidentiality, others applaud the move as a step toward a more open government.[1]

One of the major issues that the courts should take into consideration when deciding the impact of cameras in the courts is how it will affect the trial participants: the defendant, the lawyers, the judges, the jury and the witnesses. Some argue that televised coverage has some impact on these participants. However, it is not clear whether that impact is positive or negative. According to David A. Anderson, a professor of law at the University of Texas School of Law, evidence shows that the more contact the public has with the judicial system, the less respect they have for the system and its actors. Anderson uses the O.J. Simpson trial as an example to demonstrate that the public felt that "celebrities receive favorable treatment ... less respect for lawyers... less respect for the criminal justice system... less respect for the media."[2]

One of the positive aspects of Simpson's trial coverage was the number of public opinion polls that were administered and the wealth of information that these polls provided. Americans were asked about their opinions and perceptions of the trial. Specifically, the public was asked how they viewed the major trial participants in the Simpson trial, as well as their attitude toward the criminal justice system as a whole.[3]

Nonetheless, there is a consensus among researchers that there is a need for more empirical analysis in order to determine the true effect of cameras within the courtroom. More studies must be focused on the impact of televising court proceedings and their affect on the public. Ralph Roberts' analysis of the Simpson data seems to indicate that there is a correlation between cameras in the courtroom and public loss of confidence in the justice system.[4] While the Simpson data can in no way be relied on as specific evidence, it can be utilized as a starting point in researching an important factor-- public opinion.

Given the state of public perception about the judicial branch of government and the criticism of additional media coverage of this branch in the form of courtroom television, do the benefits outweigh the harm? To answer that, we must first see if the alleged harm of cameras is real or imagined.

THE ACCURACY OF RESEARCH RESULTS ON
THE EFFECTS OF TELEVISED TRIALS

While more studies concerning the effects of televised trials on public opinions are needed, it is as important to study the results of televised trials on various court participants. There has been very little empirical analysis by the legal community to assess the effects of televised trials. Eugene Bordiga's study[5] attempted to observe the effects of the media on potential witnesses and jurors by exposing one group to electronic media coverage, one group to conventional media coverage, and one group to no media coverage. The study concluded that the electronic media may not impair witness recall or the ability to give credible testimony, and that the electronic media group recalled more information than either of the other groups. Naturally, everyone will react differently under different circumstances. As a result, the conclusions of studies like this one can only be made in general terms.

The empirical studies conducted thus far do not establish that the camera adversely affects the trial participants.[6] Despite the lack of empirical evidence to support it, Justice Harlen made the following statement in *Estes v. Texas* relating to potential adverse effects of cameras on trial participants:

> Courtroom television introduces into the conduct of a criminal trial the element of professional showmanship', an extraneous influence whose subtle capacities for serious mischief in a case of this sort will not be underestimated by any lawyer experienced in the elusive imponderables of the trial arena. In the context of a trial of intense public interest, there is certainly a strong possibility that the timid or reluctant witness, for whom a court appearance even at its traditional best is a harrowing affair, will become more timid or reluctant when he finds that he will also be appearing before a "hidden audience" of unknown but large dimensions. There is certainly a strong possibility that the "cocky" witness having a thirst for the limelight will become more "cocky" under the influence of television. And who can say that the juror who is gratified by having been chosen for a front-line case, an ambitious prosecutor, a publicity-minded defense counsel, and even a conscientious judge will not stray, albeit unconsciously, from doing what "come naturally" into pluming themselves for a satisfactory television 'performance'?[7]

THE IMPACT OF THE SIMPSON CASE

Not since Watergate have average Americans engaged in such matter-of-fact conversations about the limits of the Fourth Amendment, the definition of hearsay and the purpose of preliminary hearings. Many believe that this would not have been possible without cameras. Millions watched the Simpson trial not only in the United States but all over the world, and many eagerly awaited and watched as the jury returned its verdict. According to some of the viewers, watching the trial provided them with an opportunity to learn more about the adversial system and its operation. Other viewers developed a cynical view about the criminal justice system and how it operates. Opponents of cameras in the courtroom view the Simpson case as a landmark event to further their support or disapproval of televising sensational cases.

According to a survey taken by the New York County Lawyers' Association, ninety-one percent of New York State judges believed that coverage of the Simpson trial damaged the public perception of the judicial system.[8]   However, Gallup poll data revealed that most of the participants in the proceedings were viewed favorably, except for Johnnie Cochran and O.J. Simpson.[9] A majority of CBS poll takers found that the presence of a camera had an effect on the trial proceedings.[10] A majority of Newsweek poll takers perceived the effect of the Simpson case to have been a negative one on the public.[11] ABC's poll at the beginning of the trial proceedings revealed that 7 out of 10 poll takers thought that the trial should not be televised.[12] After the trial's conclusion, a majority of the participants had less confidence in the trial proceedings.   Based on the survey results at the time, some researchers concluded that the public opinion in the Simpson trial seems to indicate that there is a correlation between televising trials and the public's loss of confidence in the judicial system.[13]

The backlash against cameras in the courtroom struck just as cameras were gaining a solid foothold in traditionally off-limits courtrooms. At the time of Judge Lance Ito's decision to allow the high profile 1995 Simpson trial to be televised live, federal judges were wrapping up a successful three-year experiment with cameras in their courtrooms. The Federal Judicial Center recommended relaxing the ban on cameras in federal courts. However, by the time it came up for consideration, the Simpson media circus was well under way. According to a Los Angeles Superior Court judge, there was no question that after O.J. the door slammed shut. Many judges were concerned about what they had seen. There was a very strong reaction, and they did not want the media to come in and run their courtrooms.   A post-Simpson California study reached similar conclusions. The study was ordered by then-Governor Pete Wilson, who wanted cameras barred from California courts. But, instead of confirming Wilson's suspicions that cameras were responsible for courtroom anarchy, the survey found that the only judges who oppose cameras in the courtroom had little or no experience with cameras. According to some judges, it is a perception that is based more on myth than reality.[14]

Furthermore, they claim that the polls revealed that the public believed that cameras in the courtroom do have some type of influence on the proceedings, however, the extent of that influence is not clear.[15] It is suggested, however, that currently the public confidence in trial proceedings has returned to their previous levels.[16]

THE EXPERIENCE OF VARIOUS JURISDICTIONS

On or about 1974, states began to authorize, by statutes and/or rules, the audio visual recording and televising of in-court proceedings, including trial court proceedings. The substance of the statutes and/or rules varied by state. Some authorized coverage on an experimental basis; others on a permanent basis. All included a variety of procedural protections for trial court participants, restrictions on the kind and scope of coverage, and restrictions on type of equipment to be used.

As part of the movement during the past two decades to allow in-court coverage of trial court proceedings, 29 jurisdictions have formally studied and evaluated the effects of the televising of such proceedings; some jurisdictions having conducted more than one such evaluation. The studies have examined the impact of audio-visual coverage on the dignity of the proceedings, the administration of justice, and the effect of in-court cameras upon trial participants, including witnesses, jurors, attorneys, judges and other interested parties. The evidence assembled by all of these studies demonstrates that television coverage does not disrupt trial court proceedings or impair the administration of justice. Moreover, these studies demonstrate that televised coverage of trials provides substantial benefits to the public.

For example, in 1977, the Florida Supreme Court initiated a pilot program allowing "the electronic media [to] televise and photograph" civil and criminal judicial proceedings in all courts of the State of Florida, subject to specific restrictions on types of equipment, light and noise levels, camera placement and audio pickup, and subject to the "reasonable orders and direction of the presiding trial judge in any such proceeding".[17] In conjunction with the Florida Experiment, "all media participants in the program, all parties hereto, and all participants and judges" were requested to furnish to the Florida Supreme Court a "report on their experience under the program."

When the Florida Experiment ended on June 30, 1978, the Florida Supreme Court received and reviewed briefs, reports, letters, resolutions, comments and exhibits. The Court also conducted its own independent, separate surveys of witnesses, jurors, court personnel (excluding judges), and attorneys. Responses were sought from individuals who had participated in or were associated with trials in which audio-visual coverage had been permitted, and all responses were to remain anonymous. Prior to their distribution, the questionnaires were reviewed by the Supreme Court, the Judicial Planning Unit of the Office of the State Courts Administrator and interested academicians. Finally, the Florida Conference of Circuit Judges conducted a separate survey of trial court judges who had participated in televised proceeding.[18] After reviewing this material, the Florida Supreme Court concluded that the Florida Code of Judicial Conduct "should be amended to permit access to the courtrooms of this state by electronic media subject to standards adopted by this Court and subject also to the authority of the presiding judge at all times to control the conduct of the proceedings before him to ensure a fair trial to the litigants." More specifically, the Court found the following:

(i)   "It is essential that the populace have confidence in the [judicial] process, for public acceptance of judicial judgments is manifestly necessary to their observance."

(ii)   "Technological advancements have so reduced size, noise and light levels of the electronic equipment available that cameras can be employed in courtrooms unobtrusively."

(iii)   Electronic equipment presents "no ... discernible effect" on "the decorum of the proceedings."

(iv)   Assertions that "lawyers will 'grandstand' or 'play to the cameras' to advance their own self-interests" were "unsupported by any evidence."

(v)   Assertions that "judges will engage in 'posturing' - particularly at election time" - were "unsupported by any evidence."

(vi)   Assertions that "witnesses will either assume a stage presence and 'ham it up' or will be intimidated as not to be able to present fairly their testimony" were "unsupported by any evidence."

(vii)   Assertions that "jurors will be either be distracted from concentrating on the evidence and the issues to be decided by them or, because of their identification with the proceedings, they will fear for their personal safety, be subjected to influence by members of the public, or attempt to conform their verdict to community opinion" were "unsupported by any empirical evidence."

(viii)   Assertions that "the presence of electronic media in the courtroom will make that case appear to the participants to be a cause celebre and, therefore, prevent an objective and dispassionate presentation and resolution of the issues" were "unsupported by any empirical evidence."

(ix)   Despite the fact that before the pilot program "the overwhelming majority of trial court judges of this state [were] generally unsympathetic to the experiment," "it was the opinion of an overwhelming majority (90-95%) of respondents to the survey of the Florida Conference of Circuit Court Judges that jurors, witnesses, and lawyers were not affected in the performance of their sworn duty in the courtroom."

(x)   Witnesses and jurors were no more likely to be adversely influenced by exposure to televised proceedings than by exposure to the print media.

(xi)   Retrials or separate, subsequent trials of co-defendants were no more likely to be adversely affected by "accurate, direct broadcast of the events occurring in the courtroom" than by print media coverage or out-of-court filming and broadcast of trial participants.[19]

In 1978, Wisconsin appointed a committee to evaluate the use of audio and video for one year in the courtroom. They polled 181 circuit judges and gave questionnaires to jurors, witnesses, judges and attorneys. In addition, the committee used law students as observers. Of the 55 judges that answered, 44 supported televised trials, stating that they did not believe televised coverage promoted an unfair trial. The questionnaires resulted in the majority believing that TV coverage had no bearing on the trial outcome, and most were oblivious to the cameras. The committee concluded that broadcasting trials would be in the public's interest. The committee also proposed twelve rules to govern the use of audio and video, and asked the State Supreme Court to adopt their rules which provided that judges have a wide discretion to assure fair trials. Since July 1, 1979, Wisconsin trial and appellate courts have allowed radio, TV, and photograph coverage of civil and criminal trials.[20]

The Minnesota's Supreme Court in January 1978 allowed coverage of trials by cameras on an experimental basis. In March of 1981 various media groups petitioned the court to either make a permanent rule or a two year experiment that would allow television coverage of trial and appellate court proceedings. In January of 1982 the Minnesota Advisory Commission on Cameras in the Courtroom replied that TV technology had become advanced enough so as not to be obtrusive, although the Commission noted that there was no evidence to support the idea that cameras were either detrimental or beneficial to the judicial process. According to the Commission, it was difficult to reach any conclusion based on data which consisted of opinions, theories, and personal prejudices. The Commission did not make a permanent ruling on this issue, but authorized experimentation until January 1994. Presently, televised trial coverage is allowed on a case-by-case basis and cameras have been allowed in Minnesota appellate courts since April 20, 1981.[21]

Following a two-year study by an advisory committee of the Iowa Supreme Court, Iowa began its experiment with camera coverage of trial proceedings in January 1980. Four years and 190 trials later, surveys of jurors found that an overwhelming number of them viewed camera coverage as having little effect on trial participants, and no effect on the performance of judges or witnesses. Camera are now permitted in Iowa on a permanent basis with a presumption, in each case, in favor of televised trials.[22]

In 1983, Arizona, following a one-year experiment, reported that over 90% of judges interviewed stated that the presence or amount of media equipment did not affect the dignity or conduct of the proceedings. Moreover, 93% of jurors surveyed stated in response to questionnaires that the presence of media equipment did not distract them. Ninety-two percent of witnesses reported that once they learned that television coverage was taking place, it did not change their attitude about the proceedings, and 92 percent stated that the presence of cameras would not affect their willingness to testify again.

Following a one-year experiment, the Chief Court Administrator of the State of Connecticut reported in 1983 that the experiment "has been a success. We believe that the introduction of electronic coverage by the media into Superior Court proceedings has been accomplished without threatening the rights of parties or without interfering with the orderly disposition of cases." Moreover, the Administrator determined that cameras in the courtroom "afford the people of Connecticut with an excellent opportunity to learn more about the operations of their judicial branch of state government. For many of them, this has been their first glimpse of the court system. Providing this opportunity is consistent with the objective of the Judicial Department to increase the public's awareness and understanding of their courts."

The Alaska Judicial Council, after a three-year experiment, reported that television cameras in the courtroom have had virtually no effect on the courtroom behavior of participants. Judges have noted that there is no grandstanding by attorneys, and, if anything, the realization that they may appear on the evening news has improved attorneys' behavior. Most often participants forget that the cameras were there after the first few moments and instead concentrated on the reason they were all in the courtroom." Moreover, the study observed that "[m]any of the judges interviewed in the course of this study originally had grave reservations about the presence of cameras in their courts. Paradoxically, these were the same judges who were placed in situations where they had to face cameras in their courts on a daily basis and the result was most surprising to them .... Perhaps the surest sign of the success of the Media Plan is the case with which judges, attorneys, court personnel and the public have accepted the changes. News cameras have become a daily presence in the court buildings and the courtrooms. Trial proceedings frequently appear on the television news and similar photos are in the daily newspapers. Far from creating a courtroom spectacle, cameras in the courtroom have become accepted tools for bringing elements of our justice system into the everyday lives of the public. [23] Of particular interest is the experience in California. It was among the first states to conduct a statewide evaluation of film and electronic coverage of court proceedings. A one year experiment in 1980 and 1981 - subsequently summarized and evaluated in a several-hundred-page report prepared by an independent consulting firm - was a success. Participants reported little awareness of, and little distraction caused by, the presence of cameras. Indeed, fully ninety percent of the judges and attorneys surveyed said that the presence of cameras did not interfere at all, or interfered only slightly, with courtroom dignity and decorum. Most judges and attorneys surveyed also agreed that camera coverage did not affect the behavior of the various participants. As a result of the report, in 1984, California enacted Rule 980, which permitted extensive coverage of criminal and civil trials.

The 1980 California report was among the more comprehensive studies conducted on the perceived effects of televised trials on the proceedings themselves. But the California story did not end there. Three weeks after the O.J. Simpson criminal case concluded in 1996, the Chief Judge of the California Supreme Court appointed a special Task Force on Photographing, Recording, and Broadcasting in the Courtroom (the "Task Force") to evaluate whether Rule 980, should be amended. As part of its charge, the Task Force considered the views of judges, media representatives, victims' rights groups, public defenders, prosecutors and other representatives of the bar. The Task Force also evaluated surveys and reports from other jurisdictions. It took into account numerous objections raised by opponents of camera coverage, and also the view "that the American judicial system was designed to be as open as possible," and that "[p]rograms such as Court TV have provided access to judicial proceedings for millions of people who would otherwise have little opportunity to observe the courts in action."

The Task Force concluded in 1996 that cameras should continue to remain in California's courtrooms. It determined that "society's interest in an informed public, recognized in the planning and mission of the Judicial Council, is an important objective for the judiciary, which would be severely restricted by a total ban. Today's citizen relies too heavily on the electronic media for information; yet actual physical attendance at court proceedings is too difficult for the courts to countenance a total removal of the public's principal news source."

The Task Force found that judges who had actually had experience with cameras in their courts favored continued camera coverage of California trials. Ninety-six percent of those judges reported that the presence of a video camera did not affect the outcome of a trial or hearing in any way. In addition, a large majority of them reported that the camera did not affect their ability to maintain courtroom order and control of proceedings, and further reported "[n]o decrease in persons' willingness to serve as jurors as a result of video broadcast media in the courtroom." They also reported that "there were not more attempts to offer unnecessary motions, evidence, or witnesses in case" covered by the electronic media. In early 1996, the California Judicial Council voted to adopt almost all the Task Force's recommendations. Effective January 1, 1997, new Rule 980 went into effect, setting forth a variety of factors sufficiently inclusive to provide additional guidance to trial courts considering future coverage requests.

The State of New York had a long history of grappling with this issue. In 1982, the Chief Judge of New York State, with the approval of the Associate Judges of New York Court of Appeals, promulgated a set of rules authorizing an experimental program for audio-visual coverage of civil trials, to become effective if the Legislature removed the bar contained in Section 52 of the Civil Rights Law. However, despite the broad movement in many states to allow cameras in courts, the Legislature did not act until five years later.

In 1987, the New York Legislature suspended the enforcement of Section 52 of the Civil Rights Law by authorizing an 18-month experiment of audio-visual coverage of criminal and civil trial court proceedings pursuant to Section 218 of the Judiciary Law (First Experiment). The First Experiment began on December 1, 1987 and was to expire on May 31, 1989.

In enacting the First Experiment, the Legislature noted that:

It was the experience of an earlier generation that bright lights, large cameras and other noisy equipment intruded upon the dignity and decorum of the courtroom and tended to create an atmosphere unsuited to calm deliberation and impartial decision-making.

In enacting the First Experiment, the Legislature found that:

various improvements in the technology of photography and of the audio and video broadcast media, in addition to the development of procedural safeguards as provided for in various state programs, make it feasible to permit in this state, on an experimental basis, audio-visual coverage of court proceedings without disruptive effect.

The First Experiment authorized, and the rules promulgated thereunder provided, implementing procedures for cameras in trial court proceedings, subject to procedural protections for the parties and other participants, regulations limiting the kind and scope of coverage, and regulations regarding the placement and nature of equipment.

Under the First Experiment, the presiding trial judge, in deciding whether to permit audio-visual access, was obligated to consider the type of case involved, any harm to participants, the effect on the fair administration of justice or on the rights of the parties, the effect of any law enforcement activity, and whether the proceeding involved lewd or scandalous matters, although consent of the participants was not required.

The First Experiment required the Chief Administrative Judge to evaluate the First Experiment and submit a report to the Legislature. On or about March 1988, Chief Administrative Judge Albert M. Rosenblatt submitted the required report (Rosenblatt Report). The Rosenblatt Report was based upon over 1,000 written evaluations submitted by judges, lawyers, witnesses and news media representatives who had participated in court proceedings in which audio-visual coverage was permitted.

The Rosenblatt Report concluded, *inter alia*, that 84% of New York judges were favorable to televised coverage, that no judge believed such coverage made it difficult for jurors to ascertain the truthfulness of testimony and that no one (whether favorably or unfavorably inclined with regard to televising court proceedings) had commented that the presence of cameras influenced the ultimate outcome of any trial. The Rosenblatt Report recommended that the First Experiment be made permanent.

Following the submission of the Rosenblatt Report, the Legislature amended Section 218 of the Judiciary Law, continuing the experiment of permitting audio-visual coverage of civil and criminal proceedings in trial courts (Second Experiment). The Second Experiment was to continue for two additional years beyond the expiration date of the First Experiment, until May 31, 1991.

The Second Experiment, as had the First Experiment, required the submission of a report to the Legislature by the Chief Administrator on the effect of the experiment. As part of this study, a temporary advisory committee was created, consisting of two social scientists with extensive experience in research methodology, two communications experts, and one legal expert.

On or about March of 1991, Chief Administrative Judge Matthew T. Crosson submitted a report to the Legislature evaluating the Second Experiment (Crosson Report). Like the Rosenblatt Report, the Crosson Report concluded that the experiment had been successful and recommended that the Second Experiment be made permanent, with certain minor changes added to the new statutory language.

Despite the recommendations set forth in both the Rosenblatt Report and the Crosson Report, and despite the participant evaluations upon which those reports were based, the Legislature failed during the 1992 legislative session either to make Section 218 permanent, to continue the experiment or otherwise to facilitate the continuation of televised trial court proceedings. On June 1, 1991, audio-visual coverage of trial court proceedings in this State ceased.

On or about June 1992, the Legislature re-enacted Section 218, and re-instated the experiment for two-and-a-half more years until January 31, 1995 (Third Experiment). As part of the Third Experiment, Section 218 removed the bar of Section 52 of the Civil Rights Law up to and including January 31, 1995.

As part of the Third Experiment, Section 218 adopted most of the procedural protections, restrictions on kind and scope of coverage, restrictions on types of equipment and the manner in which that equipment is deployed during trial court proceeding as were previously provided by former Section 218 and the rules promulgated thereunder.

As part of the Third Experiment, however, Section 218 was amended in several respects to provide additional procedural protections for witnesses, defendants in criminal cases, family members of parties or victims, and to ensure the orderly conduct of the proceedings.

As part of the Third Experiment, Section 218 created a 12-member committee, chaired by then-Judge Burton Roberts (the Roberts Committee), to review audio-visual coverage of court proceedings. The Committee of three members appointed by the Governor, three (including the Chair of the Committee) appointed by the Chief Administrator of the Courts, three appointed by the majority leader of the Senate, two appointed by the Speaker of the Assembly, and one appointed by the minority leader of the Assembly.

Section 218 accorded the Roberts Committee with "the power, duty and responsibility to evaluation, analyze and monitor" the Third Experiment. The Roberts Committee was also empowered to require assistance from bar associations. Finally, the Committee was required to recommend to the Legislature, the Governor and the Chief Judge "as to the efficacy" of the Third Experiment, and "whether it should be continued."

In carrying out its mandate, the Roberts Committee adopted the following methods: It solicited and compiled comments and observations of trial judges throughout the State who presided over proceedings in which audio-visual coverage was permitted during the Third Experiment. It solicited complaints, instances of statutory violations and other concerns relating to audio-visual coverage of court proceedings from members of the Criminal Justice Section of the New York State Bar Association and from the New York State District Attorneys Association. It collected, compiled data from and analyzed all applications for audio-visual coverage made during the Third Experiment. It reviewed and analyzed prior studies and surveys relating to audio-visual coverage of court proceedings, including the Rosenblatt and Crosson Reports, as well as studies conducted in other jurisdictions. It reviewed and analyzed information regarding audio-visual coverage statutes and rules from other jurisdictions. It conducted two public hearings, at which 46 witnesses testified, and it reviewed written submission prepared by other organizations and individuals who did not testify before the Committee. It met as a group on several occasions to discuss and debate the issues relating to audio-visual coverage of court proceedings.

On or about May 1994, the Roberts Committee submitted a 106-page report to the Legislature, the Governor and the Chief Judge (Roberts Report). The Roberts Report, by a 12-1 vote, concluded that the benefits of the Third Experiment had been "substantial" and that the First, Second and Third Experiments had been a "success". The Roberts Committee recommended that Section 218 be permanently enacted.

In determining that Section 218 should be permanently enacted, the Roberts Committee concluded that:

(i)   "No criminal conviction in New York has ever been reversed or set aside on the ground that audio-visual coverage interfered with the defendant's right to a fair trial."

(ii)   Because "relatively few people ever attend court proceedings," and because "vast numbers of citizens rely on television as their primary source of information about our society ..., [t]elevision coverage of court proceedings, therefore, exposes greater numbers of citizens to our justice system.

(iii)   Cameras in trial court proceedings enhance public education of the judicial and criminal processes by "engender[ing] a deeper understanding of legal principals and processes."

(iv)   Cameras in trial court proceedings have led to "increased public respect for the justice system."

(v)   Cameras in trial court proceedings have helped "energize debate over" the "major substantive issues" (such as "domestic violence, date rape, freedom of speech") that cases frequently present "because citizens have examined the issues as they have arisen in the lives of real people whom they have seen and heard."

(vi)   Cameras in trial court have enabled the public, to greater effect than previously possible, to monitor whether "justice is handed out fairly and impartially."

(vii)   "[R]eporting on court proceedings, both by newspaper and broadcast reporters, frequently is more accurate and comprehensive when cameras are present."

(viii)   "Unlike the rudimentary technology of yesteryear, cameras now function in the courtroom without disruption or distraction. Improvements in technology have rendered cameras no more, and possibly less, conspicuous than the newspaper reporter with pencil and notebook and the courtroom artist with crayon and sketch pad."

(ix)   There is "no concrete evidence" that cameras in trial court proceedings have inclined trial judges to act any more unfairly or harshly toward criminal defendants than any such judge would act without cameras present. "[A] judge whose interest is not in seeing that justice is done by in pleasing the majority will be inclined to do so even if only the print media are covering the proceedings. Camera coverage, in fact, could more effectively expose judges who demonstrate a pattern of lack of impartiality."

(x)   Cameras in trial court proceedings have not "affect[ed] adversely the performance of attorneys" in representing their clients.

(xi)   Cameras in trial proceedings have had minimal, if any, impact on the "vast majority of witnesses who have testified with cameras present" and the Roberts Committee reported learning that "no prosecutor or defense attorney ... has lost a witness because of camera coverage."

(xii)   "The suggestion that camera coverage adversely affects jurors is also erroneous." All juror surveys reveal that "camera coverage does not influence their role in the proceedings."

(xiii)   "A review of applications for audio-visual coverage made during the [Third Experiment] reveals that it is simply not true that the media have sought to cover only 'sensational' proceedings." Moreover, audio-visual coverage of high-profile or "sensational" cases also serves to educate the public. "Coverage of those cases reveals the reality of the courtroom as distinctly as does the coverage of other cases."

(xiv)   Audio-visual coverage of trial court proceedings is a "superb" educational tool for judges, attorneys and students, who can enhance their knowledge and courtroom skills by studying the recordings of the proceedings."

(xv)   The Roberts Committee, after inquiring of the New York State Bar Association, the New York State

District Attorneys Association, witnesses at public hearings and judges who had presided over proceedings in which audio-visual coverage of proceedings occurred, found only two minor violations of Section 218 of the Judiciary Law during the Third Experiment, despite the hundreds of applications for audio-visual coverage made during that time.

The Third Experiment had been scheduled to sunset on January 31, 1995 - in what turned out to be in the middle of the O.J. Simpson criminal trial in California. On February 1, 1995, the Legislature re-enacted Section 218, authorizing yet another experiment for two-and-a-half more years (Fourth Experiment). As part of the Fourth Experiment, Section 218 again removed the bar of Section 52 of the Civil Rights Law up to and including June 30, 1997.

As part of the Fourth Experiment, Section 218 adopted exactly the same procedural protections, restrictions on kind and scope of coverage, restrictions on types of equipment and the manner in which that equipment is deployed during trial court proceedings as were previously provided by former Section 218 and the rules promulgated thereunder.

But, given that some had concluded that cameras had caused the perceived problems at the Simpson trial, the Legislature provided for yet another committee to review audio-visual coverage of court proceedings. The Committee was chair by Fordham Law School Dean John Feerick (Feerick Committee).

As with the prior New York experiments, Section 218 accorded the Feerick Committee with "the power, duty and responsibility to evaluate, analyze, and monitor" the Fourth Experiment.[24] The Office of Court Administration and all participants in proceedings in which audio-visual coverage was to be permitted, including judges, attorneys and jurors, were required to cooperate with and assist the Feerick Committee in evaluating the impact of audio-visual coverage of court proceedings. The Feerick Committee was mandated to request assistance from bar associations. Finally, the Committee was required to issue a report to the Legislature, the Governor and the Chief Judge "evaluating the efficacy" of the Fourth Experiment and "whether any public benefits accrue from the [Fourth Experiment], any abuses that occurred during the [Fourth Experiment], and the extent to which and in what way the conduct of participants in court proceedings changed when audio-visual coverage is present."

In carrying out its mandate, the Feerick Committee adopted the following methods: It designed and conducted a written survey of over

350 trial judges throughout the State to assess the experience of New York judges with cameras in the courtroom under the Fourth Experiment. It commissioned the Marist Institute for Public Opinion to survey public opinion in New York on the issue of cameras in the courtroom. It contacted 150 bar associations in New York requesting information about the experience of their members with respect to the Fourth Experiment. It heard testimony from over 50 witnesses at five public hearings, including judges, civil and criminal trial lawyers who had participated in televised trials, crime victim advocates, law enforcement officials, media scholars, jurors and representatives of the print and electronic media. It received numerous communications and letters from the public commenting on the issue of cameras in the courtroom. It collected data from the Office of Court Administration regarding applications for audio-visual coverage made during the Fourth Experiment. It reviewed samples of televised courtroom footage. It contacted jury consultants to obtain information about their experience with the impact of cameras in the courtroom on jurors and other trial participants. It obtained and reviewed information on the experience of cameras in the courtrooms in fifty states and in the federal courts.

On or about April 1997, the Feerick Committee submitted its report to the Legislature, the Governor and the Chief Judge (Feerick Report). Despite the backlash of the Simpson case against televised trials, the Feerick Report reaffirmed them. The Feerick Report concluded that "[a]lmost 10 years of experience argue in favor of allowing cameras in the courts on a permanent basis." It recommended, "[i]n light of the long period of examination of this subject by prior committees and this Committee, ... that Section 218 of the Judiciary Law be amended to permit audio-visual coverage on a permanent basis, with all of the safeguards of the current legislation for defendants in criminal proceedings, parties in civil proceedings, witnesses, jurors, crime victims, children and others." It found that such an approach "respects the public value of openness, the public nature of a trial, and the constitutional principle of a fair trial." Finally the Feerick Report determined that the "benefits that flow from televised coverage of the judicial process are so important that *they ought not to be sacrificed by barring cameras from the courtroom across-the-board*" (emphasis added).

In determining that Section 218 should be permanently enacted, the Feerick Committee also concluded that:

(i)   Research had not revealed any appellate decision "overturning a judgment, verdict, or conviction based on the presence of cameras at trial."

(ii)   "Our review of the [Fourth] [E]xperiment .... did not find that the presence of cameras in New York interferes with the fair administration of justice."

(iii)   "[O]ne of the greatest benefits derived from the presence of cameras in the courtroom is enhanced public scrutiny of the judicial system. The majority of judges who responded to the Committee's survey and a wide array of witnesses who testified at the Committee's hearings agreed that the presence of television cameras in the courtroom enhances public scrutiny of judicial proceedings."

(iv)   Television coverage of court proceedings "enables the public to learn more about the workings of the justice system, to see directly the conduct of particular cases, and to become more familiar with legal concepts and developments. The fact that many view television coverage as a form of entertainment does not deprive it of educational content, since education and entertainment are not mutually exclusive."

(v)   "[T]elevision coverage has drawn the public's attention to major societal problems, such as domestic violence and child abuse, and has served a cathartic purpose for the families of some homicide victims."

(vi)   "Video and photographs have become important tools in presenting news to the public, many of whom now rely on televison as their principal source of information about public affairs."

(vii)   "The record developed by this Committee does not show that the fears regarding the impact of cameras on trial participants have been realized in New York during the experimental period."

(viii)   "[M]any judges believe that witnesses' testimony is unchanged in the presence of cameras."

(ix)   "[W]itness intimidation is neither borne out by the record in New York nor sufficiently strong to warrant barring cameras from the courtroom across-the-board. Such witness concerns are adequately addressed, in our view, by all of the current safeguards in Section 218 and in the implementing rules" (emphasis added).

(x)   Claims that jurors will watch televised coverage of their case and will be influenced either by commentary about the case or by evidence ruled inadmissible and not presented to the jury are unsupported. "No one has drawn the Committee's attention to a specific case in New York in which jurors had improper communications regarding a television case or in which jurors disregarded a judge's instructions not to watch televised coverage of the proceedings. Nor has it been suggested to us that the outcome of a particular case in New York was altered by the presence of cameras."

(xi)   "[M]ost judges felt that compared to similar cases covered only by the print media, lawyers made about the same number of motions, objections and arguments in camera-covered cases and presented about the same amount of evidence and witnesses."

(xii)   "[W]e have no basis from our review to conclude that lawyers in camera-covered cases in New York State have failed to serve their clients and the public responsibly. The evidence from the record before this Committee is that they have met their professional obligations."

(xiii) "There was ample testimony and public comment that cameras raised some judges' performances and had a positive impact on judicial demeanor."

(xiv)   "In the end, we are left with a record heavily weighted with opinions which suggest that judicial conduct may improve rather than worsen in the presence of cameras. There is no basis in this record to conclude that judges will not faithfully discharge their responsibilities if courtrooms are open to cameras. The evidence before this Committee is that they have met their obligations with a high degree of competence."

(xv)   "[W]e believe that openness and the public access to information about trials afforded by television works as a safeguard, not a threat, to the defendant's rights."

(xvi)   "Openness of public institutions, including the judiciary, is a key ingredient in our democracy. Among the many values served by openness are promoting public confidence in government, providing the public with information about the workings of the judiciary, assuring the fairness of court proceedings, and satisfying the appearance of justice."

(xvii)   "Although televised coverage could, at times show the judicial system in an unfavorable light, we do not view that as a detriment. Rather, to the extent that such coverage offers an opportunity for improving the judicial system, we view it as a strength of our democratic system."

(xviii) "The Committee's record includes strong evidence of compliance with the requirements and safeguards of Section 218 by representatives of the electronic news media. Reporters and photographers who testified before the Committee appeared to understand and respect the solemnity and dignity of the courtrooms they covered."

Despite the Feerick Committee's support for televised coverage of trial proceedings and recommendations to make Section 218 permanent, the Legislature failed to act; audio-visual coverage of trial court proceedings ceased on June 30, 1997, and Section 52 sprang back to life. No legislative action has since occurred.

In the wake of the decision by the Legislature, no trials held in the courts of New York were televised until early 2000. At that time, Albany Supreme Court Justice Judge Joseph Teresi permitted Court TV to televise *People v. Boss*, the highly publicized homicide trial of four New York City police officers accused of shooting Amadou Diallo.

The Court permitted the televising of the trial after having granted a motion by Court TV to intervene to seek to televise the trial and an application to do so. In so ruling, the Court struck down Section 52 as unconstitutional under both the First Amendment and Article I, Section 8.[25] Justice Teresi characterized the *per se* ban of Section 52 as a "monument to politically created procrastination and inaction [that] arises not from scholarly debate but rather .... the failure of the Legislature to maximize the press and public's legitimate constitutional access to the courts."[26] The court noted both the doctrinal transformation in the law and the evolution in technology and, invoking the "re-examination" implicitly invited by Justice Harlan in *Estes*, declared that "[in] the year 2000 ... an absolute ban on audio visual coverage in the courtroom [is] unconstitutional."[27]

The trial was televised without incident, despite the enormous publicity it generated (even before the determination to permit its televising) and the political passions it aroused. In the wake of Justice Teresi's decision in *Boss*, a number of other trials in other parts of the State were permitted to be televised, the result of individual determinations in those cases that Section 52 was unconstitutional. Other courts have refused to permit trials to be televised, and refused to declare Section 52 unconstitutional.

The few trials that have been televised in New York in the last few years lend further support to the findings of the Feerick Committee and the reports that preceded it. No verdict has been reversed or vacated because of the presence of television cameras. Judicial dignity has not been impaired. Witnesses have not been intimidated from testifying. Jurors have not been unable to perform their duties. The only thing that has occurred is that, in these few cases, much more of the public has been able to see the justice system, first-hand, at work.

In the case of *Boss*, televising the trial acted as a kind of counterpoint to the O.J. Simpson trial in California: citizens were able to watch justice conducted with dignity and order in a high-profile trial that was thought to reflect racial and ethnic divisions, and in which the result - an acquittal of officers publicly accused of racial bias - was controversial. As the Chief Administrative Judge of New York wrote in May of 2000: "the *Boss* trial suggested [that] televised access to court proceedings can promote respect for the legitimacy of our justice system - even when whole segments of society disagree with a particular outcome. When the public is given the opportunity to see and weigh the evidence for itself, it can be expected to make reasonable judgments."

In this way, *Boss* belied the notion that the in-court coverage of the Simpson trial was the problem in that particular case, but, rather, that the problem was with the way the trial proceedings themselves were conducted. Indeed, *Boss* vindicated the 1996 observations of former Second Circuit Chief Judge Jon O. Newman who, as paraphrased by the *Washington Post*, was of the view that "cameras had nothing to do with the deficiencies of the Simpson case, such as its length, lack of judicial control and grandstanding by prosecutors and defense attorneys."

On May 25, 2000, however, the Appellate Division of the Fourth Department issued an order declaring as impermissible the intervention procedure that the press, including Court TV, had been invoking to gain access to trial court proceedings such as *Boss*, and to obtain individual declarations of the unconstitutionality of Section 52. In *Santiago v. Bristol*[28] the court issued an order granting a writ of prohibition barring a Monroe County Court Judge from enforcing an order he had entered to permit the televising of a death penalty trial in Rochester on the basis of his determination that Section 52 was unconstitutional. The court ruled that the trial judge had exceeded his authority by having permitted intervention by the press and stated that "[r]ather than moving in County Court for an order permitting audiovisual coverage of [the] trial, [the press] should have commenced a declaratory judgment action in Supreme Court challenging the constitutionality of the statute and rule barring such coverage."[29]

THE FEDERAL COURTS

After a two-year pilot program in six federal district courts evaluating the effect of cameras in civil proceedings, the Federal Judicial Center reported in November 1993 that "[o]verall, attitudes of judges toward coverage ... were initially neutral and became more favorable after experience with electronic media coverage under the pilot program." Moreover, "[j]udges and attorneys who had experience with electronic media coverage under the program generally reported observing little or no effect of camera presence on participants in the proceedings, courtroom decorum, or the administration of justice." In 1994, based on all the data gathered during the two-year pilot program, the research staff that had analyzed the data recommended that the Judicial Conference "authorize federal courts of appeals and district courts nationwide to provide camera access to civil proceedings in their courtrooms, subject to Conference guidelines". The recommendation was based on the determination that the in-court presence of the electronic media "did not disrupt court proceedings, affect participants in the proceedings, or interfere with the administration of justice." Although the Judicial Conference of the United States declined to adopt the recommendation, in 1996, federal courts in New York State ruled that the Judicial Conference did not have statutory authority to decide whether cameras could be permitted in federal trial courts.[30]   As of now, Rule 1.8 of the Southern and Eastern Districts of New York permits judges to decide for themselves in each case whether to permit civil trials to be televised, and legislation is currently pending in both houses of Congress to permit each federal court to decide for itself whether to permit particular trials to be televised.[31]

Decisions on whether cameras should be allowed in United States Federal courts are made by the Judicial Conference, which meets twice a year to discuss and set policy. The Conference is a 28 member body made up of the Chief Judges of each circuit, plus representatives from other

Courts. The Chief Justice of the Supreme Court, William Rehnquist, presides at the conference.

The Conference sponsored a pilot program from 1991-94 to test cameras in federal courtrooms. In the three-year pilot project, cameras were allowed in many federal courts with very positive results. Most judges had no problem with the cameras and reported that the media were largely cooperative, and witnesses and jurors were unfazed. When the test ended, a Subcommittee recommended in 1994 that the ban be lifted. However, the Conference declined.[32]

Sunshine bills started popping up after the pilot program ran its course. The pilot program did not provide a convincing argument for cameras in the courtroom. In 1994, the U.S. Judicial Conference's Ad Hoc Committee on Cameras in the Courtroom recommended that the Judicial Conference eliminate Canon 7A(7), which prohibits electronic camera presence in federal courtroom proceedings in order to experiment with camera presence in the federal courtrooms.[33] This experiment was conducted on a voluntary basis, and as a result, the conclusions are not entirely reliable. This experiment found that both the judges and attorneys, especially those with previous courtroom camera experience, reacted favorably to the presence of cameras during the trial proceedings. The study found that a majority of the coverage was conducted with a television reporter. The air time spent on the plaintiff was more than on the defendant. Further, it was revealed that the coverage was not highly detailed. However, the study revealed that the more extensive camera coverage did not necessarily mean that more information on trial proceedings was conveyed.[34]

The Federal Judicial Center found that district court judges with some experience with cameras in the courtroom believed that the cameras had a minor effect on the trial and trial participants. Judges reported better experiences than they had anticipated and became more supportive of cameras in the courtroom after their experiences. Judges also reported that the significant potential benefit of cameras in the courtroom is found in the educational value that it provides the public. Although the benefits were recognized only moderately under the experimental program, judges were more willing to allow cameras in their courtrooms if the media promised gavel-to-gavel coverage of the case.[35]

DISTRICT JUDGES

Federal Judicial Conference ("FJC") analysis of responses about the effects of electronic media coverage focused on judges who had experienced electronic media coverage under the program. In general, district judges who had experience with electronic media coverage under the pilot program believed electronic coverage had only minor effects on the participants or proceedings. In the follow-up questionnaire, their median ratings indicated that all but one potential effect occurred "to little or no extent" or "to some extent."[36] Table 1 shows all of the judges' responses to the follow-up survey about specific effects of coverage.

When FJC compared the results in Table 1 to results from the initial questionnaire (not displayed here), FJC analysis showed that district judges who had experience with electronic media coverage rated nine of seventeen potential effects significantly lower (i.e., as occurring to a lesser extent) on the follow-up questionnaire than on the initial questionnaire.[37] These effects included the following items relating to electronic media coverage: "violates witnesses' privacy"; "distracts witnesses"; "makes witnesses more nervous than they otherwise would be"; "signals to jurors that a witness or argument is particularly important"; "causes attorneys to be more theatrical in their presentation"; "disrupts courtroom proceedings"; "motivates attorneys to come to court better-prepared"; "increases judge attentiveness"; and "prompts judges to be more courteous." Thus, judges apparently experienced these potential effects to a lesser extent than they had expected.

In contrast, when the FJC compared ratings of conventional coverage effects between the initial and follow-up surveys they found no significant differences. This suggests that the differences in ratings of effects of electronic media coverage between the initial and follow-up questionnaires were attributable to experience with electronic media coverage and not to some more general shift in judges' attitudes toward the media.

Table 1. Ratings of Effects by District Judges Who Experienced
Electronic Media Coverage Under the Program, by Percentage*

Effect	To little or no extent	To some extent	To a mod-erate extent	To a great extent	To a very great extent	No opinion
Motivates witnesses to be truthful	61	7	7	2	0	22
Violates witnesses' privacy	37	34	10	7	5	7
Makes witnesses less willing to appear in court	32	22	15	2	2	22
Distracts witnesses	51	22	15	2	2	7
Makes witnesses more nervous than they otherwise would be	24	37	22	5	0	12
Increases juror attentiveness	46	22	7	7	2	15
Signals to jurors that a witness or argument is particularly important	51	15	10	5	7	12
Increases jurors' sense of responsibility for their verdict	49	15	15	10	0	12
Prompts people who see the coverage to try to influence juror- friends	54	10	7	0	0	27
Motivates attorneys to come to court better prepared	32	32	15	10	7	5
Causes attorneys to be more theatrical in their presentation	29	37	20	2	5	7
Prompts attorneys to be more courteous	44	20	15	17	2	2
Increases judge attentiveness	63	10	15	10	2	0
Causes judges to avoid unpopular						

Table 1 (continued)

Effect	To little or no extent	To some extent	To a moderate extent	To a great extent	To a very great extent	No opinion
decisions or positions	88	2	5	2	0	2
Prompts judges to be more courteous	56	22	15	7	0	0
Disrupts courtroom proceedings	83	15	0	2	0	0
Educates the public about courtroom procedure	12	20	12	24	30	2

* *Note*: The figure in each cell represents the percentage of responding judges (N = 41) who selected that answer.

Taken from the Federal Judicial Center's Report on the Electronic Media Coverage of Federal Civil Proceedings - An Evaluation of the Pilot Program in Six District Courts and Two Courts of Appeals. (1994)

With respect to overall attitudes toward electronic media coverage of civil and criminal proceedings, district judges (including those who personally experienced coverage and those who did not experience coverage, but presumably observed the effects of coverage on their colleagues and on the court as a whole) exhibited significantly more favorable attitudes toward electronic media coverage of civil proceedings in the follow-up questionnaire than they had in the initial questionnaire. The median response to this question in the initial questionnaire was a 3, indicating "I have no opinion on coverage," while the median response in the follow-up questionnaire was a 2, representing "I somewhat favor coverage." After the program had been in place, thirty-six judges had more favorable attitudes toward electronic coverage of civil proceedings than they had reported in the initial questionnaire, fifteen had less favorable attitudes, and sixty-one reported the same attitude that they had in the initial questionnaire.

District judges also indicated less opposition to coverage of criminal proceedings in the follow-up questionnaire, moving from a median of 4 in the initial questionnaire (indicating "I somewhat oppose coverage") to a median of 3 (indicating "I have no opinion on coverage"). In the follow-up questionnaire, thirty-five judges reported more favorable attitudes toward criminal coverage than they had in the initial questionnaire, seventeen reported less favorable attitudes, and sixty-one reported the same attitude they had initially.

APPELLATE JUDGES

Experience with electronic media coverage appears not to have changed the appellate judges' ratings of the effects of cameras. In both the initial and follow-up questionnaires, appellate judges' median ratings of effects were generally 1 (indicating the effect occurs "to little or no extent") or 2 (indicating the effect occurs "to some extent"). The following table shows responses of appellate judges with electronic media experience to the questions in the follow-up survey about the effects of coverage.

Table 2. Ratings of Effects by Appellate Judges with Experience in the Program, by Percentage*

Effect	To little or no extent	To some extent	To a moderate extent	To a great extent	To a very great extent	No opinion
Prompts attorneys to come to oral argument better prepared	52	26	0	17	0	4
Causes attorneys to be more theatrical in their presentation	48	30	9	4	4	4
Causes attorneys to change the emphasis or content of their oral argument	39	43	9	0	4	4
Increases judges' attentiveness at oral argument	70	26	4	0	0	0
Prompts judges to be more courteous in questioning attorneys	57	35	9	0	0	0
Causes judges to change the emphasis or content of their questions at oral argument	65	30	4	0	0	0
Disrupts courtroom proceedings	74	22	0	4	0	0
Educates the public about the work of the court of appeals	17	30	30	9	9	4

*Note: The figure in each cell represents the percentage of responding judges (N = 23) who selected that answer.

Taken from the Federal Judicial Center's Report on the Electronic Media Coverage of Federal Civil Proceedings - An Evaluation of the Pilot Program in Six District Courts and Two Courts of Appeals. (1994)

JUDGES WITH ELECTRONIC MEDIA EXPERIENCE UNDER THE PILOT PROGRAM

Twenty judges with the greatest experience with electronic media under the pilot program (as measured by the number of cases covered in which they presided on an appellate panel or presided as a district court judge) were interviewed. This group comprised judges from each of the pilot courts and included four appellate judges, fifteen district judges, and one bankruptcy judge. The database showed that these twenty judges were involved in sixty-seven proceedings covered under the program. The greatest number of covered cases in which any one judge was involved was five for district judges and five for appellate judges.

Experienced judges were asked a number of questions about their practices in allowing electronic media coverage under the pilot program; their perceptions regarding the effects of electronic media on attorneys, jurors, witnesses, themselves, and on courtroom decorum and the administration of justice; and their overall attitudes toward electronic media coverage.

1. BENEFITS AND DISADVANTAGES OF ELECTRONIC MEDIA COVERAGE

Judges were asked what they saw as potential benefits and potential disadvantages of electronic media coverage of court proceedings, and whether they thought these effects were realized under the pilot program. Nearly all judges thought that *educating the public* about how the federal courts work was the greatest potential benefit of coverage, and most thought this benefit could be more fully realized with electronic media rather than traditional media. However, most judges said the educational benefit had been realized only to a moderate extent or not at all under the program. Several judges expressed the view that the education function was best served through extended coverage of proceedings rather than brief "snippets" of coverage. The potential disadvantage of electronic media coverage most frequently mentioned by judges was the possibility of distorting or misrepresenting what goes on in court, although generally they did not feel this problem had occurred under the program.

2. PRACTICES IN RULING ON APPLICATIONS

Most of the judges interviewed had never denied media coverage. Those who denied coverage did so because the nature of the proceeding was particularly sensitive or the proceeding was being held in chambers. In reaching decisions on such applications, about half of the judges either solicited the views of counsel and/or parties, or at least notified counsel of the prospect of camera coverage. Most judges also reported giving attorneys an opportunity to object to coverage, with several mentioning they have overruled objections on this issue on one or more occasions. Judges who heard attorney objections on the issue generally reported that this took only a small amount of their time. When asked, most judges expressed the view that media coverage would be reduced considerably if parties or witnesses had an absolute right to refuse coverage in a case.

3. WITNESS PRIVACY ISSUES

District judges were asked whether they thought witness privacy concerns presented a problem for electronic media coverage in civil cases. Most said this was not a major problem in civil cases and that the presiding judge in a particular case would be able to address the problem if it arose. One judge thought that even though witness privacy could be an issue in some instances, "the public's right to know outweighs the privacy issue."

4. EFFECTS OF ELECTRONIC MEDIA ON TRIAL PARTICIPANTS

When asked about the effects of electronic media coverage on various trial participants, most judges who had experienced electronic media in their courts reported no major or detrimental effects. Nearly all such district judges said they saw no significant effect of electronic media presence on jurors, with two indicating that jurors noticed the cameras for the first few moments of the trial but then ignored their presence. One district judge said that he had closely observed the result of a jury trial over which he presided and had spoken with jurors after the trial to determine whether the presence of a camera had had an effect. His conclusion was that the jurors were not concerned about the camera "nor was the result out of line." Most district judges explained the presence of cameras to jurors at the beginning of a trial, informing them that they would not be photographed, that the presence of cameras for a particular portion of a trial should not be considered significant, and that jurors should not watch coverage of the trial on television. All district judges indicated they were not aware of any instances in which jurors had viewed televised coverage of trials in which they were sitting as jurors.

Most district judges also did not observe an effect of cameras on witnesses. One judge pointing out that, because of the increasing use of video depositions, many witnesses are already "used to having cameras poked in their faces." Two judges said they thought witnesses were more affected than other trial participants, but they did not think the effect was strong. Most district and appellate judges found electric media to have no effect or a positive effect on the performance and behavior of counsel. As one judge said, "[counsel] shouldn't do anything for cameras they wouldn't do for me or the jury." Similarly, most judges thought they themselves were not affected by the presence of cameras, or that they were affected in a positive way (e.g., by being more courteous to counsel or more vigilant regarding proper courtroom procedures).

5. COURTROOM DECORUM AND THE ADMINISTRATION OF JUSTICE

District and appellate judges were also asked whether the presence of electronic media negatively affected courtroom decorum, or interfered with the administration of justice. All but one judge who responded to the decorum question said that the presence of electronic media did not negatively affect courtroom decorum. The judge who did report a negative effect described a case involving "a lot of politicians" in which counsel "played to the TV" and their "arguments were overly zealous and exaggerated." Two judges said that courtroom decorum could be even better preserved if cameras could be installed permanently in courtrooms in concealed locations.

With respect to the effects on the administration of justice, all but one judge thought the presence of electronic media had no effect. One judge was concerned that the click of a still camera at certain points in a proceeding "puts an exclamation point on certain testimony," but thought this was usually not a problem in civil cases.

6. EFFECTS ON SETTLEMENT

District judges were asked whether, to the best of their knowledge, the prospect of camera coverage affected the possibility of settlement in any cases before them. Although the majority of judges said they had not seen a negative effect on settlement, four judges believed that there was an adverse effect in one or more of their own cases. One judge reported having seen this adverse effect happen in other judges' cases, while another said that in settlement discussions with the parties in a case "there might have been a time or two when a party was being outlandish . . . and I might have suggested [that] would look interesting on TV."

7. EXPERIENCES WITH THE MEDIA

Judges were also asked about their working relationship with representatives from the electronic media. All judges who had experience with cases involving pooling of camera coverage were satisfied with this arrangement, and most said that issues concerning pooling were not brought to the attention of the court. Two judges pointed out that the camera pooling resulted in fewer media representatives being present in the courtroom, because members of the press who would normally be in the courtroom choose to watch the proceedings elsewhere so that they could continue other activities without disturbing the court (e.g., chat, make phone calls). Judges in courts for which a media coordinator had been hired were also pleased with how that system worked. All experienced judges also said—often very enthusiastically—that members of the media generally complied with the Judicial Conference guidelines and with any additional restrictions imposed by presiding judges. However, one appellate judge was concerned about the "noisy shutters" of still cameras in a quiet courtroom, while another appellate judge relayed an episode where a still photographer used a "bright flash" that he found distracting.[38]

LAWYERS' VIEWS ON THE TOPIC

After the pilot program had been in operation for over two years, questionnaires were sent to lead plaintiff and defense attorneys from 100 cases covered by electronic media during the first two years of the program. All 32 cases covered by extended-coverage networks were included in the sample, and the remaining 68 cases were selected randomly from among other cases covered under the program. Questionnaires were returned from 110 out of 191[39] attorneys surveyed (58%), with respondents divided fairly equally between plaintiff and defense (or appellee and appellant) attorneys.[40]

The FJC asked attorneys the following questions: (1) did the court adequately considered their views and the views of their clients in deciding whether to approve coverage requests; (2) did potential witnesses refuse to testify because of the prospect of camera coverage; (3) what effects of electronic media coverage did they observed; (4) did electronic media coverage affect the fairness of the proceedings; (5) overall, did they favor electronic media coverage of civil proceedings; and (6) did their views toward electronic media coverage change as a result of participation in the program.

Overall, 72 out of 109 attorneys responding (66%) indicated they somewhat or greatly favor electronic media coverage of civil proceedings. Fourteen (13%) said they had no opinion on coverage, while the remaining [41] (21%) were somewhat or greatly opposed to electronic media coverage. In response to a separate question about whether experience with coverage had changed their views, 29 out of 104[42] attorneys responding (28%) reported they were more favorable toward electronic coverage now than they had been prior to having experience with it, 4 (4%) said they were less favorable, and 71 (68%) said their opinions had not changed.

Sixty-three percent of attorneys responding to the survey reported that they had been given adequate time to notify their clients after learning of the prospect of camera coverage, and most (76%) indicated they had been given an opportunity to object to coverage, although few (8%) had actually registered an objection. The majority of both district and appellate court attorneys responding thought the court had given adequate consideration to the views of counsel and of the parties in deciding whether to allow electronic media coverage. Fifty-eight percent of attorneys in the district courts and 83% of attorneys in the appellate courts did not believe their clients would have chosen to refuse coverage if given an absolute right to do so. Only one attorney reported having a witness or witnesses decline to testify because of the prospects of camera coverage.

When asked whether the presence of cameras affected the overall fairness of the proceeding, 97% said camera presence had no effect on fairness, three said camera presence increased the fairness of the proceeding, and four said it decreased the fairness of the proceeding.

Table 3 shows the number of attorneys selecting each answer in response to questions about effects of electronic media coverage in the case in which they participated. The table shows that attorneys with experience under the program who expressed an opinion generally indicated that various effects occurred "to little or no extent." These results are consistent with questionnaire results of judges who experienced electronic media coverage under the program.

Table 3. Attorney Ratings of Electronic Media Effects in Proceedings in Which They Were Involved, by Percentage*

Effect	To little or no extent	To some extent	To a moderate extent	To a great extent	To a very great extent	No opinion
Motivate witnesses to be more truthful than they otherwise would be (N = 70)*	58	3	2	0	0	38
Distract witnesses (N = 66)*	52	18	9	5	0	17
Make witnesses more nervous than they otherwise would be (N = 66)*	46	21	12	5	2	15
Increase juror attentiveness (N = 53)*	26	6	8	6	0	55
Distract jurors (N = 54)*	30	9	6	4	0	52
Motivate attorneys to come to court better-prepared (N = 97)	71	11	7	4	1	6
Cause attorneys to be more theatrical in their presentations (N = 103)	78	7	9	2	3	2
Distract attorneys (N = 103)	73	20	6	1	0	1
Prompt attorneys to be more courteous (N = 103)	80	12	3	1	0	5
Increase judge attentive-						

Table 3 (continued

Effect	To little or no extent	To some extent	To a moderate extent	To a great extent	To a very great extent	No opinion
ness (N = 101)	54	17	10	6	1	12
Prompt judges to be more courteous (N = 101)	62	12	8	4	3	11
Disrupt the courtroom proceedings (N = 103)	77	10	8	3	0	3

* *Note*: The figure in each cell represents the percentage of responding attorneys selecting that answer. Items marked with an asterisk were presented only to attorneys in district court cases; other items were presented to attorneys in both district and appellate court cases.

Taken from the Federal Judicial Center's Report on the Electronic Media Coverage of Federal Civil Proceedings - An Evaluation of the Pilot Program in Six District Courts and Two Courts of Appeals. (1994)

REVIEW OF STATE STUDIES OF ELECTRONIC MEDIA EFFECTS ON JURORS AND WITNESSES

In response to an inquiry from the Committee on Court Administration and Case Management, the FJC reviewed the results of studies others had done on the effects of electronic media on jurors and witnesses. The studies report that the majority of jurors and witnesses who experienced electronic media coverage did not report negative consequences or concerns. These findings are consistent with what judges and lawyers in the pilot courts observed about jurors and witnesses in those courts.

The FJC summarized the results from studies conducted in state courts (Arizona, California, Florida, Hawaii, Kansas, Maine, Massachusetts, Nevada, New Jersey, New York, Ohio, and Virginia) of the potential effects of electronic media on witnesses and jurors.[43]   For witnesses, researchers have looked at such effects as distraction, nervousness, distortion or modification of testimony, fear of harm, and reluctance or unwillingness to testify with electronic media present.   For jurors, researchers examined such effects as distraction, effect on deliberations or case outcome, making a case or witness seem "more important," and reluctance to serve with electronic media present. Most state evaluations have studied jurors and witnesses through surveys.   In California researchers also observed the behaviors of jurors and witnesses in proceedings covered and not covered by electronic media.

In all of the state courts whose evaluations are discussed below, electronic media coverage was allowed in criminal as well as civil cases, the majority of which was criminal.   As pointed out by several judges interviewed in the Pilot Program study, certain effects could be expected to occur to a greater extent in criminal cases than in civil cases (e.g., a witness' fear of harm from being seen on television). Thus, it might be expected that the findings of these studies would be more negative than findings from studies focused solely on experiences in civil cases.

EFFECTS ON WITNESSES

1.   DISTRACTION

A concern of many is that witnesses in cases covered by electronic media will be distracted and unable to focus on their testimony. A number of state evaluations addressed this issue in surveys and found that, only a small number of witnesses reported being distracted, and that the vast majority reported no distraction at all or only an initial distraction.

2.   NERVOUSNESS

Another concern is that witnesses will be made nervous by the presence of electronic media, that this nervousness will make them uncomfortable, and that jurors will, as a result, find it difficult to judge the veracity of their testimony. In state studies that asked witnesses about nervousness, the vast majority said that they were not at all nervous or were only slightly nervous due to the presence of electronic media during their testimony. In addition, jurors in a 1991 New York survey were asked whether the credibility of witnesses was affected by their relative insecurity or tenseness caused by audio or visual coverage. The majority of jurors indicated this did "not at all" affect the credibility of witnesses, and most indicated that the presence of audio and visual media did not in fact tend to make witnesses appear tense or insecure. Similarly, over 90% of responding jurors in Florida and New Jersey surveys said the presence of electronic media had "no effect" on their ability to judge the truthfulness of witnesses.

Finally, in addition to surveying witnesses, the consultants who conducted the California study systematically observed proceedings in which electronic media were and were not present. They concluded that witnesses were equally effective at communicating in both sets of circumstances.[44]

3.   DISTORTION OR MODIFICATION OF TESTIMONY

One of the more serious expressed concerns is that witnesses who testify will distort or modify their testimony because of the presence of electronic media. In state evaluations in which this issue was addressed, most witnesses reported that the presence of electronic media had no effect on their testimony and did not make it more difficult for them to testify. A small number of witnesses indicated an inhibitory effect.

4.   FEAR OF HARM

Several surveys in state studies asked witnesses—most of whom had testified in criminal trials—whether the presence of electronic media caused them to fear that they would be harmed. Most witnesses surveyed said they had no fear of harm stemming from electronic media coverage of a proceeding in which they testified, although a minority said they did fear harm to some extent.

5.   RELUCTANCE TO TESTIFY WITH ELECTRONIC MEDIA

Surveys in several states asked witnesses if they were reluctant to testify at all because of the presence of electronic media. In general, about 80% to 90% of witnesses said the presence of electronic media did not affect their desire to participate or would not affect their willingness to serve as a witness in a future proceeding, a finding closely parallel to the attorney survey responses in the FJC study.[45]

EFFECTS ON JURORS

As in the federal pilot program, most state programs did not allow electronic media to film individual jurors. In some programs, the jury could be shown by camera, but no individual juror could be shown in an identifiable way. Other kinds of problems have, however, been posited.

1.   DISTRACTION

If the presence of cameras were distracting to jurors, this could decrease their ability to concentrate on testimony, potentially affecting the outcome of the proceedings. The state court results, however, suggest that this is not a problem for the majority of jurors. In California, results of the observational portion of the study indicated that jurors in proceedings covered by electronic media were slightly more attentive to testimony than jurors in proceedings not covered by electronic media. In addition, when asked about their level of distraction from the electronic media presence, most jurors responding to surveys in state court evaluations indicated they were not distracted or were distracted only at first.

2.   EFFECT ON DELIBERATIONS OR OUTCOME

Some commentators on electronic media in the courtroom fear that coverage will influence jurors' decisions—for example, by creating more public pressure to decide the case in a particular way. At least four state studies have surveyed jurors about this issue and generally reported in the vast majority of cases there was no influence of electronic media coverage on jurors' deliberations and that jurors did not feel pressured by the media to decide the case in a particular way. In addition, the California researchers found that jurors who had experience with electronic media coverage were less likely to think it would affect the outcome of trials than did jurors who did not have experience with electronic media coverage.

3.   HIGHLIGHTING IMPORTANCE OF A CASE OR WITNESS

Another concern about cameras in the courtroom is that cameras will distort the importance of a case or, if present only for a portion of the proceedings, that cameras will make jurors think certain witnesses and testimony are more important than others. The state court results on this issue indicate that the majority of jurors do not think the presence of electronic media signals that a case or witness is more important, although a minority do think it lends importance to the case (very few think it makes a witness more important).

4.   RELUCTANCE TO SERVE AS A JUROR

There is some concern that allowing camera access to proceedings will make it more difficult to impanel juries because some prospective jurors may try to avoid jury duty in an effort to avoid being covered by electronic media. Again, the state court results suggest that this fear is not likely to be a problem, with the vast majority of jurors reporting that the presence of electronic media would not affect their willingness to serve in a future proceeding.

The results summarized above are consistent with FJC findings from the judge and attorney surveys; that is, for each of the several potential negative effects of electronic media on jurors and witnesses, the majority of respondents indicated that the presence of cameras does not effect jurors and witnesses, while a minority indicated only a slight effect on jurors and witnesses. The state court findings, to the extent credible, lend support to the findings and the recommendations made in the initial report.

Although indications from even a small number of participants that cameras have negative effects can be a cause for concern, perhaps these concerns are addressed adequately by the federal court guidelines. These guidelines give the judge trying the case discretion to limit or prohibit, if necessary, coverage of any proceeding or of a particular witness or witnesses. In addition, coverage of jurors is prohibited (see Appendix II). The Research project staff of the Federal Judicial Center has made several recommendations on these topics to its board. (See Appendix V for these recommendations).

POST PILOT PROJECT INITIATIVES

After a successful three-year pilot project in six federal district courts and two appellate courts, the Conference decided in 1994 to disband the experiment. Despite these findings, the Judicial Conference ignored the evidence and issued a ban on cameras in all federal courts. This was later amended in March of 1996, two years later, whereby the Conference authorized coverage only in the appeals courts. Surprise and disappointment was the reaction of some of the federal judges around the country, who had no significant problems with electronic coverage.

The House Judiciary Committee gave the issue a push later by passing a measure that would allow federal judges to permit television cameras in their courtrooms. The bill would merely authorize the right to include cameras, not require them.

The Sunshine in the Courtroom Act could foster a wealth of legal education complementary to what is provided by television, radio and photographic coverage of state courtroom proceedings in 47 states. Coverage of the state courts tends to focus on criminal trials. This legislation, which would be naturally geared to civil litigation, is the main focus of Federal courts. The media advocates had hoped that the Judicial Conference of the United States would have institutionalized cameras in the Federal courts.

Not everyone is so sure that the judges will continue to resist the electronic age. According to some constitutional law experts, the move to allow judges to decide whether or not to allow cameras in federal courtrooms is an essential first step. Bill sponsors complain that in an open democracy, people must be well informed. When it comes to courts, they believe that the majority of the public is not informed about the courts.

Chapter 7

CONCLUSION

Are we better off with or without comprehensive, gavel-to-gavel television coverage of trials? The question is whether public information about trials is to come solely from second-hand summaries on the news, "spin control" press conferences, prejudicial and inflammatory characterizations by interested third parties; or whether the public will be permitted, as well, to observe the entirety of the actual in-court proceedings under the control of the Court. As Supreme Court Justice Anthony Kennedy stated in testimony to Congress:

> You can make the argument that the most rational, the most dispassionate, the most orderly presentation of the issue is in the courtroom and it is the outside coverage that is really the problem. In a way, it seems somewhat perverse to exclude television from the area in which the most orderly presentation of the evidence takes place.[1]

History refutes the claims that televised coverage of trials constitutes a *unique* risk to the administration of justice, to the right of a fair trial, or to the dignity of the court. The risk appears to be no greater than that posed by public and press access to reporting upon trials. Long before television was invented, "trials of the century" occurred regularly, with citizens receiving information in whatever form it was obtainable, including gossip, innuendo and tabloid speculation. After the advent of television, the problem of accurate information continues without cameras in the courtroom. In such case, information about what happens inside the courtroom comes from the second-hand summaries of the few members of the media permitted inside who then pick and choose the information to report, often describing the facial expressions and gestures of participants, and attributing motives and meaning to their actions and statements. Press conferences are routinely held, offering summaries of in-court events, often at odds with each other. "Sound bites" from out of court interviews are regularly played, often juxtaposed against photographs, taken out of court, of participants. Televising trials, showing the proceedings themselves under the control of the presiding judge, by definition permits citizens to make their own judgments about proceedings.

IS OPENING THE JUDICIAL BRANCH THE ANSWER?

Court TV is a national cable legal news network dedicated to reporting on the legal and judicial systems of the United States, the fifty states, and the District of Columbia. Since its creation in 1991, Court TV's cornerstone has been to televise gavel-to-gavel coverage of civil and criminal trials.

By stationing a single camera inside a courtroom, Court TV seeks to enable viewers to observe the proceedings as though they themselves were in the courtroom. Court TV represents that it does this to inform and educate the public in the most accurate fashion possible, differentiating its coverage from the sound bites and "spin" frequently attending out-of-court coverage of judicial proceedings - the attorney and party press conferences and out-of-court interviews, the second-hand summaries that not only (of necessity) pick and choose the information "worthy" of being reported -- but whose authors attribute motives and meaning to the actions and statements of participants, reporting their conclusions to the public for it simply to accept. Court TV permits citizens to watch for themselves the moment-to-moment work of the judicial process in action. Court TV has covered a wide variety of criminal trials, that have raised important social, economic, political and cultural questions.

Prior to and throughout each proceeding it covers, Court TV works with the presiding judge and/or court personnel to help ensure that all requirements concerning equipment placement and camera coverage are satisfied. It employs a single, stationary camera, which produces no noise and requires no lighting other than existing courtroom lighting. The camera is placed away from the proceedings and, if necessary, it can be operated by remote control by a Court TV technician. Wiring is unobtrusive. Microphones are small and are never operated in such a way as to record conversations between attorneys and clients; they are turned off during all parts of the proceedings that are not part of the public record. As a matter of policy, Court TV does not photograph jurors in any jurisdiction where it not permitted to do so, and then, only with the permission of the presiding judge. As a matter of policy, Court TV edits out the names of jurors and the addresses of witnesses.

What is the harm in such unfiltered coverage?[2] As the Supreme Court has stated:

> [T]he right of access to criminal trials plays a particularly significant role in the functioning of the judicial process and the government as a whole. Public scrutiny of a criminal trial enhances the quality and safeguards the integrity of the fact-finding process, with benefits to both the defendant and to society as a whole . . . And in the broadest terms, public access to criminal trials permits the public to participate in and serve as a check upon the judicial process - an essential component in our structure of self-government.[3]

Accordingly, proponents of cameras further believe the camera increases respect for the system by showing the public what actually happens in a trial, as opposed to the fictional accounts portrayed by *Law & Order*, *Perry Mason*, or tabloid television shows like *Hard Copy*. According to John Coughenour, a Federal judge in western Washington, "the best way we could increase trust and confidence in our court system is to allow in the cameras and show the public what is being done."[4]

So, do cameras help or hurt? Mostly, they seem to help. But there is a time and a place for every technological advancement, and some reporting tools are more intrusive and distracting than others. Perhaps the best approach for the time being is the one many of the nation's state courts already follow -- leaving it up to the judge in each case to decide when to welcome cameras. This may be most of the time once the camera becomes as normal as the notepad. What once seemed like an astonishing development is becoming a commonplace part of protecting defendants from secret trials and letting people know how their legal system is being run.[5]

The California experience demonstrates that the very jurisdiction in which the outcry of the Simpson trial was the loudest was unpersuaded to reject years of positive experience with televised proceedings. It reaffirms an undisturbed body of twenty-five years worth of cumulative empirical evidence, which points to only one conclusion: It is now demonstrable, as a matter of fact, that (to use Justice Harlan's phrase) there is no "reasonable likelihood" that the presence of an in-court camera "disparages the judicial process"; and it is now demonstrable that cameras in the courtroom possess great social value.

State court judges generally have welcomed TV cameras into their courtrooms. The way state judges see it, the disruptions sometimes caused by cameras are outweighed by the benefit of humanizing the courts to the public. The Federal bench, however, does not want to see or be seen. Is this a good thing in a democratic society? Judges may need to be shielded from some forces that might intrude on the decision-making process. However, this should not extend to Federal judges who are appointed for life.[6] These days people primarily get their information from television and the Internet. If the public is to understand how our federal judicial system works, that is how they will learn about it in the 21st century. Cameras can provide the whole story of a trial, not just an edited version filtered through a reporter's eyes or the pen of a court artist. If we believe in open government, judicial credibility and mass public participation, the federal courts cannot be excluded from modern means of communication.[7]

Television coverage of legal proceedings over the years has been limited until the early 90's. With the emergence of Court TV, the landscape changed and brought increased television news coverage. However, studies since the early 90's by the ABA and Court TV reveal a public that is skeptical of television news snippets and prefer unfiltered access. So, comprehensive broadcasts like Court TV stand to enhance public perception and education. Also, public perception of the judicial system is negative in many respect unrelated to broadcasting. Surely the more that is known about the system, the greater the chances for an improved image or for improvement.

Whatever arguments might reasonably be made to keep cameras out of trial courts, most surely do not apply to appellate courts, including the United States Supreme Court. There are no witnesses in appellate proceedings -- just the lawyers for each side and a panel of judges. So why has the Supreme Court been so adamantly opposed camera coverage of oral arguments before the Court, which, by the way, is open to the public? Why would Justice David Souter tell a Congressional Appropriations Subcommittee that "the day you see a camera come into our courtroom it's going to roll over my dead body?"[8] Many Americans are not aware of the television blackout by the federal courts because they have followed saturation television coverage of notorious cases that have occurred in state courts. In an era when the media is so powerful, the First Amendment may have more defenders than the Sixth. Without public access to records and meetings, we can never be sure that abuses are not occurring. As former Chief Justice Warren Berger wrote in 1980, "People in an open society do not demand infallibility from their institutions, but it is difficult for them to accept what they are prohibited from observing". But as committed as we say we are to openness and to citizen oversight, it is unfortunate that we do not see more of our government in action. This is especially the case with our courts, which remain too secretive, too forbidding and too hostile to citizen and media access. While scrutiny of the executive and legislative branches of government has increased in recent years with independent prosecutors, constant media attention, freedom of information laws and C-Span coverage, the judiciary is still elusive.[9]

One of the greatest benefits derived from the presence of cameras in the courtroom is enhanced public scrutiny of the judicial system. The majority of judges who responded to the various surveys described in earlier chapters agreed that the presence of television cameras in the courtroom enhances public scrutiny of judicial proceedings with little negative impact.

Television coverage of court proceedings enables the public to learn more about the workings of the justice system, to see directly the conduct of particular cases, and to become more familiar with legal concepts and developments. The fact that many view television coverage as a form of entertainment does not deprive it of educational content, since education and entertainment are not mutually exclusive.

Television coverage also has drawn the public's attention to major societal problems, such as domestic violence and child abuse. It also has served as cathartic purpose for the families of some homicide victims.

Claims that jurors will watch televised coverage of their case and will be influenced either by commentary about the case or by evidence ruled inadmissible and not presented to the jury are unsupported. Cameras can raise some judges' performance and have a positive impact on judicial demeanor. Openness of public institutions, including the judiciary, is a key ingredient in our democracy. Among the many values served by openness are promoting public confidence in government, providing the public with information about the workings of the judiciary, assuring the fairness of court proceedings, and satisfying the appearance of justice.

Although televised coverage could, at times show the judicial system in an unfavorable light, this is not necessarily a detriment. Rather, to the extent that such coverage offers an opportunity for improving the judicial system, it should be viewed as a strength of our democratic system.

APPENDIX I

COURT TV TRIALS AND HEARINGS AIRED FROM 1999-2001

ADAMS, DENO, TISDALE AND FARLEY v. DICKERSON - Taped from Mobile, AL. Waitress Tonya Dickerson was given a lottery ticket as a tip at the Mobile, Alabama Waffle House. After a day of waiting tables, she went home to discover that the ticket was worth $10 million. Four coworkers, who also received lottery tickets as tips, sued for a share, claiming they entered a verbal contract with Dickerson to divide the bounty. Dickerson claimed a verbal contract doesn't apply to amounts more than $5,000. The jury found for the plaintiffs and ordered Dickerson to share the jackpot. (6/99)

ARIZONA v. JACQUELINE CALIRI - Taped from Phoenix. Court TV aired Caliri's first trial, which ended in a hung jury. She was convicted during the retrial and was sentenced to life imprisonment. ORIGINAL SUMMARY: Phoenix police say Jacqueline Caliri's abusive marriage drove the 39-year-old mother of three into the arms of a younger man and left her angry enough to kill. With the help of her new lover, Caliri allegedly hired a hitman in July 1998 to "get rid of" her husband of 20 years. The defense says the state's motive misses the mark because the Caliris were on the verge of reconciling for the sake of their children. If convicted, Caliri faces the death penalty. (11/01)

CALIFORNIA v. COLEMAN - Live from Inglewood. Gary Coleman was accused of punching an autograph seeker in the eye at a store in South Central Los Angeles in July 1998. Tracy Fields claimed the 30-year-old actor, who now works as a security guard at a shopping mall, got upset when she asked him to personalize the autograph for her son. Coleman claimed Fields swung at him first. Coleman pleaded guilty to disturbing the peace just after closing arguments. He received a 90-day suspended sentence and was ordered to take 52 anger management classes. (2/99)

CALIFORNIA v. JOHNSON - Taped from San Diego. The retrial of Suzanne Johnson, who faced felony child abuse and murder charges in the death of an infant in her care. Johnson was convicted of felony child abuse and was sentenced to 25 years to life. (3/99)

CALIFORNIA v. WILSON - Taped from Vista. A Wisconsin drifter, who told police he planned to keep killing until he was caught , stood trial for slashing the throat of a 9-year-old boy. Brandon Wilson, 20, targeted Matthew Cecchi after he saw Cecchi walk into a restroom while his aunt waited outside. Wilson followed the child inside, grabbed him and then stabbed him. Wilson pleaded guilty to first-degree murder with special circumstances of lying in wait, but he also pleaded not guilty by reason of insanity. Wilson was found to be sane and convicted of murder and was sentenced to death. (9/99)

CLINTON IMPEACHMENT TRIAL - Live from Washington, DC. Coverage of President Bill Clinton's impeachment trial. (1/99)

COLORADO v. YBANEZ - Taped from Castle Rock. Fearing exile at military school by his parents, Nathan Ybanez, 17, killed his mother. Authorities said Ybanez and his friend beat Julie Ybanez with their fists and fireplace tongs as she pleaded for her life. Ybanez was tried as an adult; his friend has already been convicted. Ybanez was convicted of first-degree murder and was sentenced to life in prison without parole. (1/00)

ESTATE OF SAM HOLMES SHEPPARD v. STATE OF OHIO - Taped from Cleveland. Sam Reese Sheppard, son of Dr. Sam H. Sheppard of "The Fugitive" fame, sued the state of Ohio for wrongful imprisonment of his father. Sheppard said the years in prison led to this father's premature death at the age of 46. The jury found for the State of Ohio and rejected the attempt by the late doctor's estate to have him declared officially innocent of the crime. (2/00)

FLORIDA v. ALBRITTON - Taped from Bradenton. Paula Albritton was convicted of using a cadaver in a voodoo ritual to revive her lagging funeral home business. She was sentenced to one year in prison. (5/99)

FLORIDA v. BOLIN - Taped from Dade City. After two previous convictions were overturned, Oscar Bolin once again faced the death penalty for murdering Teri Lynn Matthews in 1986. Bolin was convicted and sentenced to death. (12/01)

FLORIDA v. BOWEN - Taped from Tampa. Bernice Bowen's boyfriend, Hank Carr, killed her 4-year-old son when his rifle allegedly went off accidentally.   When police came looking for her boyfriend, Bowen allegedly helped him flee.   Prosecutors claim the couple devised a getaway plan that went awry - Carr fatally shot three officers before turning the gun on himself.   Bowen was convicted of being an accessory after the fact to first-degree murder, manslaughter and escape and was sentenced to 22 years. (6/99)

FLORIDA v. JUAN "TORO" CARDENAS - Taped from Bradenton, FL. Juan Cardenas, 18, was charged with dropping a 22-pound rock on Julie Laible's car. Laible, who was an assistant professor at the University of Alabama, was killed instantly when the rock smashed her skull, as a frantic passenger tried to maneuver the car to safety. Cardenas argued reasonable doubt, but was convicted of second-degree murder. (04/00)

FLORIDA v. CONAHAN - Taped from Punta Gorda. Daniel Conahan, 45, suspected of being responsible for six murders dubbed the "Hog Trail Killings," faced the electric chair in the first trial related to those murders. Prosecutors claimed Conahan lured a 21-year-old man to a desolate wooded area where he raped, killed and dismembered him. Police believe Conahan coerced transients into sex and nude photographs by plying them with money, drugs and alcohol. Conahan was convicted of first-degree murder and was sentenced to death. (11/99)

FLORIDA v. CRAIN - Live from Tampa. The body of 8-year-old Amanda Brown has never been found but it didn't stopped prosecutors from seeking the death penalty against convicted child molester Willie Crain, who was accused of her kidnapping and murder. Amanda's mother testified that Crain, whom she met two days prior at a bar, drugged her before falling asleep with her and Amanda. By dawn, Amanda and Crain vanished. Crain maintained that he left while Amanda slept, and that someone else is responsible. Crain was convicted of first-degree murder and kidnapping. (9/99)

FLORIDA v. EGAN - Live from Orlando. Shirley Egan, 68, was charged with the attempted murder of her daughter, Georgette Smith after allegedly overhearing that her daughter and boyfriend were planning to put her in a nursing home. Smith was shot in the neck and then died after requesting to be taken off life support. The sickly Egan could have faced murder charges. Egan, who is also accused of trying to kill Smith's boyfriend, claims the shooting was accidental.   In Smith's emotional deathbed deposition, Smith forgives her mother and insists the shooting was indeed accidental. Egan was acquitted. (8/99)

FLORIDA v. FRIEDMAN - Live from Fort Lauderdale. Teacher Beth Friedman was accused of having a sexual relationship with her middle school student and providing him with alcohol and drugs. Friedman was found guilty of a misdemeanor charge and will be sentenced in February 2002. (11/01)

FLORIDA v. GREEN - Taped from Clearwater. Carlos Green, 24, said he thought the teenagers who continuously harassed him outside his barber shop planned to rob him, so he told them to leave the premises. They refused. As Green's arguments with the teens escalated, he produced a gun and shot at the youths, killing one. Green claims he shot in self-defense. Green was charged with second-degree murder but was convicted of the lesser included offense of manslaughter. Because of his previous record, the judge exceeded the sentencing guidelines and sentenced Green to 30 years in prison instead of the maximum recommended 21 years. (10/99)

FLORIDA v. HAMDEH - Live from Miami. Khaled Abu Hamdeh, a Palestinian shop owner, stood trial for killing a black employee after arguing about $20. The defendant claimed he shot Charles Nelson, his clerk and security guard, in self-defense after Nelson first threatened to shoot him; however, Nelson was unarmed. Hamdeh was convicted of second-degree murder and was sentenced to 15 years in prison. (2/99)

FLORIDA v. MARAMAN - Taped from Dade City. Sylvia Marman, 35, claimed she was in a cloud of alcohol and Valium when she killed a longtime family friend, who taunted Maraman about sexually molesting her daughter, then 12. Maraman, herself a victim of sexual abuse, said she snapped. She shot Arthur Danner, 73, 6 times at point-blank before reloading and shooting him 6 more times. Maraman was convicted of murder. Maraman was convicted of second-degree murder with a firearm and was sentenced to 25 years. (5/00)

FLORIDA v. MCINTYRE - Live from Vero Beach. Police Officer Molly McIntyre investigated her own son's possible link to the strangulation murder of his ex-girlfriend. Now Patrick McIntyre, 26, claimed that during a private jailhouse meeting set up by police, his mother coerced his confession to collect a $7,500 reward. Prosecutors claimed the confession was voluntary because the meeting was a family affair, not a police investigation. McIntryre was convicted of first-degree murder and was sentenced to 3 concurrent terms of life in prison without parole. (2/99)

FLORIDA v. MISENER - Taped from Clearwater. Brett Misener faced attempted murder charges for using a controversial dietary supplement to poison a female clubgoer who ignored him. He's accused of spiking his water bottle with Renewtrient, a derivative of the popular date rape drug GHB, and giving it to a woman he had just met. The victim suffered a coma. Misener claimed the substance was legal at the time he bought it and the woman knew what she was drinking. Misener was convicted of drug possession and culpable negligence; he was sentenced to 7 years and fined $50,000. (5/00)

FLORIDA v. NUNEZ - Live from Ft. Lauderdale. Emilio Nunez stood trial for gunning down his estranged wife. As a video camera crew rolled tape, Nunez executed his wife at point-blank range near the grave of the couple's 15-year-old daughter who had committed suicide days earlier. Nunez claimed it was a crime of passion. Prosecutors used the video, which shows Nunez pumping 12 bullets into his wife, then fleeing the cemetery. Nunez blamed his wife for his daughter's suicide because he believed his wife's lover had impregnated their daughter. Nunez was convicted of first-degree murder and was sentenced to 25 years to life in prison. (1/00)

FLORIDA v. PINKSTAFF - Live from Daytona Beach. James Pinkstaff, owner of the Pampered Pooch doggie salon, was accused of brutally beating a Yorkshire terrier during a routine grooming session. The defense contended the dog died from a seizure. Pinkstaff was acquitted. (1/99)

FLORIDA v. POSTMA - Live from Bradenton. Jackie Postma, a mother of three, was convicted of second-degree murder for plotting her huband's death with her lover. She was sentenced to life in prison. (7/01)

FLORIDA v. REYNOLDS - Taped from Fort Lauderdale. Jacqueline "Nikki" Reynolds was tried for murdering her mother. The prosecution claimed that Nikki, who had told her boyfriend she was pregnant, killed her mother after she forced Nikki to tell him she wasn't expecting. Her boyfriend then left her. Nikki claimed she is insane as she attempted suicide shortly before the attack. The jury was deadlocked and a mistrial was declared; she will be retried. (7/99)

FLORIDA v. RICH - Taped from Miami. Bruce Rich, 51, stood trial for first-degree murder for killing his parents for their life insurance policy and will. Prosecutors were skeptical about Irving and Blanche Rich's murder-suicide almost from the beginning. Blanche Rich was shot twice, and no suicide note was found. Police also ruled out robbery because no signs of forced entry were found, and nothing was taken from the home. Rich denied the allegations. He was convicted of first-degree murder and was sentenced to life in prison. (3/00)

FLORIDA v. RICHARDSON - Taped from Miami. After a jury deadlocked his first trial, prosecutors retried a county court judge for allegedly soliciting oral sex from an undercover cop posing as a prostitute. Judge Reginald Richardson testified at the first trial that he stopped his vehicle to speak to the female officer because she flagged him down, and he thought she was in some type of danger. Richardson, 45, a father of three married to a schoolteacher, denied that he solicited sex and that he tried to avoid arrest by using his judicial influence. (11/99)

FLORIDA v. ROBERT BOLTUCH - Live from Fort Lauderdale, FL. Robert Boltuch, then 23, faced the death penalty for shooting at an interracial couple, killing 20-year-old college student Jody-Gaye Bailey. Witnesses testified that Boltuch, who was drunk, made racist comments hours before the murder. The victim's fiancee, Christian Martin, 20, also took the stand as an eyewitness. The jury recommended a life sentence for Boltuch. The judge sentenced Boltuch to an additional 30 years to life for attemped second-degree murder. (01/00)

FLORIDA v. SALDANA - Taped from Orlando. Prosecutors claimed Ruben Saldana, head of the Miami International Posse's Orlando chapter, disapproved of the gang's superiors and wanted to take over the state syndicate. He plotted the murder of the gang's "godfather" and a high-ranking officer. Two gangsters responsible for the execution testified against him. Saldana denied ordering the hits, claiming to be a victim of spiteful members who opposed his plans to legitimize the gang's illegal activities. Saldana was convicted of manslaughter and was sentenced to 15 years. (3/00)

FLORIDA v. SIMPSON - Live from Miami. Prosecutors charged football great O.J. Simpson with misdemeanor battery and felony burglary charges for allegedly hitting a motorist during a road rage incident. Simpson was acquitted of all charges. (10/01)

FLORIDA v. TACL - Taped from Bronson. Joseph Tacl and his son, Michael, faced charges for growing marijuana. Joseph Tacl claimed it eased his chronic back pain and that Florida's approved medical necessity defense applied both to himself and his family. His son admitted to helping cultivate the plants. Joseph and Michael Tacl were convicted of illegal cultivation and possession of marijuana. Joseph was sentenced to 36 months probation and Michael received 18 months probation. (8/99)

FLORIDA v. TREXLER - Priscilla Trexler, 54, may look like the grandmother-next-door, but prosecutors say she deserves the death penalty for hiring a hitman to kill her former son-in-law. Prosecutors allege Trexler wanted her granddaughter's father dead because she suspected him of abusing the child. Trexler is expected to testify and deny the allegations levied by her hair stylist, who hired the alleged hitman. The hitman, now serving a life sentence, also may testify. Jurors convicted Trexler of being a principal to first-degree murder. The same jury recommended a life sentence, which the judge immediately imposed. (6/01)

FLORIDA v. VILLELLA - Taped from Daytona Beach. A funeral director, Mark Villella was convicted of fatally stabbing his adulterous wife and hiding and burying her corpse in a casket that contained a "customer." He was convicted of murder and sentenced to life in prison. (10/01)

FLORIDA v. WALKER - Taped from Bradenton. Thomas Fuller, a popular Methodist minister, was shot in the back by John Walker, his uncle-in-law. Prosecutors claimed Fuller had admonished Walker about meddling into the Fuller family's private affairs. Fuller claimed Walker became obsessed with the Fuller family and wanted to become the family patriarch. The defense argued the shooting was accidental. Walker was convicted of attempted murder and was sentenced to 4 years. (3/99)

FLORIDA v. WILSON - Taped from Sumter County. Secily Wilson, a reporter/anchor with the Fox Network affiliate in Tampa, was charged with resisting arrest for allegedly kicking and scratching a highway patrolman who pulled her over for speeding. She denied she resisted the officer, but does admit to becoming "upset" because the officer, who she said overreacted, pointed his gun and pepper spray at her. Wilson was acquitted. (1/99)

GA. v. SOLOMON SENTENCING - Anthony T.J. Solomon, 17, will be sentenced for opening fire in his high-school hallway and wounding six students in 1999. In November, Solomon pleaded both guilty and guilty by reason of insanity for the Colombine copycat crime. At the sentencing, the judge will decide which plea to accept. There will be victim impact statements from the six injured students and their families, as well as testimony by the mental health experts who evaluated Solomon. Solomon received 40 years in prison of his guilty but mentally ill plea. (11/00)

GEORGIA v. ANDERSON - Taped from Atlanta. A verbal dispute between neighbors led to a shooting death. The argument began when oil from Willie Brewster's driveway ran onto Mozel Anderson's property. After tensions escalated, Anderson drew a gun and shot her neighbor. Anderson claimed that she is insane. Anderson was convicted of murder and aggravated assault and was sentenced to life in prison. (2/99)

GEORGIA v. BAUGH - Dionne Baugh, 32 faces life in prison for the 1996 murder of prominent African-American businessman Lance Herndon. Prosecutors will likely claim that the beautiful Jamaica native bludgeoned Herndon, 41 because he would not resume their affair. Although police always suspected Baugh, they had no evidence linking her to the crime until her 1998 divorce proceedings, during which she apparently incriminated herself. Herndon was the CEO of a growing computer consulting firm and had been named 1995's "Entrepreneur of the Year" by President Clinton. Baugh was convicted of murder and sentenced to life in prison. (7/01)

GEORGIA v. LEWIS, et al. - Live from Atlanta. NFL Pro Bowl linebacker Ray Lewis was charged with murder in the fatal stabbing of 2 young men outside an Atlanta nightclub. Lewis and his entourage were seen speeding away from the club in a stretch limousine around 3am on January 31, following a Super Bowl bash. Two of his friends who were in the limousine were also charged. Lewis pleaded guilty to obstruction of justice, a misdemeanor, and was sentenced to 12 months probation. As part of the plea, Lewis testified against his co-defendants, Joseph Sweeting and Reginald Oakley, who were acquitted. (56/00)

IOWA v. ANFINSON - Taped from Des Moines. Heidi Anfinson frantically called police, saying she awoke from a nap to discover her 2-week-old son, Jacob, missing from his playpen. When police found the infant's body pinned under 25 pounds of rocks at the bottom of a nearby lake, Anfinson was arrested and charged with murder. She later confessed that the baby drowned accidentally in the bathtub, and she panicked and tried to hid the body in the lake. The jury was deadlocked and the judge declared a mistrial; her retrial is scheduled for February 7, 2000. (10/99)

IOWA v. ENGHOLM - Taped from Adel (not aired as of 1/29/02). Kari Engholm, 34, went to work at the Dallas County Hospital on a hot, sunny day in June 2001 when she left her 7-month-old daughter, Clare, in the back of her minivan. Engholm, chief executive officer of the hospital, discovered Clare dead in the backseat nine hours later. An autopsy showed that Clare died of overheating. The prosecution charged Engholm with neglect of a dependent person and involuntary manslaughter. The defense said that she simply made a mistake. Engholm, who faced 12 years in prison, was found not guilty. (12/01).

IOWA v. RAYMOND PEEBLER - Raymond Peebler was accused of animal abuse after kicking a neighbor's dog on June 17, 2001. According to prosecutors, Peebler, 50, kicked John Wilt's 16-week-old Yorkshire terrier when the 6-pound puppy walked onto Peebler's lawn. The dog, named Cascade, died the following day. The defense believed Peebler was defending his property. Peebler and Wilt had reportedly been involved in a continuing dispute. Peebler faced up two years in prison if convicted. (8/01)

KENTUCKY v. AARON LAMAR HARDIN - Aaron Lamar Hardin, 15, was found guilty of killing his younger brother last December. Hardin and his younger brother Andre, 13, were wrestling for a video game joystick when Hardin allegedly became so angry that he shot his brother in the head. Charged as an adult, Hardin is facing murder and weapons possession charges. Hardin told police he did not mean to kill his brother. He said, "It was like I picked [the gun] up and it went off." He faces up to 50 years. He will be sentenced June 4, 2001.

KING v. JOWERS - Live from Memphis. Surviving family members of Martin Luther King Jr. sued a former Memphis restaurant owner who claims he participated in the 1968 assassination of the civil rights leader. Loyd Jowers claims he and several other men were involved in both the murder and the plot to frame James Earl Ray, but he has no evidence to prove his story. The King family, represented by Ray's former attorney, took Jowers to court to prove that he was indeed involved in a conspiracy. The jury found for the plaintiff. (11/99)

LENFESTEY v. HELD - Taped from Ft. Lauderdale, FL. Suffering from depression following a hot air balloon crash, Lynn Lenfestey admitted herself into the Coral Ridge Psychiatric Hospital. When she tried to check out, the medical staff allegedly forced her to stay, violating Florida's Patient Rights law. Lenfestey, 50, who was pro se, claimed the hospital, which has since closed, made her a prisoner for 8 days so it could collect insurance money. The defendant was found not liable. (2/99)

MASSACHUSETTS v. WARREN BUSH - Warren Bush, a 55-year-old construction company owner, faced 20 years in prison after a little girl died at one of his work sites. Jacquelyn Moore, 4, was playing in a drainage ditch when the walls collapsed around her, crushing her. Her mother and neighbors frantically tried to save her, but she was buried too long and suffocated. Prosecutors say Bush left the site in a dangerous condition and charged him with manslaughter. His lawyer say Bush is a responsible family man who is being unfairly prosecuted for an accident. He was acquitted. (7/01)

MASSACHUSETTS v. DIRK GREINEDER - Was world-renowned physician Dirk Greineder so obsessed with Internet porn and prostitutes that he'd kill to keep it a secret? Prosecutors say Greineder, 59, fatally beat and stabbed his wife, Mable, 58, during an early morning walk after she learned of his alternative lifestyle. Greineder maintains that Mable was attacked by an unknown assailant. Greneder, a prominent allergist and asthma specialist, was on the advisory board at Harvard Medical School. He was given a mandatory sentence of life in prison. (6/01)

MASSACHUSETTS v. SHARPE - Live from Lawrence. Dr. Richard Sharpe, a cross-dressing millionaire physician, was accused of murdering his wife Karen while her brother and two other people watched. Sharpe, who pleaded not guilty by reason of insanity, was convicted and sentenced to life in prison. (10/01)

MICHIGAN v. ABRAHAM - Live from Pontiac. In 1997, prosecutors charged 11-year-old Nathaniel Abraham with first-degree murder, the first time in U.S. history that such a young person faced trial as an adult.

Abraham, now 13, was accused of shooting a man outside a convenience store with a stolen rifle. He later confessed. The defense claimed he was firing at trees for target practice. Abraham was convicted of second-degree murder and was sentenced to juvenile detention; he will be released when he turns 21 years old. (10/99)

MICHIGAN v. BOOMER - Live from Standish. Timothy Boomer, 24, was canoeing with friends in rural Michigan when he was jostled out of the boat and fell into the river. Wet and a little drunk, Boomer began to swear at his friends. A family with 2 small children canoeing nearby claimed the swearing lasted several minutes and was highly offensive. Police also witnessed the incident and cited Boomer under a century-old law prohibiting cursing before women and children. The ACLU took on Boomer's case. Boomer was convicted of cursing in the presence of children. (6/99)

MICHIGAN v. DAVID KRUPINSKI - Police Officer David Krupinski, 23,, was charged with manslaughter for shooting a deaf and mute man in August 2000. After responding to a call about a dispute, Krupinski and three other policemen were approached by Errol Shaw, 39, who was holding a rake. The defense said that Shaw held the rake like a baseball bat, threatening Krupinski. The prosecution said Krupinski was "unreasonable to resort to fatal force." Shaw's mother said she repeatedly told officers about her son's disabilities; the officers denied her claim. Krupinski faced a 15-year prison term. (7/01)

MICHIGAN v. KEVORKIAN - Live from Pontiac. Jack Kevorkian stood trial for the murder of Thomas Youk, who was battling Lou Gehrig's disease. Prosecutors charged Kevorkian after viewing tapes of Youk's death, which was televised in November on "60 Minutes." Kevorkian was convicted of second-degree murder and delivering a controlled substance and was sentenced to 10 to 25 years. (3/99)

MICHIGAN v. LESKO - Taped from Mount Clemens. In 1994, Albert Lesko, 43, and his wife Cindy, 30, were in the middle of a messy divorce and custody battle for their two children. But that does not mean Lesko killed Cindy in Oct. 1994, Lesko's attorneys said. Cindy's body was never found. Prosecutors believe Lesko killed his wife because she was going to testify against him on a drug charge. Lesko, who was charged with first-degree murder and faced life in prison without parole, was acquitted. (10/01)

MICHIGAN v. RANDOLPH - Taped from Pontiac. Prominent African-American attorney Thomas Randolph was charged with murdering his wife in January 1982. Prosecutors say the 58-year-old hired a hitman to kill Sharron Randolph, a former police officer. Randolph was never charged with the crime until 2000, when the alleged hitman's niece came forward to tell prosecutors that her uncle and Randolph planned the murder to collect on Sharron Randolph's life insurance policy. Randolph was convicted and sentenced to life in prison without parole. (10/01)

MICHIGAN v. SCHMITZ - Live from Pontiac. Jonathan Schmitz, who killed Scott Amedure after an appearance on The Jenny Jones Show, had his second-degree murder conviction overturned by a state appellate court in September 1998. The court decided that Schmitz's lawyers should have been allowed to remove a juror before the trial began. Schmitz was retried for second-degree murder; his attorneys asked a jury to convict Schmitz of voluntary manslaughter. Schmitz was convicted of second-degree murder. (8/99)

MICHIGAN v. STARR - Taped from Pontiac. Debra Lynn Starr had Paul Lingnau shot in 1984 to prevent him from testifying against her in a fraud suit. Prosecutors claimed Starr gave a male friend her stepfather's gun and convinced him to shoot Lingnau. The gun was never found and the shooter was never identified. Starr told several friends about the murder and rumors eventually reached the police. Starr was convicted of first-degree murder and was sentenced to life without parole. (5/99)

MICHIGAN v. TAYLOR - Taped from Detroit. Davario Taylor, who made it to college after growing up in the inner city projects, was charged with murder after a confrontation with his mother's drug dealing boyfriend. Taylor claimed he grabbed Willie Davis' gun and shot him in self-defense after Davis threatened him with a pistol. Prosecutors said Taylor was determined to get rid of Davis and killed him in cold blood. Taylor's mother originally told prosecutors that she had killed Davis but her son later confessed to police. Taylor was acquitted. (2/99)

MISSOURI v. DAVIS - Taped from Kansas City. Kim Davis faced the death penalty for the dragging death of 6-year-old Jake Robel. Davis was in the middle of stealing Robel's mother's car when the woman tried to yank her son out of the backseat to save him. The woman missed and Davis drove away, dragging the boy, who was dangling behind the vehicle strapped to his car seat, to death. (9/01)

MISSOURI v. JOHNSON - Taped from Marshfield. Jeremiah Johnson was charged with first-degree murder for killing his sister while high on LSD. After 51 hours of deliberations, Johnson was convicted and sentenced to life in prison. (8/01)

NEVADA v. MURPHY AND TABISH - Live from Las Vegas. Authorities said Sandy Murphy, a former topless dancer, and her beau, Rick Tabish, forced heroin down former casino owner Ted Binion's throat and then watched him die. Two days later, Tabish was caught digging up $4 million in silver that Binion had buried in an underground vault. Defense attorneys argued the evidence was circumstantial; there were no witnesses. They also claimed that Binion asked Tabish, a business associate, to remove the silver as a favor. Both were convicted of all charges and were sentenced to life in prison with the possibility of parole in 20 years. (3/00)

NEVADA v. JESSICA WILLIAMS - Live from Las Vegas: Jessica Williams, 21, allegedly plowed into and killed six teenagers last March. Clark County authorities say that Williams was under the influence of marijuana and ecstasy when her minivan careened off the highway, across a dirt median where several high school students were picking up trash. Defense attorneys plan to argue that the law under which Williams is charged is unconstitutional because prosecutors do not have to prove that the defendant was impaired at the time of the accident. She was sentenced on 3/30/01.

NEW JERSEY v. FLYNN - 1/12/01 Flynn was sentenced to 30 years to prison for killing her husband (manslaughter). She must serve 25 years and 6 months before she is eligible for parole. CTV did not cover her sentencing. Live from Toms River, NJ. Sylvia Flynn, 56, said she killed her husband, John Flynn, in self-defense. In August 1998, Flynn placed a 911 call from her cell phone and claimed she was scared to go home because John promised to beat her. But instead of providing Flynn with an escort, police told her it was safe to go home. Within minutes of returning, she shot her husband five times. Prosecutors claimed the murder was an act of revenge for an affair John was having. Flynn, who claimed battered woman's syndrome, was convicted of aggravated manslaughter. She will be sentenced January 12. (1/01)

NEW JERSEY v. NEULANDER - Live from Camden. Rabbi Fred Neulander, founder of one of New Jersey's largest synagogues, faces the death penalty for plotting his wife's 1994 murder. Driven by an affair with a local radio host, Neulander allegedly paid two men to bludgeon his wife Carol to death in their home. Neulander was originally charged with conspiracy to commit murder, but the charge was upgraded to capital murder in June 2000 when two men pleaded guilty to killing Carol and agreed to testify against Neulander. The rabbi claims that his wife was killed during a robbery and denies involvement. A deadlocked jury prompted the judge to declare a mistrial (10/01).

NEW MEXICO v. YAZZIE - Taped from Santa Fe. A Wayland Baptist University student was accused of raping a 19-year-old fellow student. The woman, Fred Yazzie's friend, said she was in his room because he was upset and needed to talk. The two started drinking; she passed out. Yazzie allegedly raped her after she woke up. The defense claimed it was consensual sex. The jury was deadlocked on the rape charges but convicted Yazzie of motor theft. (2/00)

NEW YORK v. BOSS, MCMELLON, CARROLL AND MURPHY - Live from Albany. Four New York City police officers were accused of shooting and killing West African immigrant Amadou Diallo. The officers, members of the elite Street Crime Unit, were each charged with two counts of second-degree murder and one count of reckless endangerment and faced 25 years to life if convicted. Prosecutors claimed the officers, who were looking for a rape suspect at the time, fired 41 shots at the unarmed Diallo. The defendants believed Diallo was reaching for a gun when they shot him. The four defendants were acquitted. (2/00)

NORTH CAROLINA v. RAE CARRUTH - Former Carolina Panthers wide receiver Rae Carruth, 26, faces the death penalty for allegedly plotting to kill his pregnant girlfriend in November 1999. Caruth's son Chancellor was delivered via Cesarean section the night his mother, Cherica Adams, 24, was gunned down in her car. Carruth claims he had nothing to do with the murder, but prosecutors say he conspired with three men to kill Adams because he did not want the baby she was carrying. Van Brett Watkins, a co-defendant who has admitted to shooting Adams, will testify against Carruth. 1/19/01 Carruth acquitted of murder charges, but found guilty of conspiracy to commit murder, shooting into an occupied vehicle and using an instrument to destroy an unborn child. 1/22/01 Carruth sentenced to more than18 years in prison. Attorney Rudolph says Carruth will appeal. (10/00)

NORTH CAROLINA v. HUNICHEN - Taped from Raleigh. A young Tennessee couple thought they met God's messenger in a traveling preacher, Rev. Howard Hunichen. In February 1999, Lisa and Kenn Fortner and their 3 children left their home and moved in Hunichen's apartment. Weeks later, while Hunichen was changing their 7-month-old son's diaper, the infant rolled off a bed and suffered permanent brain damage. Authorities were not convinced the injuries were an accident. Hunichen was convicted of felony child abuse and was sentenced to a maximum of 6 years in prison. (3/00)

NORTH CAROLINA v. MARVIN - Live from Manteo. Melissa Marvin had one too many margaritas for lunch on April 6, 1999, and on her way home, ran a red light, killing four vacationing teens. Another teen survived after undergoing extensive surgery. Now, Marvin, a 29-year-old waitress, is charged with 4 counts of second-degree murder and driving while impaired. Marvin, who has two prior arrests for driving under the influence, had a blood alcohol level of .21 at the time of the accident. Marvin was convicted of second-degree murder and was sentenced to 60-75 years in prison. (1/00)

NORTH CAROLINA v. PRUETT AND MARSH - Jason Pruett and Andrew Marsh face involuntary manslaughter charges of providing alcohol to teen girls who were later involved in a fatal auto wreck. Pruett, 22, and Marsh, 21, face 20 months in prison for buying alcohol for 17-year-olds Michelle Mull and Amanda Ross. Ross crashed her car the night of Jan. 20, 2000, after she and Mull drank liquor at Pruett's house. Ross suffered minor injuries, but Mull was killed. The two men have not revealed a defense, and they are not expected to plead. Ross faces separate charges in another county. (7/01)

OHIO v. STEVEN BOZSIK - Taped from Medina, OH. Steven Bozsik, a 41-year-old engineer, was accused of shooting his adulterous wife seven times because she planned on leaving him after Christmas Day for her lover. Bozsik claimed he was unaware of any affair and told detectives that he and his wife had just rekindled the spark in their marriage the weekend before she was killed. Investigators, however, found an e-mail to a personal ad, from that weekend, in which Bozsik told a woman he and his wife would soon be divorced because of her affair. Bozsik was convicted and sentenced to life with no possibility of parole for 20 years. (1/00)

OHIO v. PUDELSKI - Taped from Cleveland. Prosecutors claimed 30-year-old computer programmer John Pudelski is a murderer. In March 1999, his wife found their 12-day-old baby dead. There were no visible signs of trauma; however, police began to suspect foul play after the coroner found a 4-inch skull fracture that was likely inflicted by a violent blow. Pudelski's wife claimed her husband was a cold and controlling man, as did his mother-in-law. The defense claimed the baby died from complications suffered during birth. Pudelski was convicted of murder and received a mandatory sentence of 15 years to life in prison without the possibility of parole. (12/99)

OHIO v. ROACH - Live from Cincinnati. Police officer Stephen Roach shot to death an unarmed black teenager. Roach says he fired because he thought the young man was reaching for a gun. The shooting sparked days of riots in the city, the worst in 30 years. Roach was charged with negligent homicide and obstructing official business. He was acquitted of all charges. (9/01)

PRICE v. SHINN - Live from Columbia, SC. For years, George Shinn, owner of the Charlotte Hornets, spun lies. But rumors about Shinn as a predator and a playboy surfaced in 1997 and shattered his image as a Christian family man. Shinn's name appeared in tabloids after a wealthy doctor's wife, Leslie Price, accused him of raping her at his lakeside home. Two other women, including a former Hornets cheerleader, also came forward with allegations that Shinn sexually harassed them. Unable to get the state to press charges, Price sued Shinn. Shinn claimed Price, now divorced, was after his money. The jury found Shinn not liable. (12/99)

SHANNON v. THE ESTATE OF CHARLES KURALT - Taped from Virginia City, MT. When "On the Road" reporter Charles Kuralt died in July 1997, he took a scandalous secret to his grave. Kuralt's widow, however, eventually learned of her husband's double life when his longtime mistress sued for ownership of a Montana fishing retreat. Patrick Shannon contended he promised her the property in a letter. The judge ruled that Shannon is entitled to the 90-acre estate. (3/00)

SOLIAH BAIL HEARING - Live from Los Angeles, CA. After nearly 24 years of evading authorities and murder conspiracy charges, Kathleen Soliah, the one-time member of the 1970's Symbionese Liberation Army radical group who lived under an assumed name and as a "typical mom" in Minnesota, confronted her past at a bail hearing. The hearing came less than a week after she signed an extradition waiver in Minnesota and acknowledged her identity. The judge set bail at $1 million. (7/99)

SOUTH CAROLINA v. CUTRO - Taped from Columbia. Daycare operator Gail Cutro was retried for the 1993 murders of two infants in her care and permanently injuring a third. In 1994, Cutro was convicted for one murder and given a life sentence; however the state Supreme Court overturned her conviction in 1998. In the retrial, prosecutors claimed a pattern of abuse, saying Cutro has Munchausen's Syndrome by Proxy. The jury was deadlocked and a mistrial was declared. Prosecutors will retry the case for the third time. (8/99)

SOUTH CAROLINA v. GEORGE -- Taped from North Charleston. Lorne George was one of four youths charged in the ambush killings of a 50-year-old man and a pregnant 16-year-old he'd taken in. George, then 16, was the gunman and was charged with 3 counts of murder, including one for killing the fetus. The quartet had stalked David Powers and stolen his mail, believing he had money stashed away. George was convicted of all charges and was sentenced to two consecutive life terms. (8/99)

SOUTH CAROLINA v. HILLIARD - Taped from Orangeburg. Tyrone Hilliard, then 17, claimed he shot and killed Duwayne Lee in self-defense after Lee and his "gang" came looking for trouble. Prosecutors insisted this was a case of cold-blooded murder. The defense said Lee and his friends allegedly chased Hilliard and his brother home from a gas station and threatened them with a gun and baseball bat and Hilliard fired only after Lee shot at him. Hilliard was acquitted. (5/99)

SOUTH CAROLINA v. POOLE - Taped from Conway. Renee and William Poole were strolling on a secluded strip of Myrtle Beach in June 1998, when a masked gunman ambushed them. Within seconds, Renee was stripped of her jewelry, and William was shot dead. Days later, while looking for the masked gunman, police uncovered a plot by Renee to murder her husband. Prosecutors claimed Renee and her lover, Brendon Frazier, planned the beach walk and the shooting. Renee, who was charged with murder, turned down a plea deal. She maintained she played no role in the murder. Frazier was identified as the gunman and will be tried separately. Poole was convicted of murder and conspiracy and was sentenced to life in prison. (1/00)

SOUTH CAROLINA v. ROBERTSON - Taped from York. James Robertson, a schizophrenic college dropout and math genius was accused of brutally murdering his parents in 1997 for a $500,000 inheritance. James and Meredith Moon, his girlfriend, were each charged with two murder counts; however, as part of a plea bargain, Moon testified at Robertson's trial. The defense claimed his mental illness and heavy drug use caused him to commit the murders.   Robertson was convicted of murder and armed robbery and was sentenced to death. (6/99)

SOUTH CAROLINA v. SALTZ - Taped from Columbia.   After a four-month search, police found a 12-year-old runaway's skeletal remains in the woods by his house. Only a rope tied to a tree near the remains suggested foul play.   Tipped off by three teens, police interviewed 19-year-old Michael Saltz, Jr. for 7 hours before he allegedly confessed. Saltz maintained the confession was coerced.   Saltz was convicted of murder and was sentenced to 42 years. (6/99)

TENNESSEE v. DAVIS - Live from Fayetteville. Honors student and Eagle Scout Jacob Davis, 18, was just a few days from graduation when he allegedly shot classmate Nick Creson in a dispute over a girl. Davis then sat beside his shotgun until police arrived. Davis was enraged that his girlfriend slept with Creson. During pillow talk, she told Creson that Davis was a virgin; Creson then spread the word to their classmates. Davis used a diminished capacity defense; however, he was convicted of first degree murder and was sentenced to life in prison with parole eligibility after 51 years. (7/99)

TENNESSEE v. HUSKEY - Live from Knoxville. Thomas Huskey, an alleged serial killer, nicknamed "Zoo Man" by local prostitutes because he likes having sex by the Knoxville Zoo, was charged with raping and murdering four women.   Huskey's lawyers claimed he suffers from multiple personality disorder and that one of his alter egos committed the murders. Prosecutors claimed he is faking his illness. There was a hung jury and a mistrial was declared. (1/99)

TENNESSEE v. MCKINNEY - Live from Memphis. A popular police officer moonlighting as a nightclub bouncer was shot the day after Christmas by a disgruntled patron. While Officer Don Williams struggled to stay alive, community members raised money to pay his medical bills; he died a month later. Prosecutors charged parolee Timothy McKinney with the murder after an extensive manhunt. McKinney claimed he was framed. McKinney was convicted of first-degree murder and attempted second-degree murder. (7/99)

TENNESSEE v. NICHELSON - Live from Memphis. Patrolman Peter Nichelson fatally shot a 17-year-old African-American male in the head during a car chase. Nichelson, who stood trial on second-degree murder charges, claimed he was trying to restrain Gossett when his gun fired accidentally. Nichelson was convicted of criminally negligent homicide and was sentenced to one year's probation. If he successfully completes probation, the charge will be removed from his record. (3/99)

TENNESSEE v. PARNELL - Taped from Memphis. Edward Parnell was charged with murder in the death of his 19-month-old son, who starved and froze to death at home. Authorities said the parents had food in the home and money in the bank. John Parnell was convicted of aggravated child abuse and criminal negligence and was sentenced to 20 years. (5/99)

TEXAS v. SHARMA - Taped from Houston. A Hindu prayer leader faced life in prison for using his position to exploit an impressionable young woman. Bhogeshwerand Sharma, 36, told a 20-year-old woman she needed to "cleanse" her womb with his "holy sperm" after she had sex with her boyfriend. Sharma was charged under a Texas sexual assault statute that makes it a felony for a clergy member to cause another person to submit to sex by exploiting a person's emotional dependency. Sharma argued that Hinduism is more an ethical system of beliefs than a faith in some god. Sharma was convicted and was sentenced to 10 years probation and was ordered to pay a $10,000 fine. (8/99)

TEXAS v. WALKER - Taped from Houston. Richard Miller Walker faced life in prison for fatally shooting his wife Anneeka. Walker, the son of the former president of Gulf Oil, was convicted and sentenced to 75 years in prison. (10/01)

TRAUTMAN v. MANATEE MEMORIAL HOSPITAL AND JOHN JOHNSON - Taped from Bradenton, FL. A jury acquitted John Johnson, a hospital nurse who allegedly raped Penny Trautman. She sued Johnson and the hospital where the assault occurred for emotional and psychological suffering. Trautman said the assault could have been prevented had the hospital done a background check on Johnson, who had a history of sexually assaulting women under his care. The defendants denied the rape and claimed that a background check would not have revealed that Johnson was a potential rapist. The jury found the defendants not liable. (6/99)

WASHINGTON v. CASEY - Taped from Wenatchee. John Casey, the husband of a Washington doctor, was accused of murdering his wife in October 1998, while the two were cleaning his hunting rifle. Prosecutors alleged that the Caseys, the parents of three children, were having marital problems that drove John to murder his wife. The state also argued that John stood to gain "significant" benefits from life insurance policies on his wife. Casey claimed the shooting was accidental. Casey was convicted of second-degree murder and was sentenced to 20 years in prison. (8/99)

WASHINGTON v. WHALA - Taped from Yakima. Jason Whala, 13, lost his temper while baby-sitting his 19-month-old cousin and killed him because the toddler wouldn't stop crying. Whala used a wrestling move on the infant, slamming him against the ground and landing on his head. Whala was convicted of second-degree murder. (1/00)

WEST VIRGINIA v. JACOB BEARD - Taped from Sutton, WV. In 1993, Jacob Beard was sentenced to two life sentences for allegedly killing Nancy Samotero, 19, and Vicki Durian, 22, who were on their way to a counterculture gathering in West Virginia. Beard was granted a new trial after convicted serial killer Joseph Paul Franklin confessed to the murders during a 1997 television interview. Prosecutors maintained that Beard was guilty and said that the confession was nothing more than a ploy by Franklin to gain more fame. In the second trial, Beard was acquitted of all charges. (1/00)

APPENDIX II

GUIDELINES FOR THE PILOT PROGRAM ON PHOTOGRAPHING, RECORDING, AND BROADCASTING IN THE COURTROOM. (APPROVED BY THE JUDICIAL CONFERENCE OF THE UNITED STATES, SEPTEMBER 1990. REVISED JUNE 1991.)

1. General Provisions

(a) Media coverage of federal court proceedings under the pilot program on cameras in the courtroom is permissible only in accordance with these guidelines.

(b) Reasonable advance notice is required from the media of a request to be present to broadcast, televise, record electronically, or take photographs at a particular session. In the absence of such notice, the presiding judicial officer may refuse to permit media coverage.

(c) A presiding judicial officer may refuse, limit, or terminate media coverage of an entire case, portions thereof, or testimony of particular witnesses, in the interests of justice to protect the rights of the parties, witnesses, and the dignity of the court; to assure the orderly conduct of the proceedings; or for any other reason considered necessary or appropriate by the presiding judicial officer.

(d) No direct public expense is to be incurred for equipment, wiring, or personnel needed to provide media coverage.

(e) Nothing in these guidelines shall prevent a court from placing additional restrictions, or prohibiting altogether, photographing, recording, or broadcasting in designated areas of the courthouse.

(f) These guidelines take effect July 1, 1991, and expire June 30, 1994.

2. Limitations

(a) Coverage of criminal proceedings, both at the trial and appellate levels, is prohibited.

(b) There shall be no audio pickup or broadcast of conferences which occur in a court facility between attorneys and their clients, between co-counsel of a client, or between counsel and the presiding judicial officer, whether held in the courtroom or in chambers.

(c) No coverage of the jury, or of any juror or alternate juror, while in the jury box, in the courtroom, in the jury deliberation room, or during recess, or while going to or from the deliberation room at any time, shall be permitted. Coverage of the prospective jury during voir dire is also prohibited.

3. Equipment and Personnel

(a) Not more than one television camera, operated by not more than one camera person and one stationary sound operator, shall be permitted in any trial court proceeding. Not more than two television cameras, operated by not more than one camera person each and one stationary sound person, shall be permitted in any appellate court proceeding.

(b) Not more than one still photographer, utilizing not more than one camera and related equipment, shall be permitted in any proceeding in a trial or appellate court.

(c) If two or more media representatives apply to cover a proceeding, no such coverage may begin until all such representatives have agreed upon a pooling arrangement for their respective news media. Such pooling arrangements shall include the designation of pool operators, procedures for cost sharing, access to and dissemination of material, and selection of a pool representative if appropriate. The presiding judicial officer may not be called upon to mediate or resolve any dispute as to such arrangements.

(d) Equipment or clothing shall not bear the insignia or marking of a media agency. Camera operators shall wear appropriate business attire.

4. Sound and Light Criteria

(a) Equipment shall not produce distracting sound or light. Signal lights or devices to show when equipment is operating shall not be visible.

Moving lights, flash attachments, or sudden light changes shall not be used.

(b) Except as otherwise approved by the presiding judicial officer, existing courtroom sound and light systems shall be used without modification.

Audio pickup for all media purposes shall be accomplished from existing audio systems present in the court facility, or from a television camera's built-in microphone. If no technically suitable audio system exists in the court facility, microphones and related wiring essential for media purposes shall be unobtrusive and shall be located in places designated in advance of any proceeding by the presiding judicial officer.

5. Location of Equipment and Personnel

(a) The presiding judicial officer shall designate the location in the courtroom for the camera equipment and operators.

(b) During the proceedings, operating personnel shall not move about nor shall there be placement, movement, or removal of equipment, or the changing of film, film magazines, or lenses. All such activities shall take place each day before the proceeding begins, after it ends, or during a recess.

6. Compliance

Any media representative who fails to comply with these guidelines shall be subject to appropriate sanction, as determined by the presiding judicial officer.

7. Review

It is not intended that a grant or denial of media coverage be subject to appellate review insofar as it pertains to and arises under these guidelines, except as otherwise provided by law.

GUIDELINES ADDENDUM:

The Judicial Conference Committee on Court Administration and Case Management made a number of recommendations in a June 1991 report to the Judicial Conference Executive Committee. The recommendations, sub-sequently approved, include:

(1) That the Executive Committee endorse the [CACM] Committee's interpretation that the ban on the changing of film included in guideline 5(b), does not include the changing of video cassettes.

(2) That the Executive Committee approve an expansion of the experiment to permit the Southern District of New York to allow the use of two cameras during court proceedings.

(3) That the Executive Committee direct the Committee on Court Administration and Case Management to notify courts that strict adherence to the guidelines approved by the Conference is a condition for participation as a pilot.

APPENDIX III

OBTAINED FROM THE 1999 NATIONAL SURVEY, HOW THE PUBLIC VIEWS THE STATE COURTS, NATIONAL CENTER FOR STATE COURTS AND THE HEARST CORPORATION.

Sources of Information Regarding News and the Courts

Technological advances have increased the number of sources people rely on for news and entertainment, and the number of sources of information about courts. For example, the Internet has provided an "online" electronic source of information (35% of respondents report using a computer to go online sometimes or regularly, while 65% did so hardly ever or never).

Figure 1: How often do you rely on these sources for news?

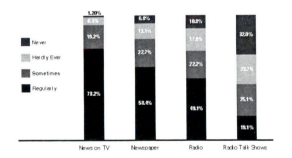

This section examines what sources respondents relied on to obtain information about courts. Results reflect the influence of the burgeoning number of court-related shows that are "reality-based" (e.g., *Judge Judy* and *People's Court*) and their impact on perceptions about courts as compared to "news" programs.

Figure 2: Where do you most frequently get information about the courts?

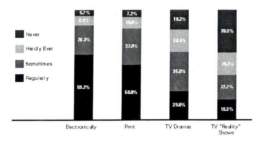

- Overall, more than of 92% of respondents indicated they watch news on television "Sometimes" or "Regularly."
- More than one-half of respondents indicated reliance on electronic and print sources for information about courts.
- African-Americans and Hispanics were significantly more likely to rely on "reality-based" productions such as *Judge Judy* for information about the courts.

After television, newspapers were the second most common source of news. While radio news programs were often cited as a regular source of news, reliance upon radio talk shows was far less common. Respondents indicated heavier reliance on electronic "news" sources over electronic "entertainment" such as TV dramas and "reality-based" shows as sources for information about the courts. One-quarter of the public reports that they receive information from TV dramas and comedies with a legal theme regularly and another 36% say that they sometimes do. This is a modest increase from the significance of TV dramas found in the 1983 survey by The Hearst Corporation.

Where do you most frequently get information about courts?

TELEVISION DRAMA

Frequently	19%
Sometimes	32%
Rarely/Never	49%

Source: 1983 Hearst Survey

Media Portrayal of Courts

- Overall, respondents do not believe the media's portrayal of the courts is accurate.

Figure 3: "The media's portrayal of courts is mostly accurate."

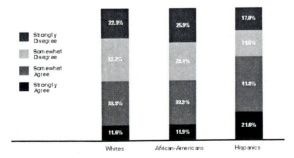

ALL RESPONDENTS

Strongly Agree	Somewhat Agree	Somewhat Disagree	Strongly Disagree
13%	35%	31%	22%

As compared to Whites/Non-Hispanics, Hispanics were more likely to agree with the statement "The media's portrayal of the courts is mostly accurate." Likewise, respondents with a high school education or less were more likely to agree with the statement "The media's portrayal of the courts is mostly accurate."

APPENDIX IV

OBTAINED FROM ELECTRONIC MEDIA COVERAGE OF FEDERAL CIVIL PROCEEDINGS: AN EVALUATION OF THE PILOT PROGRAM IN SIX DISTRICT COURTS AND TWO COURTS OF APPEALS, (1994), FEDERAL JUDICIAL CENTER.

RECOMMENDATIONS OF THE RESEARCH PROJECT STAFF ON ACCESS GENERALLY

Recommendation 1: The research project staff recommended that the Judicial Conference authorize federal courts of appeals and district courts nationwide to provide camera access to civil proceedings in their courtrooms, subject to Conference guidelines (as discussed below). This recommendation was based on information obtained in response to questions presented by the Judicial Conference and addressed in their report and did not imply any position on legal or constitutional issues.

> Explanation: The converging results from each of the inquiries suggested that members of the electronic media generally complied with program guidelines and that their presence did not disrupt court proceedings, affect participants in the proceedings, or interfere with the administration of justice. To the extent decisions about expanding access would rest on these considerations, the results supported expansion.

ON GUIDELINES

Recommendation 2: The research project staff recommended that if the committee and Conference had decided to continue or expand the program, the guidelines in effect for the pilot program remain in effect, subject to the modifications recommended in the Center's initial report (and set forth as Recommendations 3, 4, and 5 below).

> Explanation: As reported, judges, court staff, and media representatives all indicated that the guidelines were very workable and provided judges with the discretion needed to deny or limit electronic media coverage based on the circumstances of a particular case.

Recommendation 3: The research project staff recommended that the guidelines be modified to call for a standard practice of informing counsel or a party appearing *pro se* that an application for media coverage has been received. They did not recommend that there be guidelines for ruling on these applications.

> Explanation: Some attorneys responding to their survey complained that they were not informed about electronic media coverage prior to appearing for a hearing or trial. Because most judges are willing to entertain attorney and party objections, a notice requirement seemed reasonable. However, experience in the pilot program suggested that conditions that might warrant denial of an application were so specific that guidelines would have to be so general as to provide little help. The inevitably general guidelines would then be likely to produce unnecessary motion activity. The basic questions arising from the assertion of personal right to privacy and the public right to know should be left for decision in the normal course of litigation.

Recommendation 4:   The research project staff recommended that the guidelines be modified to reflect the committee's determinations regarding the eligibility of extradition and habeas proceedings for electronic media coverage.

> Explanation: From the telephone interviews they had learned that the issue of whether habeas proceedings could be covered was raised in several of the pilot courts. If the program was continued or expanded, they would recommend that the committee's determinations on these issues be incorporated into the guidelines so they will not be raised anew by media representatives unaware of the committee's determinations.

ON FACILITIES

Recommendation 5: The research project staff recommended that the guidelines be revised to permit two television cameras in trial courtrooms and appellate courtrooms.

> Explanation: The absence of problems reported from the Southern District of New York suggested that permitting two cameras in trial courtrooms did not cause additional disruptions. In addition, permitting two television cameras in the trial courtroom encourages coverage by extended-coverage networks, which provide the type of coverage that most judges favor. The majority of cases covered under the program by extended-coverage networks were in courts (both trial and appellate) that allow two television cameras, and representatives from extended coverage networks indicated in interviews that the ability to use two cameras was important when providing "gavel-to-gavel" coverage of proceedings. In comparing the type of coverage provided by extended-coverage networks to the type of coverage analyzed in the content analysis, it would appear that extended coverage likely served a greater educational function, which is a function judge interviewees identified as the greatest potential benefit of allowing electronic media access to the courts. Judges would retain discretion under the guidelines to limit the number of cameras in a particular case.

Recommendation 6: The research project staff recommended that media organizations be invited to submit to the Committee on Court Administration and Case Management proposals for constructing and regulating use of permanent camera facilities in federal courthouses.

> Explanation: In several interview and questionnaire respondents (including judges, court administrators, attorneys, and media representatives) expressed the view that electronic media coverage of proceedings would be least intrusive if cameras were installed permanently in federal courtrooms. Most who raised the issue suggested this be done at media expense.

APPENDIX V

PERCEPTIONS OF THE U.S. JUSTICE SYSTEM, AMERICAN BAR ASSOCIATION, FEBRUARY 24, 1999.

Opinions

CONFIDENCE IN INSTITUTIONS/PROFESSIONS

Respondents were asked about their level of confidence in various institutions in American society, such as organized religion or the legal profession/lawyers, using a 5-point scale with the end points of "extremely confident" and "not at all confident."

While confidence in the overall U.S. justice system is only at 30%, confidence in the different components within the system varies widely. For example, 50% of the respondents said they are extremely or very confident in the Supreme Court. Interestingly, only 34% said the same of the Federal Courts. Confidence in judges is only fair, with 32% of the respondents being extremely or very confident. Confidence in the U.S. Congress is even lower, at 18%, an only 14% of respondents said they are extremely or very confident in lawyers. In fact, the only category generating less confidence than the U.S. Congress and lawyers is the media at 8%.

The converse of this information confirms that this negative perception is held by a majority of respondents. Sixty percent (60%) are only slightly confident or have no confidence in the media. Further, almost half of respondents (42%) lack confidence in lawyers. On the positive side, the U.S. Supreme Court and the local police are the two components of the justice system that have the lowest percentage of "no confidence" votes.

In contrast to most components of the justice system, the local police, doctors and accountants have been able to garner a fairly healthy amount of confidence.

	Extremely/ Very Confident %	Somewhat Confident %	Slightly/Not At All Confident %
U.S. Supreme Court	50	35	15
The Local Police	47	33	20
Medical Profession/ Doctors	46	39	15
Accounting Profession/ Accountants	39	44	15
Organized Religion	37	30	31
Federal Courts other than U.S. Supreme Court	34	45	21
Judiciary/Judges	32	46	22
U.S. Justice System in General	30	43	27
State and Local Courts	28	47	25
The Public Schools	27	38	35
The Executive Branch of the Federal Government -- Office of the President; Departments of Commerce, Defense, Etc.	26	36	37
The Executive Branches of State/Local Government -- Office of Governors, Mayors, Etc.	24	50	26
The State Legislatures	19	54	27
Your State's Prison System	19	41	39
U.S. Congress	18	47	35
The Legal Profession/ Lawyers	14	44	42
The Media	8	32	60

Comparison of Confidence Levels in Current and Previous Study

An assessment of confidence levels in these same categories and professions was previously done twenty years ago in a study by

Yankelovich (1978). Although the methodology was different (in-person interviews versus telephone interviews), the sample is comparable (general population) and the question was worded the same. Additionally, the institutions, for the most part, remained the same. The current study included some additional professions:

- the U.S. justice system in general
- the accounting profession/accountants
- the judiciary/judges
- the legal profession/lawyers

The Yankelovich study had also asked about confidence in American business and organized labor, which were not included in the current study.

Changes in perceptions are evident. The level of confidence in the U.S. Supreme Court has improved since 1978, as has the level of confidence in the local police, federal courts (besides the U.S. Supreme court), and state and local courts. On the other hand, the public has significantly lower confidence in doctors, organized religion, public schools, U.S. Congress, and most notably, the media (29% down to 8%).

	Extremely/Very Confident	
	Yankelovich (1978)	MARC (1998)
	(1931)	(1000)
	%	%
	A	B
U.S. Supreme Court	36	50 A
The Local Police	40	47 A
Medical Profession/Doctors	50 B	46
Accounting Profession/Accountants	NA	39
Organized Religion	41 B	37
Federal Courts other than U.S. Supreme Court	29	34 A
Judiciary/Judges	NA	32
U.S. Justice System in General	NA	30
State and Local Courts	23	28 A
The Public Schools	37B	27
The Executive Branch of the Federal Government -- Office of the President; Departments of Commerce, Defense, etc.	27	26

The Executive Branches of State/	21	24a
Local Government -- Office of		
Governors, Mayors, Etc.		
The State Legislatures	21	19
Your State's Prison System	17	19
U.S. Congress	23 B	18
The Legal Profession/Lawyers	NA	14
The Media	29	8

Capital letter indicates significant difference at the 95% confidence level; lower case
letter indicates significant difference at the 90% confidence level.

Opinions About the U.S. Justice System

In order to understand what drives people's confidence, opinions about the
U.S. justice system were collected through a series of fifty attitude
statements. These statements were about the justice system in general and
about the components of the system, namely, the courts, judges, lawyers,
and the police.
The attitudes statements will be discussed in several different ways:

- By identifying how respondents feel about the U.S.
  justice system.
- By how people's level of knowledge may be
  influencing their attitudes and opinions.
- By what attitudes are driving confidence in the justice
  system and its various components.

Attitude Statements on Which the Majority of Total Respondents Agree

Overall, in spite of its problems, the justice system is still perceived to
be the best in the world; eighty percent (80%) of the respondents strongly
agree or agree with this statement. Looking back at the confidence rating
of the justice system (only 30%), people seem to be saying that they know
the justice system has its problems, but that it is still the best available
option. This could also be the difference between how it is considered
conceptually and how it actually operates.

Along these same lines, people also tend to believe in the jury system,
with a majority of respondents (78%) believing that it is the most fair way
to determine the guilt or innocence of a person accused of a crime. In fact,
most people (69%) agree that juries are the most important part of the
judicial system.

It is encouraging that most people believe that lawyers are easily accessible (69%) when they are needed. However, they also believe that lawyers spend too much time getting criminals released on technicalities (68%).

On the other hand, ninety percent (90%) of respondents strongly feel that wealthy people or companies often wear down their opponents by dragging out the legal proceedings. As a result, it is not surprising to find that most people think going to court takes too long (78%) and is too costly (77%). Further, the courts are considered to be too lenient, finding technicalities to let criminals go free (74%) and providing too many opportunities to appeal decisions (72%). These may be some of the reasons why confidence in the system overall is relatively low.

	Strongly Agree/ Agree	Strongly Agree
	%	%
In spite of its problems, the American justice system is still the best in the world	80	26
The jury system is the most fair way to determine the guilt or innocence of a person accused of a crime	78	17
Juries are the most important part of our judicial system	69	19
It would be easy to get a lawyer if I needed one	69	10
Lawyers spend too much time finding technicalities to get criminals released	68	20
Wealthy people or companies often wear down their opponents by dragging out the legal proceedings	90	40
It takes courts too long for courts to do their jobs	78	28
It costs too much to go to court	77	24
The courts let too many criminals go free on technicalities	74	26
The courts offer convicted criminals too many opportunities for appeal	72	26

Note: Question was answered on a 5-point scale; Strongly agree to Strongly disagree. Scores reported are top-2-box: Strongly Agree/Agree

Most people believe judges should have flexibility in sentencing convicted criminals, but they also clearly believe that lack of jail space should not be one of the criteria used for determining sentences.

	Strongly Disagree %	Strongly Disagree/ Disagree %
Lack of jail space should be considered by judges when sentencing criminal defendants	22	70
Judges should have no leeway in how they sentence convicted criminals	13	70

Note: Question was answered on a 5-point scale; Strongly agree to Strongly disagree. Scores reported are bottom-2-box: Strongly Disagree/Disagree

Opinions of Specific Components of the U.S. Justice System

All of the attitude statements were asked on a rotated basis within their respective component section and across different component sections. For example, one person would have rated all of the attribute statements on the court first, and the next person would have had a different component first, such as lawyers. Or, two people could have rated the courts first, but they would have rated the statements in a different order. These rotations were done to prevent response bias. The statements, while asked by component section, are analyzed here in related topic groupings:

- overall system attitudes
- how groups of people are treated
- sentencing/criminals in court
- court/judges/lawyers doing their jobs.

Overall System Attitudes

As previously noted, a majority of people strongly agree or agree that the American justice system is the best worldwide. The jury system is perceive to be both fair and the most important part of the judicial system. Respondents also believe that it would be easy to get a lawyer if needed and that, in general, it is easy to access legal services. In contrast, about half the people believe the justice system needs a complete overhaul and that there should be fewer lawyers. Some of this may be a function of people believing the profession does not adequately discipline lawyers. While most do not believe the courts are puppets of the political system, a substantial group of people (31%) believe this.

This suggests that while, in general, people believe in the U.S. justice system, they do not believe it is perfect, and improvements should be considered in specific areas.

<u>Judges</u>

Most people are confident in the qualifications of judges and believe judges are adequately compensated. They are split as to whether or not judges fulfill their role as civic-minded citizens through community service.

	Strongly Agree/ Agree %	Neither Agree Nor Disagree %	Slightly Disagree/ Disagree %
Most judges are extremely well qualified for their jobs	54	20	25
Judges are not paid enough given how much work they do	14	31	51
Most judges do not contribute enough to their community through donations of time, legal services, or money	33	38	36

<u>Lawyers Being Civic Minded</u>

The public is split on its views of lawyers, their motivations and their civic-mindedness. On the positive side, about half the people believe that some costs for lawyers' services are reasonable and that lawyers do not choose cases based on the publicity they may receive. On the other hand, most people do not believe that lawyers work harder and longer hours than most others, that the best lawyers are selected to serve as judges or that lawyers try to make divorces simpler and less painful.

Otherwise, almost as many people agree as disagree that most lawyers are motivated to both serve the public and do what is right for their clients.

Further, as with judges, people seem to feel lawyers should contribute to their communities, but that they are only doing a moderately good job in this area.

It is clear from people's lack of confidence in the profession and their questioning of lawyers' motives and efforts that some public relations is in order. Importantly, many people seem to think that the legal profession should have some altruistic or civil servant aspects to it. They believe lawyers should have in mind the welfare not only of their clients but also of the public. In essence, lawyers are put on a pedestal and are held to very high standards of moral conduct.

There is a division among the people who have used lawyers. A comparison between those who said they were very or somewhat satisfied with the service they received and those who said they were very or somewhat dissatisfied shows that those with positive experience have a more positive outlook regarding lawyers, rating them higher on trying to serve public interests well. In contrast, those with negative experience believe lawyers are more concerned with self-promotion than with their client's best interests. This group also more strongly disagrees that costs for lawyers' services are reasonable.

	Strongly Agree/ Agree %	Neither Agree Nor Disagree %	Slightly Disagree/ Disagree %
Some costs for lawyers' services are reasonable	53	9	37
Lawyers work harder and longer hours than do people in most other jobs	28	15	57
Most lawyers try to serve the public interests well	47	16	36
Most lawyers choose their cases based on how much publicity they will get	29	20	50
Most lawyers are more concerned with their own self-promotion than their client's best interests	45	22	33
The best lawyers are selected to			

	Strongly Agree/ Agree %	Neither Agree Nor Disagree %	Slightly Disagree/ Disagree %
serve as judges	27	22	50
Lawyers try to help make divorce simpler and less painful	28	21	50
Most lawyers do what is right for their clients, and still do what is good for the public	41	18	40
A lawyer from a smaller firm takes more interest in his or her client than does a lawyer from a larger firm	43	27	28
Most lawyers do not contribute enough to their community through donations of time, legal services, or money	43	31	23

Sources of Information About the Justice System

Respondents were read a list of information sources and asked, for each source, how important it was for obtaining information on the justice system. A 5-point scale was used: Extremely important = 5, Not at all important = 1.

We previously noted that a majority of respondents (89%) have had experience with the courts. Therefore, it is not surprising that personal experience (63%) is considered the most important source for obtaining information about the justice system. Jury duty (57%) is another important source and is, in fact, a form of personal experience. This gives credence to the adage "you have to see it to believe it."

Closely following personal experience are school or college courses (59%) and books/library (58%). After these sources, there is a big gap in importance, as the next most important sources are lawyers (43%) and materials available from the court (43%). It is worth noting that out of all of these information sources, the one which the justice system can directly impact is materials available from the court.

The next grouping of important sources include television news (41%), family members (40%), TV shows like 20/20, 60 Minutes, Dateline (37%), local daily newspapers (36%), national newspapers (35%), and

radio news (31%). These information sources concentrate on reporting news of the day, including current experience people have with the justice system.

Sources of information that are considered least important are various forms of entertainment, such as movies, television dramas and court programs like People's court. The lower importance ratings of these media as a source of information about the justice system parallels confidence levels in the media. As discussed previously, the level of confidence in the media is low, with a majority of respondents (60%) indicating they were slightly or not at all confident in it.

Additionally, as discussed previously, it was evident that the role and type of case people had experience with affected their perception of the justice system. With regard to perception of importance of these information sources, there are no significant differences between those with positive versus negative active court experience, with two exceptions. Those with negative experience rate court programs on TV and information from a family member significantly more important sources of information than do those with positive experiences. One possible explanation would be that this group believes their court experience should have proceeded more along the lines of the court proceeding they saw on TV.

	Total
Base:	(1,000)
	%
Extremely/Very Important	
Personal experience	63
School or college course	59
Books/library	58
Lawyers/attorneys	43
Materials available from the court	43
Television news	41
Family Member	40
Television news shows like 20/20, 60 Minutes, Dateline	37
Local daily newspaper	36
National newspapers	35
Radio news	31
High profile cases	28
Internet	23
Word of mouth	22

	Total (1,000)
Base:	%
Extremely/Very Important	
Television trials like Court TV	20
Magazines	16
Radio/TV talk shows	15
Court programs like People's Court/Judge Judy	11
Television dramas	9
Movies/videos	7

Note: The question was answered on a 5 point scale; Extremely important to Not at all important.

<u>Importance of Information Sources By Actual Level of Knowledge Groups</u>

Respondents with high levels of knowledge about the justice system do not consider any information source as significantly more important than their counterparts with medium or low levels of knowledge do. On the other hand, those with low levels of knowledge consider media sources of significantly higher importance. Additionally, this low level of knowledge group considers books or the library to be significantly more important sources of information than do the other more knowledgeable groups. Thus, it appears that these people know where to get the information, but have not actually taken the steps to get it.

	Actual Levels of Knowledge		
	High	**Medium**	**Low**
Base:	**(260)**	**(504)**	**(236)**
	%	%	%
Extremely/Very Important	A	B	C
Personal Experience	64	63	63
School or college courses	55	60	61
Jury Duty	54	57	59

Actual Levels of Knowledge

	High	Medium	Low
Base:	(260)	(504)	(236)
	%	%	%
Extremely/Very Important	A	B	C
Books/library	50	60 A	61 A
Lawyers/attorneys	45	41	46
Materials available from the court	37	42	53 AB
National newspapers	34	33	38
Local daily newspaper	32	34	47 AB
Television news	29	41 A	56 AB
Family member	29	41 A	53 AB
Radio news	26	29	40 AB
Television news shows like 20/20, 60 Minutes, Dateline	25	38 A	48 AB
High profile cases	22	29 A	34 A
Internet	21	24	23
Word of mouth	18	23	27 A
Magazines	15	15	20
Television trials like Court TV	14	21 A	25 A
Radio/TV talk shows	10	15	23 AB
Television dramas	4	8 A	16 AB
Court programs like People's Court/Judge Judy	3	10 A	22 AB
Movies/videos	2	6 A	16 **AB**

Note: The question was answered on a 5 point scale; Extremely important to Not at all important. Capital letter indicates significant difference at the 95% confidence level; lower case letter indicates significant difference at the 90% confidence level.

Sources of Education About the Justice System

In previous sections, we discussed levels of knowledge people actually have about the justice system. Respondents were also asked where they received that knowledge. Respondents with the highest levels of knowledge were more likely to receive education from many of these sources. For the most part, people received their education about the justice system from sources most have natural access to, such as social studies classes in grade school (83%) and high school civics or government classes (82%).

		Levels of Knowledge		
	Total	High	Medium	Low
Base:	(1000)	(260)	(504)	(236)
		% A	% B	% C
Social studies classes in grade school	83	89 B C	84 C	76
High school civics or government class	82	94 B C	82 C	68
Personal experience	67	79 B C	67 C	56
College level courses on political science	42	74 B C	36 C	17
Paralegal studies	5	7 C	4	3
Attended law school	3	8 B C	1	3
Graduated law school	2	6 B C	1	1
Any other source	11	14 C	13 C	4
None of the above	5	0	4 A	13 A B

Capital letter indicates significant difference at the 95% confidence level; lower case letter indicates significant difference at the 90% confidence level.

<u>Sources Willing to Learn From</u>

People are willing to learn from a variety of sources.
- Of those desiring to learn more, three-fourths want to learn from current judges or retired judges.
- College or law professors and teachers are also good sources, according to 70% of the respondents.
- Two-thirds of the people want to learn more from the state/local bar associations and from the American Bar Association.

	Desire to Learn More (610) %
Judges	75
Retired judges	73
College/law professors	70
Teachers	70
State/local bar association	69
American Bar Association	68
Lawyers	58
Civic groups	56
Any type of media	51
Other	6
None of the above	2

Printed with the Permission of the American Bar Association

APPENDIX VI
COURT TV NATIONAL SURVEY - FEBRUARY 10-12, 1997 - THE POLLING COMPANY AND MELLMAN GROUP

N=800 Registered Voters
Margin of Error ± 3.5%

1. Do you favor or oppose allowing a camera in courtrooms to broadcast proceedings of federal trials, or are you undecided about this?
    [If "FAVOR" or "OPPOSE", ASK:] Is that favor/oppose) strongly or not so strongly?
    [IF UNDECIDED, ASK:] Well which way do you lean?
    29% TOTAL FAVOR
    Favor strongly 19%
    Favor not so strongly........................... 7%
    undecided leans favor 3%
    Undecided 41%
    31% TOTAL OPPOSE
    undecided leans oppose......................... 3%
    Oppose not so strongly 10%
    Oppose strongly 18%

2. During the past 20 years, almost all states passed laws allowing judges to determine for themselves whether or not television cameras should be permitted in their courtrooms. However, under a 50-year old federal law, cameras are banned in federal courtrooms. Which of the following comes closer to your opinion......
    (ROTATE)
    12% We should required that all trials be televised to the public
    48% We should let each federal judge decide whether to allow cameras in their courtrooms depending on the case, just like most state judges
    31% We should ban cameras in all federal trials
    10% I don't have an opinion on this

3.   Do you favor or oppose televising the trial of the men accused of bombing the federal building in Oklahoma City, or aren't you sure about this?
[IF FAVOR OR "OPPOSE", ASK:] Is that (favor/oppose) strongly or not so strongly?
39% TOTAL FAVOR
Favor strongly 33%
Favor not so strongly............................ 6%
47% TOTAL OPPOSE
Oppose not so strongly 10%
Oppose strongly 37%
not sure/don't know 18%

4.   Do you favor or oppose the trial of CIA agent Aldrich Ames, accused on spying for the Soviet Union, or don't you have an opinion on this?
[IF FAVOR OR "OPPOSE", ASK:] Is that (favor/oppose) strongly or not so strongly?
36% TOTAL FAVOR
Favor strongly 30%
Favor not so strongly............................ 6%

42% TOTAL OPPOSE
Oppose not so strongly 9%
Oppose strongly 33%
not sure/don't know 22%

5.   Do you favor or oppose televising the Unabomber trial or aren't you sure about this?
[IF "FAVOR" OR "OPPOSE", ASK:] Is that (favor/oppose) strongly or not so strongly?
40% TOTAL FAVOR
Favor strongly 32%
Favor not so strongly............................ 8%
42% TOTAL OPPOSE
Oppose not so strongly 9%
Oppose strongly 33%
not sure/don't know 19%
Now I'm going to read a list of short statements. After each, please tell me whether you agree or disagree with what I have just read. If you are not sure, please say so and we'll go on.

[IF AGREE OR DISAGREE, ASK:] Is that (Agree/Disagree) strongly or not so strongly?

	agree strongly	agree not st	disagree not st	disagree strongly	don't know

[ROTATE BATTERY BY Q. 6 to Q. 10

SPLIT SAMPLE A

6.   If I were a lawyer in court and I knew I would be seen on television, I would be more prepared than ususal..

	49%	13%	7%	23%	9%

SPLIT SAMPLE B

7.   If I were a judge and I knew I would be seen on television, I would be more careful than usual......................

	52%	13%	11%	15%	9%

8.   Complete and unedited television coverage of trials would provide me with a more accurate knowledge of court proceedings than if I relied on the news media for this information....

....

	56%	13%	8%	16%	8%

9.   Since many new courtrooms are being built with cameras in them for transcription purposes this footage should be made public, as well

....

	42%	12%	12%	27%	8%

10.   We need to televise court proceedings to make it easier to watch over judges who take it upon themselves to change laws.......

....

	38%	10%	12%	31%	9%

11.   Americans have the right to witness court trials....................

68%	12%	4%	10%	6%

Let me read you some arguments you might hear from people who want to limit restrictions banning cameras in federal courts. After I read each one, please tell me how convincing you think it is.... Now how convincing is that argument, very convincing, somewhat convincing, not too convincing, or not at all convincing?

	Very con.	Smwt conv.	Not too conv.	Not at all	DK
12. In the over twenty years that cameras have been allowed courtroom not a single case has been reversed or overturned because of television cameras having been present	22%	27%	20%	19%	11%
13. Allowing television cameras in the courtroom permits Americans to see legal proceedings firsthand, and not through the filter of the news media........	47%	26%	12%	10%	5%
14. Televising federal trials would allow Americans to see legal trials and judges much the same as C-SPAN allows Americans to watch Congress............	40%	31%	13%	10%	6%
15. Following a two-and-a-half year study, the research and education divisions of the Federal Court system recommended judges decide for themselves whether or not to allow cameras in the courtroom	28%	28%	17%	19%	8%

Now, I would like to read you a couple of statements people have made about allowing a television camera in the courtroom. After I read each statement please tell me if a particular statement makes you more likely or less to allow a television in the courtroom. If a particular statement makes no difference to you, just say so. [IF MORE LIKELY OR LESS LIKELY, ASK:] And , is that much (MORE LIKELY/LESS LIKELY) or only somewhat (MORE LIKELY/LESS LIKELY)?

	Much ML	Smwt ML	Smwt LL	Much LL	No Diff	Don't Know

16. Television and movies glorify violence, but do not show the consequences of violence. Televising trials shows people the real consequences of violence 40%   17%   9%   13%   17%   5%

17. Celebrity trials will always attract media coverage, whether or not a trial is televised. However, televising the actual court proceedings helps focus on the legal process by allowing regular Americans to see for themselves what happens and make up their own minds about the outcome without the media's analysis...............................
.... 40%   18%   8%   18%   11%   6%

18. A recent survey found that more than three-fourths of high-school teachers would recommend watching COURT-TV to their students ....
.... 41%   20%   9%   11%   12%   8%

Switching subjects......

19. Which of the following comes closer to your opinion.....
(ROTATE)
20% Defendants should have the absolute right to prevent their trials from being televised if they do not want them televised20%
The Constitution mandates public trials and defendants should not have the right to prevent trials from being televised
39% It should be up to judges to decide whether or not a defendant's rights would be violated by televising a trial 21% I don't have an opinion on this

On a different topic ......

20. Federal judges are now appointed for lifetime terms until they retire. Do you favor or oppose a lifetime tenure system for federal judges or don't you have an opinion on this?
[IF "FAVOR" OR "OPPOSE", ASK:] Is that (favor/oppose) strongly or not so strongly?
19% TOTAL FAVOR

Favor strongly 13%
Favor not so strongly............................   6%
67% TOTAL OPPOSE
Oppose not so strongly 10%
Oppose strongly 57%
not sure/don't know 15%

THANK YOU.   THE FOLLOWING QUESTIONS ARE FOR
CLASSIFICATION PURPOSES ONLY.
21.   How many hours per week would you say you watch TV?
        1-4 .... 14%
        5-9 .... 19%
        10-19 .... 33%
        20+ 30%
        do not watch 1%
        don't know 3%

I'm going to read you a list of cable channels. For each please
tell me whether you watch that channel every day, several times
a week, once a week, or never?   If you haven't heard of a
network or don't know how much you watch that channel, just
say so and we'll go on. [ROTATE].

	everyday	sev times a week	once a week	less than once	never	dk
22. CNN, the Cable News Network ..	23%	19%	18%	11%	24%	6%
23. C-SPAN	6%	9%	13%	12%	52%	7%
24. Court-TV...	2%	5%	7%	13%	67%	7%

[IF "5" or "6" FOR "COURT TV" ABOVE, SKIP TO Q. 27]

25.   [ASK THOSE WHO WATCH Court TV] Has what you have
        seen on Court TV made the legal process easier to understand,
        more difficult to understand, or has it made no difference?
        easier 50%
        no effect 36%
        more difficult 10%
        don't know 4%
26.   [ASK THOSE WHO WATCH Court TV] Has what you have
        seen on Court TV made you more favorable towards the legal

process, less favorable toward the legal process, or has it not changed your opinion of the legal process?

more favorable 25%
no effect 48%
less favorable 21%
don't know 5%

27.   Has what you have seen on the general news media made you more favorable towards the legal process, less favorable toward the legal process, or has it not changed your opinion of the legal process?

more favorable 11%
no effect 47%
less favorable 36%
don't know 6%

28.   Have you ever been a victim of a crime?

yes 31%
no 68%
dk 1%

Split Sample A
29.   How closely did you follow the first O.J. Simpson trial - the criminal trial? Would you say you followed it very closely, pretty closely, not too closely, or not closely at all?

very 17%
pretty 28%
not too 37%
not at all 17%
don't know 2%

Split Sample B
30.   How closely did you follow the second O.J. Simpson trial - the civil trial which just ended?   Would you say you followed it very closely, pretty closely, not too closely, or not closely at all?

very 8%
pretty 14%
not too 40%
not at all 37%
don't know 2%

31. In the second O.J. Simpson trial - the civil trial - the families of Ron Goldman and Nicole Brown Simpson wanted the trial televised, just like the first one, to show the public new evidence against O.J. Simpson. The judge, however, decided NOT to televise the second trial. Do you (ROTATE) agree or disagree with the judge's decision not to televise the most recent O.J. Simpson trial? [IF "AGREE" OR "DISAGREE", ASK:] Is that (agree/disagree) strongly or not so strongly?

64% TOTAL AGREE
Agree strongly 56%
Agree not so strongly............................ 8%
30% TOTAL DISAGREE
Disagree not so strongly 6%
Disagree strongly................................... 24%
not sure/don't know 7%

32. Generally speaking, do you think of yourself as a Republican, a Democrat, an independent, or something else? [IF REPUBLICAN OR DEMOCRAT ASK:] Do you consider yourself a strong (Republican/Democrat) or a not so strong (Republican/Democrat)? [IF INDEPENDENT ASK:] Would you say that you lean more toward the Republicans or more towards the Democrats?

37% TOTAL REPUBLICAN
strong Republican 24%
not so strong Republican........................ 9%
Indep. leans Republican......................... 4%
Independent 22%
33% TOTAL DEMOCRAT
Indep. leans Democrat 5%
not so strong Democrat........................... 8%
strong Democrat..................................... 20%
dk/na/other.. 9%

33. Do you consider yourself very liberal, somewhat liberal, moderate, somewhat conservative or very conservative? [IF MODERATE, ASK:] Do you lean toward the liberal or conservative side?

26% TOTAL LIBERAL
very liberal 8%
somewhat liberal 14%

moderate leans liberal 4%
Moderate 28%
38% TOTAL LIBERAL
moderate leans conservative 4%
somewhat conservative.......................... 22%
very conservative 16%
dk/na 5%

34.   What is your age? [CODE ACTUAL AGE. REFUSED=99]

_____

35.   What was the last level of schooling you completed?
less than high school graduate 7%
high school graduate 30%
some college 28%
college graduate and beyond 26%
post graduate 7%
na 3%

36.   Do you consider yourself black, white, Hispanic, Asian, or something else?
black 7%
white 91%
Hispanic 3%
Asian .... *
other 3%
na 3%

37.   And, what is your zip code? _____ _____ _____
_____ THANK YOU FOR YOUR COOPERATION.

38.   Finally, if your member of congress were on the other end of the phone right now and you could give him or her one piece of advice concerning cameras in the courtrooms, what would that advice be?   [INTERVIEWER RECORD VERBATIM RESPONSE]

THANK YOU FOR YOUR COOPERATION.
Sex of Respondent
        male 48%
        female 52%

CENSUS DIVISION [top of sample sheet]
New England 5%
Mid Atlantic 15%
East North Central 19%
West North Central 6%
South Atlantic 17%
East South Central 11%
West South Central 8%
Mountain 5%
Pacific 14%

Printed with the permission from Court TV.

NOTES

NOTES TO CHAPTER 1

1. Some of the issues and concerns with Court TV and the presence of courtroom cameras are similar to the concerns that pertained to electronic sound recording and the introduction of computers in the courtrooms. Use of penwriters became stenotype machines, the transcripts of which were read into a tape machine which was later typed into a manuscript by a typist. With the invention of the computer came the computer assisted transcription (CAT) which had the capability of producing the record verbatim. Since court reporters can be expensive, an alternative was necessary. This was electronic sound recording (ESR) which replaced the need of court reporters. The use of video has become a popular form of court recording with its ability to document the date and time on the recording. Further, no operator is needed other than the judge, and little distractions are evident. Finally, video can scan the particular "vocal zone" for which it is situated. The National Center for State Courts (NCSC) evaluated the capabilities of the video recording system and found it to be the most reliable way to record court proceedings. For more details, see Craig M. Bradley and Joseph L. Hoffman, *"Public Perception, Justice and the "Search for Truth" in Criminal Cases, Southern California Law Review*, 69 (1996) 1267. Controversial issues were raised with video recording. For example, there was a need to protect the victims as well as to allow the defendant to confront his accuser. Some attempts at reconciling these types of problems were the use of screens which conflicted with a defendant's Sixth Amendment right to confront his accusers. The Supreme Court held that such a right was not absolute and should be determined on a case-by-ease basis. The more successful solution was the use of closed circuit television (CCTV), which allowed accuracy and reliability in the evidence and testimony without further harming the victim(s). For more details, see David P. Anderson, Jr., "Audiovisual Application in Court Management", in *Handbook of Court Administration and Management*, (1993), 425.

2. *State v. Simpson*, (1995).

3. Bob Edwards, "Many Americans are now Hooked on Court TV" *National Public Radio*, October 6, 1995, Transcript #1710-10.

4. Robert A. Pugsley, "This Courtroom is Not a Television Studio: Why Judge Fujisaki Made the Correct Call in Gagging the Lawyers and Parties, and Banning the Cameras From the Of Simpson Civil Case", *Loyola of Los Angeles Entertainment Law Journal*, 17(1997) 370.

5.   Sandra F. Chance, "Considering Cameras in the Courtroom", *Journal of Broadcasting & Electronic Media* 39 (1995) 555.

6.   Ibid.

7.   Ibid.

8.   Ibid.

9.   "Topics of the Times: Cameras in the Courts", *The New York Times*, (June 30, 1997) A10.

10. Christo Lassiter, "TV or Not TV-- That Is the Questions", *Journal of Criminal Law & Criminology*, 86 (1996) 974.

11. Angelique M. Paul, "Turning the Camera on Court TV: Does Television Trials Teach Us Anything About the Real Law?", *Ohio State Law Journal* 58, (1997) 682.

12. Paul Arenella, "Foreward: Of Lessons", *Southern California Law Review* 69 (1996) 1252.

13. S. L. Alexander, "The Impact of California v. Simpson on Cameras in the Courtroom", *Judicature* 79 (Jan.-Feb. 1996) 169.

14. Peter Arnella, 1233 (1996).

15. Seth Blomeley, "Bar chief advocates courtroom cameras to dispel legal myths", *The Arkansas Democrat-Gazette*, June 12, 1999, B2.

16. Kelli L. Sager and Karen N. Frederiksen, "Televising the Judicial Branch: In Furtherance of the Public's First Amendment Rights", *Southern California Law Review* 69(1996)1521.

17. Stephen G. Thompson, "Electronic Media in the Courtroom: Some Observations on Federalism and State Experimentation", *Ohio Northern Law Review* 9, (1982) 353.

18. 384 U.S. 333 (1966).

19. Doris Graber, "Mass Media and American Politics", (Washington, D.C.: *CQ Press*, 1997) 78.

20. Ibid.

21. Ibid., 79.

22. Ibid., See Also *Nebraska Press Association v. Stuart*, 427 U.S. 539 (1976).

23. Graber, 79.

24. Ibid.

25. Charles S. Clark, "Courts and the Media", *CQ Researcher* 4, (1994) 828.

26. Stephen A. Metz, "Justice Through the Eye of a Camera: Cameras in the Courtrooms in the United States, Canada, England, and Scotland", *Dickson Journal of International Law* 14 (Spring 1996) 675.

27. Sager, 1519.

28. Metz, 695.

29. Ibid., 676. 29.

30. Ibid. See Also Adrian Conquer, "The First Annual Symposium on Media & the Law: Free Speech v. Fair Trial", *South Dakota Law Review*, 95-96 (1996) 118.

31. Ibid. Charles Manson's case, which went untelevised, took nine months to complete, and the Hillside Strangler case lasted 23 months.

32. Ibid., 675.

33. Ray Surette, "Media, Crime, and Criminal Justice: Images and Realities", (Belmont, CA: Wadsworth Publishing, 1998) 72.

34. Ibid. Surette defines a media trial as "a regional or national news event in which the media co-opt the criminal justice system as a source of high drama and entertainment."

35. Ibid., 72, 75.

36. Ibid, 75.

37. Christo Lassiter, "Cameras in the Courtroom? A Fair Trial is at Stake", *Trial*, 31 (Mar. 1995) 68. See Also David Tajgman, *"From Estes to Chandler: The Distinction Between Television and Newspaper Coverage"*, *Comm/Ent Law Journal*, 4 (Summer 1982) 575.

38. Robert Schmidt, "House Panel Backs Courtroom Cameras", *Legal Times*, (Mar. 30, 1998) 12.

39. Robert Schmidt, "Congress Eyes Courtroom Cameras: Pilot Program Heads for House Vote", *Legal Times*, (March 23, 1998) 6.

40. Schmidt, "House Panel Backs Courtroom Cameras", 12.

41. Ibid.

42. Clark, 828.

43. Ibid.

NOTES TO CHAPTER 2

1. Jonathan M. Remshak, "Truth. Justice and the Media: An Analysis of the Public Criminal Trial", *Seton Hall Constitutional Law Journal,* 6 (1996) 1089.

2. Ibid., 1086.

3. Ibid.

4. Ibid.

5. Warren Freedman, "Press and Media Access to the Criminal Courtroom", New York: Quorum Books, 1988.

6. Remshak, 1090.

7. Henry S. Schleiff "All Courts Need Sunshine", *New York Law Journal*, (October 21, 1999) 2.

8. William J. Harte, "Why Make Justice a Circus? The O.J. Simpson, Dahmer and Kennedy-Smith Debacles Make the Case Against Cameras in the Courtroom", *Trial Lawyer's Guide*, 39 (1996) 380.

9. Susanna R. Barber, "News Cameras in the Courtroom", Norwood, N.J.: Ablex Publishing, 1987, 1.

10. Ibid.

11. Lassiter, "TV or Not TV", 936.

12. Kathleen M. Krygier, "The Thirteenth Juror: Electronic Media's Struggle to Enter State and Federal Courtrooms", *CommLaw Conspectus*, 3 (1995).

13. James M. Jennings II, "Cameras in the American Courtroom: 1935 to the Present", Master's Thesis, Ohio University (1980) 3.

14. Robert S. Stephen "Prejudicial Publicity Surrounding a Criminal Trial: What a Trial Can Do to Ensure a Fair Trial in the Face of a 'Media Circus'", *Suffolk University Law Review* 26 1068-1969.

15. David A. Anderson, "Democracy and the Demystification of Courts: An Essay", *The Review of Litigation*, 14 (1995) 629.

16. Barber, 6. See Also Paul Thaler, "The Watchful Eve", Westport, Conn.: Praeger, (1994), 23.

17. Ibid. See Also Anderson, (1995) 628.

18. Anderson, 629.

19. Ibid.

20. Barber, 6.

21. Lassiter, 936.

22. Ibid.

23. Barber, 3.

24. Ibid.

25. Ibid, 4.

26. Ibid. 3-4

27. Ibid., 4: Lassiter, 936.

28. Barber, 4.

29. Anderson, 630.

30. Stephen, 1069.

31. Anderson, 630.

32. Ibid.

33. Ibid., 630-631.

34. Barber, 7.

35. Anderson, 630.

36. Ibid.

37. Ibid.

38. Ibid., 629.

39. Jennings, 2.
40. Barber, 8; Jennings, 8.
41. Ibid.
42. Barber, 8.
43. Ibid.
44. Barber, 8; Jennings, 9.
45. Barber, 8.
46. Ibid., 9.
47. 62 A.B.A. Rep. 1134-1135 (1937), Rpt. in Barber, 9.
48. Barber, 9.
49. Jane E. Kirtley, "A Leap Not Supported By History: The Continuing Story of Cameras in the Federal Courts", *Government Information Quarterly*, 12, (1995) 369.
50. Ibid.
51. Freedman, 42.
52. Ibid.
53. Laralyn M. Sasaki, Electronic Media Access to Federal Courtrooms: A Judicial Response, University of Michigan Journal of Law Reform 23 (1990) Although some courts have cited Canon 35 as authority on the issue of cameras in the courtroom, it is important to note that ABA canons are not binding on any state or federal court unless they are codified in court rules or state statutes; they are only advisory in nature. Lassiter, "TV or Not TV" 937; Sasaki, 773; Lovorich, 443.
54. DKT # 22092, Okla. County Dist Ct. 1953.
55. Freedman, 42; Barber, 10.
56. Ibid.
57. Ibid., 43; Barber 10.
58. Ibid.
59. Ibid; *Lyles v. State*, 330 P2d 734 (Okla., 1958).
60. Freedman, 43.
61. Ibid.
62. Barber, 12.
63. Ibid.
64. Taffiny L. Smith, "The Distortion of Criminal Trial Through Televised Proceedings", *Law & Psychology Review*, 21 (1997) 266. See Also Mercy Hermida, "Trial By Tabloid", *St. Thomas Law Review*, 7 (1994) 202.
65. 373 U.S. 723 (1963).
66. Ibid., 724.
67. Ibid.
68. Ibid.

69. Ibid., 725.
70. Ibid., 726 (emphasis in original).
71. *Estes v. Texas*, 381 U.S. 532 (1965).
72. Surette, 95.
73. *Estes*, 536.
74. Ibid.
75. Ibid.
76. Ibid., 536-537.
77. Ibid., 537.
78. Ibid.
79. Sager, 1522.
80. Ibid., 1523. The Court stated: "It is contended that this two-day pretrial hearing cannot be considered in determining the question before us. We cannot agree. Pretrial can create a major problem for the defendant in a criminal case. Indeed, it may be more harmful than publicity during the trial for it may well set the community opinion as to guilt or innocence." *Estes*, 536.
81. *Estes*, 539.
82. Remshak, 1093.
83. *Estes*, 540.
84. Surette, 95; Tajgman, 504.
85. *Estes*, 544.
86. Ibid., 545-550.
87. Ibid., 544. "[E]xperience teaches that there are numerous situations in which it might cause actual unfairness — some so subtle as to defy detection by the accused or control by the judge." Ibid., 544-545.
88. *Estes*, 595.
89. See, *Chandler v. Florida*, 449 U.S. 560 (1981).
90. 384 U.S. 333 (1966).
91. Clark, 828.
92. Ibid.
93. *Sheppard*, 340, 342. The papers named several women Sheppard allegedly had affairs with, but only one affair was presented at trial. Ibid.
94. *Sheppard*, 352-353.
95. Ibid., 342-343.
96. Ibid., 343-344.
97. Ibid., 344.
98. Ibid.
99. Ibid.
100. Ibid., 354 - 355 (citations omitted).
101. Barber, 40.

102. Barber, 15.

103. Ibid.

Canon 3A (7) of the American Bar Association Code of Judicial Conduct (as amended in 1972) (rpt. in Barber, 15).

A judge should prohibit broadcasting, televising, or taking photographs in the courtroom and areas immediately adjacent thereto during sessions of court or between sessions, except that a judge may authorize:

(a) the use of electronic or photographic means for the presentation of evidence, for the perpetuation of a record, or for the purposes of judicial administration;

(b) broadcasting, televising, recording, or photographing if investitive, ceremonial, or naturalization proceedings;

(c) the photographic or electronic recording and reproduction of appropriate proceedings under the following conditions:

(i)   the means of recording will not distract participants or impair the dignity of the proceedings;

(ii)   the parties have consented, and the consent to being depicted or recorded has been obtained from each witness appearing in the recording and reproduction;

(iii)   the reproduction will not be exhibited until after the proceeding has been concluded and all direct appeals have been exhausted; and

(iv)   the reproduction will be exhibited only for instructional purposes in educational institutions.

104. Charles Whitebread and Darrell Contreras, "Free Press v. Fair Trial: Protecting the Criminal Defendant's Rights in a Highly Publicized Trial By Applying the Sheppard-Mu' Minimum Remedy", *Southern California Law Review*, 69 (1996) 1590.

105. Remshak, 1104.

106. 427 U.S. 539 (1976).

107. Ibid., 542.

108. Ibid.

109. Ibid., 543.

110. Ibid. The district court's order specifically prohibited the press from reporting: (1) the confession the defendant had made to police; (2) any statements the defendant had made to people other than the police; (3) the contents of a note the defendant had written on the night of the crime; (4) certain portions of the medical testimony at the pretrial hearing; and (5) the identity of victims of the alleged sexual assault. Ibid., 543-544.

111. Ibid., 544. The Nebraska Supreme Court prohibited the reporting of any confessions to the police; any statements to people other than the

police, excluding members of the press; and other facts "strongly implicative" of the defendant. Ibid., 544.

112. Whitebread, 1591.
113. Ibid.
114. Nebraska Press Association, 562.
115. Whitebread, 1591.
116. Ibid.
117. Barber, 44.
118. Surette, 102.
119. 443 U.S. 368 (1979).
120. Ibid., 385.
121. Ibid., 385, 394.
122. Ibid., 378.
123. Ibid., 378-379.
124. Ibid., 379-80, 391.
125. Ibid., 393.
126. Barber, 25.
127. 370 So. 2d 764 (1979).
128. Barber, 25.
129. *Post-Newsweek*, 781-782.
Florida Code of Judicial Conduct Canon 3A(7) provided: "Subject at all times to the authority of the presiding judge to (i) control the conduct of the proceedings before the court, (ii) ensure decorum and prevent distractions, and (iii) ensure the fair administration of justice in the pending cause, electronic media and still photography coverage of public trial courts of this state shall be allowed in accordance with standards of conduct and technology promulgated by the Supreme Court of Florida." Ibid., 781.
130. Lassiter, 941.
131. For a summary of these mostly constitutionally based challenges, see Radio-Television News Directors Association, News Media Coverage of Judicial Proceedings with Cameras and Microphones: A Survey of the States (1993).
132. 449 U.S. 560 (1981).
133. Ibid., 568. Two minutes and fifty-five seconds of the trial was broadcasted.
134. Ibid., 573.
135. Ibid., 575.
136. Sager, 1526.
137. *Chandler*, 582.
138. Ibid.

139. Ibid., 583.
140. Lassiter, 942.
141. 448 U.S. 555 (1980).
142. Ibid., 580.
143. Ibid., 564-575.
144. Ibid., 581.
145. Ibid., 581 footnote 18.
146. 457 U.S. 596 (1982).
147. Ibid., 610-611.
148. Ibid., 606-607.
149. 695 F.2d 1278 (1983).
150. Ibid., 1279 footnote 6, 1284.
151. Ibid., 1279.
152. Ibid., 1280.
153. Ibid., 1279.
154. Ibid., 1280.
155. Ibid.
156. Ibid.
157. See ABA Standing Committee on Ethics and Professional Responsibility, Final Draft of Recommended Revisions to ABA Code of Judicial Conduct, December 1989.
158. 467 U.S. 39 (1984).
159. Ibid., 50.
160. Ibid., 47.
161. Ibid., 47, 48.
162. Ibid., 47.
163. Ibid., 50.
164. 478 U.S. 1 (1986).
165. Ibid., 8.
166. Ibid., 14.
167. Ibid., 15.
168. 500 U.S. 415.
169. Ibid., 431.
170. Ibid., 430.
171. See Report of the Judicial Conference Ad Hoc Committee on Cameras in the Courtroom (September 1990).
172. See Report of the Proceedings of the Judicial Conference of the United States (September 1990).
173. Ibid.
174. The program was originally scheduled to terminate on June 30,1994. In March 1994, the Judicial Conference adopted a

recommendation of the Committee on Court Administration and Case Management to continue the program in the pilot courts through the end of 1994 to avoid a lapse in the program while a final Judicial Conference decision was pending.

175. Ibid., 381.

176. James C. Goodale, "Cameras, the Courts and the Missing 'Simpson' Backlash", *New York Law Journal*, 2 August 1996, 3.

177. Schmidt, "House Panel Backs Courtroom Cameras", 12.

178. Samuel H. Pillsbury, "Time, TV, and Criminal Justice: Second Thoughts on the Simpson Trial", *Criminal Law Bulletin*, 33 (January/February 1997) 3.

179. Pugsley, 371.

180. Goodale, (August 2, 1996).

181. "Klausner, Speaking at Forum, Says More Judges in County Are Barring Cameras From Courtrooms," *Metropolitan News-Enterprise*, (March 22, 1996) 1.

182. Ibid.

183. Melissa Block, Joe Palca, "TV or Not TV?" Morning Edition (NPR 10:00 am ET). Trans. #97073016-210, (July 30, 1997).

184. Alexander, 169.

185. Ibid., 170.

186. Ibid.

187. Ibid.

188. Ibid., 170-171.

189. Ibid., 171.

190. Ibid.

191. Ibid.

192. Henry Reske, "No More Cameras in Federal Courts", *ABA Journal*, (November 1994) 28.

193. Ibid.

194. Robert G. Morvillo, "Television and the Public Trial", *New York Law Journal* (Apr. 1, 1997) 3.

195. Kirtley, 375.

196. Melissa A. Corbett, "Lights, Camera, Trial: Pursuit of Justice of the Emmy?", *Seton Hall Law Review*, 27 (1997) 1542-1578.

197. Taffiny L. Smith, "The Distortion of Criminal Trials Through Televised Proceedings", *Law & Psychology Review* 21, (1997) 264.

198. Lassiter, 948.

199. Elizabeth M. Hodgkins, "Throwing Open A Window on the Nation's Court By Lifting the Ban on Federal Courtroom Television", *Kansas Journal of Law & Public Policy*, 4 (1995) 92.

200. Lassiter, 949. *See, Globe Newspaper Co. v. Superior Court*, 457 U.S. 596 (1982).

201. Lassiter, 949.

202. Lassiter, "Put the Lens Cap Back on Cameras in the Courtroom: A Fair Trial is at Stake", *New York State Bar Journal* (Jan. 1995) 10. *See* Also Smith, 265.

203. Ibid.

204. Ibid.

205. 471 N.E.2d 874 (Ohio App. 1984).

206. Elizabeth M. Hodgkins, (1995) 92.

207. *Cosmos Broadcasting* at 883.

208. Hodgkins, 92.

209. Ibid

210. Ibid.

211. Mercy Hermida, "Trial by Tabloid" *St. Thomas Law Review,* 7 (1994) 211 (citations omitted).

212. Clark, 822.

213. Ibid.

214. Melissa Grace, "Courts' bank on Cameras Retained", *The Times Union*, August 2, 1999, A1.

215. Federal judges could allow cameras in their courtroom, according to bills introduced in the House and Senate last week, *Broadcasting & Cable*, 129, No. 13 (March 29, 1999), 76.

216. William F. Doherty, "Judges aren't all smiling for camera", *The Boston Globe*, April 7, 1999, A1.

217. Erik Ugland, *Minnesota Daily*, August 20, 1999.

218. Melissa Grace, A1.

219. John Caher, "Law Day sees push for Court Cameras", *The Times Union*, May 1, 1999, B2.

220. Phil Davis, "Despite O.J., Cameras are coming to Courtrooms", *The Daily News of Los Angeles*, May 30, 1999, L12.

221. Sager, 1545.

222. Eugene Borgida, Kenneth DeBono, and Lee Buckman, "Cameras in the Courtroom", *Law and Human Behavior,* 14 (1990) 504.

223. Ibid.

224. Barber, 77-78.

225. Daniel Wise, "Report Favors TV Cameras in Court", *New York Law Journal* (Apr. 4, 1997) 3.

NOTES TO CHAPTER 3

1.   Court TV is a basic cable network that provides a window on the American system of justice through distinctive programming concerning law and justice. Founded in 1991, Court TV's cornerstone has been the televising of civil and criminal trial court proceedings. Court TV has televised all or portions of more than 740 trials and numerous other proceedings, including parole hearings, death penalty hearings, and proceedings in municipal and night courts around the United States, as well as international proceedings from the former Soviet Union, El Salvador, the former Republic of Yugoslavia and the International Court of Justice at the Hague.

2.   Courtroom Television Network, *Viewer's Guide* 24 (1992), rpt. in Harris, 806-807.

3.   Timothy Sullivan Special Project Producer, at the time of interview, interview by author, tape recording, New York, NY 1999.

4.   On February 4, 1997, Mathew Eappen, an eight-month old baby, was rushed to the Children Hospital for severe head injury. On February 9, 1997, Mathew Eappen passed away. Louise Woodward, a British nineteen-year old, worked as an au pair for the Eappen family since 1996. On March 5, 1997, Louise Woodward, was indicted by the grand jury for the murder of baby Eappen. The Woodward trial lasted for three weeks. Judge Zobel gave the jury instructions on murder in the first and second degrees. Woodward requested that the judge not instruct the jury on manslaughter. A jury first found the teenager from Elton, England, guilty of second-degree murder, an automatic life sentence offense in Massachusetts. But the state Superior Court judge who oversaw the case, Hiller Zobel, exercised his right to review the case and reduced the charge to manslaughter and her lifetime sentence was sliced to time served, the 279 days that she spent in jail while awaiting trial and while awaiting action on her post-conviction motion. The Commonwealth and Woodward both filed appeals to the Massachusetts Supreme Judicial Court. The Commonwealth argues that the judge abused his discretion in reducing the jury's verdict from murder to manslaughter conviction. Woodward argued there was error in the court ruling of finding her guilty due to conclusiveness of scientific evidence on healing. On June 16 1998, the Massachusetts Supreme Judicial Court let stand the involuntary manslaughter conviction for Woodward, rejecting appeals by prosecutors and defense attorneys.

5.   Dan Levinson, Executive Vice President, Marketing at the time of interview, interview by author, tape recording, New York, NY, 1999.

6. Ibid.
7. Ronald L. Goldfarb, "TV or Not TV: Television Justice, and the Courts", New York University Press, (1998), 126.
8. Goldfarb.
9. Goldfarb, 127.
10. Goldfarb.
11. Steven Brill, "Cameras in the Court and Original Intent", *The Connecticut Law Tribune*, (Jan. 29, 1996) 43.
12. Brill, quoted in Unger, 44; Goldfarb, 127.
13. Brill, quoted in Goldfarb, 127.
14. Brill, quoted in Thaler, *56*. Court TV has also been described as a cross between C-Span and MTV. Mark Landler, "Will Viewers Be Shouting: I Want My Court TV?" *Business Week*, 24 June 1991, 139.
15. Goldfarb, 130.
16. Goldfarb, 134.
17. Goldfarb.
18. Goldfarb.
19. Goldfarb., 136 (citation omitted).
20. Ibid.; Paul Thaler, "The Watchful Eye", Westport, Conn. Praegor, (1994) *56*.
21. Thaler.
22. Thaler, 56.
23. Thaler.
24. Thaler., *57*.
25. William Kennedy-Smith was accused of raping Patricia Bowman on March 30, 1991 at the Kennedy estate in Palm Beach, Florida. The credibility of a woman and the liberty of a man was what was at stake in the case. The Courtroom Television Network covered the case gavel to gavel. Close-ups of the six jurors wasn't permitted and the face of the victim was blurred. Judge Mary Lupo showed herself as restrained and judicious. The lead prosecutor was Moira Lasch, who seemed overtly hostile to the defense and the judge. The lead defense attorney was Professor Roy Black, who was known for his gentle folksy style. Black's partner was Mark Schnapp, a former federal prosecutor in Miami. Smith had said he would pay for the tab of nearly $1 million for his defense. The jury was impaneled and sequestered for the duration of the trial.

Some critics thought that Florida was just a randy state were everyone is "lustful, eager for sexual gratification". The prosecutor Lasch "during her cross-examination of Smith repeatedly and sarcastically reiterated her disbelief that a women would be willing to have sex with a man less than two hours after she met him". The jury did not take too long to acquit

Kennedy unanimously. Steven Brill, president of Court TV, at the time, used this case to comment that democracy is based on the rule of law and people have to have an understanding of this branch of the government. For more details see, David A. Kaplan and others, "Case No. 91-5482 Comes to Trial", *Newsweek* 18 No. 25 (December 9, 1991) 26-27 and John Taylor, "A Theory of the Case", *New York*, 25 No. 1 (January 6, 1992) 34-3 8.

    26. Ibid., 58.

    27. David A. Harris, "The Appearance of Justice: Court TV, Conventional Television, and the Public Understanding of the Criminal Justice System", *Arizona Law Review* (1993) 801.

    28. Angelique M. Paul," Turning the Camera on Court TV: Does Television Trials Teach Us Anything About the Real Law"? *Ohio State Law Journal* 58 (1997) 662.

    29. Paul.

    30. Paul, 663.

    31. Timothy Sullivan, 1999.

    32. Erik and Lyle Menendez were sons of a wealthy Cuban-American video business executive, Jose and his wife, Kitty Menendez. Everything was going well, or so it seemed, until one night in August of 1989 when something snapped in both of the brothers. On that night, both Jose and Kitty Menendez were murdered while eating ice cream. For months after the murder, but of the Menendez brothers indulged in their childhood fantasies while the murders were initially blamed on the Mafia. Erik purchased a new wardrobe that consisted on silk shirts while also attempting to play on the pro tennis circuit. Lyle bought an old childhood haunt, a cafe in Princeton, NJ. In July of 1993, the brothers confessed to the murders when their culpability was eventually discovered. The brothers maintained that their actions were a result of sexual abuse by both of their parents. The initial Menendez trial unfolded, right before the publics' eyes, on the pages of the tabloids. This type of publicity persuaded some of the jurors to believe that the boys had murdered their parents in self-defense; mistrials were declared.

    33. Krysten Crawford, "Brill Sells Stake in AMLAW, Court TV to Time Warner", *The Recorder*, (Feb. 20, 1997) 1.

    34. Interview with Dan Levinson, 1999. Also see, Valerie Block, "Court TV on Trial: Struggling Network Heals Ownership Rift", *Crain's New York Business*, (November 2, 1998) 3.

    35. Jennifer Weiner, "Cable's Court TV Goes on Trial, Sacramento Bee, (May 14, 1999) G5.

    36. Dan Levinson, 1999.

37. Glenn Moss, Vice President, Business Affairs and Affiliate Relations at the time of interview, interview by author, tape recording, New York, NY 1999.

38. Ibid.

39. *Marisol v. Guiliani*, (SDNY 1996), Application of Courtroom Television Network, Proposed Intervenor, Memorandum in Support, at 7, found at Court TV Online.

40. *Marisol v. Guiliani*, (SDNY 1996), Application of Courtroom Television Network, Proposed Intervenor, Memorandum in Support, at 7, found at Court TV Online.

41. Harris, 804.

42. Ibid., 804-805.

43. Ibid., 805.

44. Dan Levinson, 1999.

45. David A. Harris, 806.

46. Harris.

47. Rich Brown, "Court TV's Steve Brill: Witness For a Nation", *Broadcasting & Cable* 125 *(1995)* 46.

48. Betsy Vorce, Executive Vice President of Corporate Affairs, at the time of interview, interview by author, tape recording, New York, NY 2002.

49. Interviews by author, tape recording with Court TV executives, New York, NY 1999. See Also, Harris, 805; Krygier, 83.

50. Duncan Irving, Coordinating Producer, Trial Coverage, at the time of interview, interview by author, tape recording, New York, NY 1999.

51. Elaine F. Fullerton, "The Camera and Its Effect on Justice in the American Courtroom", thesis James Madison University (1996), 7 1-72.

52. Fullerton, 73.

53. Harris, 818-820.

54. M.K. Krygier, "The Thirteenth Juror: Electronic Media's Struggle to Enter State and Federal Courtrooms", *The Catholic University of America CommLaw Conspectus*, 3 (1995) 785.

55. *Marisol v. Guiliani*, (SDNY 1996), Application of Courtroom Television Network, Proposed Intervenor, Memorandum in Support, at 7, found at Court TV Online.

56. Paul, 665.

57. Paul, 667.

58. William J. Harte, "Why make Justice a Circus? The O.J. Simpson, Dahmer and Kennedy-Smith Debacles Make the Case against Cameras in the Courtroom", *Trial Lawyers Guide*, 39 (1996) 379.

59. Harte, 825.

60. Paul, 669.

61. Paul, 671.

62. Paul., 671-672.

63. Paul, 672-673.

64. Dian G. Cox, "Lights. Camera. Justice?", *The National Law Journal* (January 29, 1996) A12.

65. Harte, 412 (citations omitted).

66. Steven Brill, quoted in Debra Gersh Hernandez, "The Historical Case For Courtroom Cameras", *Editor & Publisher*, 17 February 1996, 13.

67. Warren Burger, "Cable in the Court!", *New York*, 24, no. 31(1991) 40.

68. Alan M. Dershowitz, "Court TV", *ABA Journal*, May 1994, 46.

69. Thaler, 59.

70. Ibid.

71. Roscoe C. Howard, Jr., "The Media Attorneys, and Fair Criminal Trials", *Kansas Journal of Law and Public Policy* 4 (1995) 61.

72. Timothy Sullivan, 1999.

73. Henry Schleiff, President and Chief Executive Officer at the time of interview, interview by author, tape recording, New York, NY, 1999. Henry Schleiff, "All Courts Need Sunshine", *New York Law Journal*, October 21, 1999, 2.

74. Schleiff, 1999.

75. Block, 3.

76. Doug Jacobs, Executive Vice President and General Counsel of Court TV, at the time of publication of this book, interview by author, tape recording, New York, NY 2002.

NOTES TO CHAPTER 4

1.   Karla G. Sanchez, "Barring the Media from the Courtroom in Child Abuse Cases: Who Should Prevail?", *Buffalo Law Review*, 46 (1991) 2 17-256.

2.   James Henderson, "*Sheppard v. Maxwell*, The Sufficiency of Probability", *North Dakota Law Review* 43, (1966-1967) 1-16.

3.   Hodgkins, 92. See Also Lassiter, "TV or Not TV", 944 - 945; *Gannett Co. v. DePasquale*, 443 U.S. 368 (1979) (holding that the public did not have an independent right of access to criminal trials under the Sixth Amendment).

4.   U.S. Const. Amend VI.

5. Robert Kopple, "Constitutional Law - Balancing of Free Press and Fair Trial-Inherent Prejudice From Mass Publicity", *DePaul Law Review,* 16 (Autumn-Winter 1966) 3-209.

6. Kopple, 204.

7. Hodgkins, 92.

8. Ibid.

9. Jon Share, "Televised Trials: Let's turn on those Cameras", *New Jersey Lawyer,* (May 4, 1998) 3.

10. Smith, 266. See Also Hermida, 202.

11. Smith, 266-267.

12. Floyd Abrams, "Yes: Cameras Reflect the Process, For Better or Worse", *ABA Journal,* (Sept. *1995)* 36.

13. Lassiter, "Put the Lens Cap Back on Cameras in the Courtroom", 10.

14. Nicholas Lovrich, Michael Stohr-Gillmore, Byron Daynes, David Mann, Charles Sheldon, Dennis Soden, and Glen Sussman, "Cameras in the Courtroom, In Handbook of Court Administration and Management", edited by Steven Hayes and Cole Blease Graham, Jr., New York, Dekker, (1993) 440, 446.

15. Lassiter, "TV or Not TV", 949.

16. Ibid., 950.

17. Goldfarb.

18. George Gerber, "Courtroom TV makes for low-budget entertainment", *National Public Radio,* July 12, 1994, Transcript #1387-11.

19. Ronald L. Goldfarb, (1998) "Introduction" xxiii.

20. Barber, 282.

21. All things considered, "TV in the courtroom - How is it affecting trials?", *National Public Radio,* April 6, 1993.

22. *Estes,* (Justice Harlan concurring) 595.

23. All things considered, "TV in the courtroom - How is it affecting trials?", *National Public Radio,* April 6, 1993.

24. Paul Thaler, 154.

25. In 1988 Joel Steinberg was accused in the beating death of his 6-year old daughter Lisa. Steinberg, then a lawyer from Manhatten, was convicted of manslaughter and is serving a 25-year sentence.

26. Paul Thaler.

27. Christo Lassiter, "TV or Not TV - That is the Question", *Journal of Criminal Law & Criminology,* 86 (1996) 926-1001.

28. Ralph E. Roberts, Jr., "An Empirical and Normative Analysis of the Impact of Televised Courtroom Proceedings", *Southern Methodist Law Review* 51(1998) 622.

29. William J. Harte, "Why Make a Justice a Circus? The O.J. Simpson, Dahmer and Kennedy-Smith Debacles Make the Case Against Cameras in the Courtroom", *Trial Lawyer's Guide*, 39 (1996) 389-392.

30. Harte, 389-392.

31. Harte, 389-392.

32. David A. Anderson, "Democracy and the Demystification of Courts: An Essay", *The Review of Litigation*, 14 (1995) 627.

33. Harte, *Trial Lawyer's Guide.*

34. Harte, 400-405, 415.

35. Harte, Ibid.

36. Harte, 400-405, 415. Also see, James R. Cady, Bouncing "Checkbook Journalism: A Balance between the First and Sixth Amendments in High Profile Cases", *William & Mary Bill of Rights Journal*, 4 *(1995)* 671.

37. Harte, Ibid.

38. Paul Thaler, 154.

39. Anderson *(1995).*

40. Harte, 396-400.

41. Harte, Ibid.

42. Harte, Ibid.

43. Harte, 396-400. See, Saul M. Kassin, "TV Cameras. Public Self-Consciousness, and Mock Juror Performance", *Journal of Experimental Social Psychology*, 20 (1984) 336-349. See Also, James R. Cady, *William & Mary Bill of Rights Journal*, (1995) 671-713.

44. Paul Thaler, 154.

45. David A. Anderson (1995).

46. Kathleen M. Krygier, "The Thirteenth Juror: Electronic Media's Struggle to Enter State and Federal Courtrooms", *CommLaw Conspectus*, 3 (1995) 71.

47. Mercy Hermida, "Trial by Tabloid", *St. Thomas Law Review*, 7 (1994) 197-215.

48. Harte, 392-396.

49. Harte, Ibid.

50. Harte, Ibid.

51. Harte, 392-396.

52. Peter Arnella, (1996) 1256-57.

53. Selwyn Crawford, "A Heavy Caseload: Flood of TV Shows. Birth of Media stars Reflect Public Appetite for more Information about Trials", *Dallas Morning News*, (June 6, 1999) 1J.

54. Harte, 408.

55. Susanna R. Barber, "Televised Trials: Weighing Advantages against Disadvantages", *The Justice System Journal*, 10, 3 (1985) 279-289.

56. Rosco C. Howard, Jr., "The Media. Attorneys. and Fair Criminal Trials", *Kansas Journal of Law and Public Policy* 4, *(1995)* 62.

57. Smith, 259-260.

58. Ibid., 260.

59. Ibid.

60. "Facts and Opinions About Cameras in Courtrooms", 2.

61. Lassiter, "TV or Not TV", 960.

62. *Richmond Newspapers*, 572.

63. Sager, 1533.

64. Lassiter, "TV or Not TV", 962.

65. *Estes*, (Justice Harlan concurring) 589.

66. Sager, 1533.

67. Ugland, August 20, 1999.

NOTES TO CHAPTER 5

1. National Center for State Courts and the Hearst Corporation, "How the Public Views the State Courts", 1999 National Survey. The Study was based upon interviews conducted by the Indiana University the Public Opinion Laboratory. The Survey was designed and analyzed in collaboration with University of Nebraska Public Policy Center and Scientific Resources for the Law, Inc., and was presented at the National Conference on Public Trust and Confidence in the Justice System, May 14, 1999, in Washington, D.C.

2. "National Conference on Public Trust and Confidence in the Justice System", May 14-15, 1999, Washington, D.C., sponsored by the American Bar Association Conference of Chief Justices, Conference of State Court Administrators and the League of Women Voters, in cooperation with the National Center for State Courts

3. Ibid.

4. National Center for State Courts and the Hearst Corporation, "How the Public Views the State Courts", 1999 National Survey.

5. "National Conference on Public Trust and Confidence in the Justice System", May 14-15, 1999, Washington, D.C.

6.   John Seigenthaler, Founder First Amendment Center, Vanderbilt University, "National Conference on Public Trust and Confidence in the Justice System", May 14-15, 1999, Washington, D.C.

7.   "National Conference on Public Trust and Confidence in the Justice System", May 14-15, 1999, Washington, D.C.

8.   American Bar Association Report, "Perception of the U.S. Justice System", February 24, 1999.

9.   Comments of Frank A. Bennack, Jr. at the" National Conference on Public Trust and Confidence in the Justice System", May 1999, Washington, D.C. Also see, the National Survey by the National Center for State Courts and the Hearst Corporation, "How the Public Views the State Courts", 1999.

10.   The polling company ™/Court-TV Judge Mail-in Survey, May 3, 1999.

NOTES TO CHAPTER 6

1.   Deborah Sharp, "Web-wired Courtroom Lets World Attend Fla. trial", *USA Today*, August 17, 1999, 3A.

2.   Anderson, (1995) 627.

3.   Roberts, 635.

4.   Roberts, 621-645.

5.   Borgida et al., (1990) 489

6.   Others concur. *See*, e.g., Goldfarb, 96.

7.   See, *Estes v. Texas*, 381 U.S. 532, 601 (1965) (Harlen, J., concurring, quoting amicus curiae brief of American Bar Association).

8.   Roberts, Ibid., 636.

9.   Roberts, Ibid., 636.

10.   Roberts, Ibid., 640.

11.   Roberts, Ibid.

12.   Roberts, Ibid., 641.

13.   Roberts, Ibid., 642.

14.   Davis, (May 30, 1999) L12.

15.   Roberts, 645.

16.   Roberts, Ibid., 639.

17.   The "Florida Experiment" *In re Petition of Post-Newsweek Stations*, 347 So. 2d 402, 403 (1977).

18.   *In re Petition of Post-Newsweek Stations*, 370 So. 2d 764, 767-68 (1979).

19.   *id.* at 767.

20.   Roberts, 639.

21. Goldfarb, (1998) 56-95. See Also Robert (1995) 645.

22. *See* Iowa Code Jud. Conduct, Canon 3.B.2 (West 2001).

23. The Alaska Judicial Council, "News Cameras in the Alaska Courts: Assessing the Impact", January 1988.

24. *See* Former Jud. L. § 218(a)(9).

25. *People v. Boss*, 182 Misc. 2d 700, 701 N.Y.S. 2d 891 (Sup. Ct. Albany Co. 2000).

26. 701 N.Y.S. 2d at 893, 895.

27. *Id*. at 894-95.

28. 273 A.D. 2d 813, 708 N.Y.S.2d 724 (4th Dep't 2000).

29. 273 A.D. 2d at 814, 708 N.Y.S.2d at 726 (citations omitted).

30. *See e.g., Marisol A. v. Giuliani*, 929 F. Supp. 660 (S.D.N.Y. 1996); *Hamilton v. Accu-Tek*, 942 F. Supp. 136 (S.D.N.Y. 1996).

31. *See* H.R. 2519 (int. July 17, 2001); S. 986 (int. June 5, 2001).

32. Ibid.

33. Molly Treadway Johnson and Carol Krafka, "Electronic Media Coverage of Federal Civil Proceedings - An Evaluation of the Pilot Program in Six District Courts and Two Courts of Appeals", (1994), Federal Judicial Center.

34. Electronic Media Coverage of Federal Civil Proceedings: An Evaluation of the Pilot Program in Six District Courts and Two Courts of Appeals (1994), Federal Judicial Center.

35. Ibid.

36. Median represents the midpoint of all responses. The median rating on the item "educates the public about courtroom procedures" indicated this effect occurred "to a great extent."

37. Ratings of each potential effect by judges who completed both questionnaires were compared using a Wilcoxon Signed Rank test. This analysis examined the number of judges who changed their response in each direction and enabled a determination of whether the direction and magnitude of changes in ratings between the initial and follow-up questionnaires were statistically significant.

38. Use of a flash attachment is prohibited by the guidelines.

39. No information was available for nine attorneys in the sampled cases.

40. In particular, of those attorneys responding to this item on the district court questionnaire, forty-six identified themselves as representing a plaintiff in the case, thirty-six identified themselves as representing a defendant, and two identified themselves as "other" (e.g., representing a respondent to a subpoena). Of attorneys responding to the appellate

questionnaire, eleven identified themselves as representing the appellant, eleven as representing the appellee, and one as "other."

41. Questions used in each set of interviews are on file in the Research Division of the Federal Judicial Center.

42. Not all attorneys answered every question.

43. Studies of the effects of electronic media in state courts have generally been conducted by state court administrators, special advisory committees appointed by the court, bar associations, or outside consultants. A handful of state studies other than those mentioned here address juror and witness issues; the FJC did not include all of them, however, because some reports do not provide enough detail about methods to determine what questions were asked and how, and others used methods the FJC did not consider sufficiently rigorous to rely on for this evaluation (e.g., a judge polling one jury after a trial about whether cameras affected them). But even the less rigorous studies tend to report results that are similar to the FJC findings and other state court findings. A more detailed description of the studies summarized in FJC report is on file with the Research Division of the FJC.

44. In an experimental study comparing the effects of conventional and electronic media coverage on mock witnesses and jurors, researchers at the University of Minnesota found that witnesses who were covered by electronic media reported being more distracted and more nervous about media presence than witnesses who were covered by conventional media. There was no difference between the two conditions, however, in mock juror perceptions of the quality of witness testimony, including ratings of the extent to which the testimony was believable. *See* Eugene Borgida et al., "Cameras in the Courtroom: The Effects of Media Coverage on Witness Testimony and Juror Perceptions", 14 *Law & Hum. Behav.* 489 (1990).

45. In FJC attorney survey, they asked attorneys who participated in proceedings covered by electronic media whether they had any witnesses who declined to testify because of the prospect of electronic media coverage. Out of sixty-eight district court attorneys responding to this question, sixty-three (63%) reported they had no witnesses who declined to testify, one reported he had, and four reported they couldn't say.

NOTES TO CHAPTER 7

1. Hearings Before a Subcommittee of the House Committee on Appropriations, 104th Cong., 2d Sess. 30 (1996).

2.   Don Kaplan, "Judgment Day - Push to get Cameras back in New York Courtrooms", *The New York Post*, (August 10, 1999) 079.

3.   *Globe Newspaper Co. v. Superior Court of Norfolk*, 457 U.S. 596, at 606.

4.   Bill Hall, "Do Court Cameras bring out the worst in lawyers?", *Lewiston Morning Tribune*, (August 4, 1999) 10A.

5.   Ibid.

6.   Scott Graham, "Only a Cloistered Federal Judge Would Be Whistling 'Dixie'", *The Recorder*, August 13, 1999, 4.

7.   Marianne Means, "Let the Sun Shine on Supreme Court", *Chattanooga Times*, (August 15, 1999) H6.

8.   Ugland, August 20, 1999.

9.   Ibid.

INDEX